Appropriating Kartini

Appropriating *Kartini*

Colonial, National and Transnational Memories
of an Indonesian Icon

EDITED BY
PAUL BIJL · GRACE V.S. CHIN

ISEAS YUSOF ISHAK
INSTITUTE

First published in Singapore in 2020 by
ISEAS Publishing
30 Heng Mui Keng Terrace
Singapore 119614

E-*mail*: publish@iseas.edu.sg
Website: <http://bookshop.iseas.edu.sg>

The responsibility for facts and opinions in this publication rests exclusively with the authors and their interpretations do not necessarily reflect the views or the policy of the publisher or its supporters.

ISEAS Library Cataloguing-in-Publication Data

Names: Bijl, Paul, editor. | Chin, Grace V.S., editor.
Title: Appropriating Kartini: colonial, national and transnational memories of an Indonesian icon/edited by Paul Bijl and Grace V.S. Chin.
Description: Singapore : ISEAS – Yusof Ishak Institute, 2020.
Identifiers: ISBN 978-981-4843-91-1 (paperback) | ISBN 978-981-4843-92-8 (pdf)
Subjects: LCSH: Kartini, Raden Adjeng, 1879-1904. | Women social reformers—Indonesia. | Nationalism and collective memory—Indonesia. | Indonesia—Civilization.
Classification: LCC DS625 A65

Cover photo: The cover image of this book is entitled "Kartini: Door duisternis tot licht" (Kartini: Through darkness into light). Copyright © 2016 by Apeep Qimo, the founder of Rumah Kartini, Jepara, Indonesia. Used with permission of the maker. All rights reserved.

Typeset by Stallion Press (S) Pte Ltd

CONTENTS

ACKNOWLEDGMENTS

Both editors are thankful to KITLV/Royal Netherlands Institute of Southeast Asian and Caribbean Studies, Leiden for supporting their work on this publication. Paul Bijl was also supported by NWO/Netherlands Organisation for Scientific Research.

Chapter 5 is reprinted from "Unpacking a National Heroine: Two Kartinis and Their People", by Danilyn Rutherford from *Indonesia* Journal. Copyright © 1993 by Cornell University. Used with the permission of the author and publisher. All rights reserved. Minor alterations have been made to conform to ISEAS' style.

Chapter 7 is reprinted from "Colonial and Postcolonial Silence: Listening to Kartini in the Netherlands", by Paul Bijl. In *Beyond Memory: Silence and the Aesthetics of Remembrance*, edited by Alexandre Dessingué and Jay M. Winter. London: Routledge, 2015, pp. 15–30. Copyright © 2015 by Taylor & Francis. Used with the permission of the author and publisher. All rights reserved. Minor alterations have been made to serve the purposes of the present volume and to conform to ISEAS' style.

THE CONTRIBUTORS

Paul Bijl teaches comparative literature at Utrecht University in the Netherlands. He has written *Emerging Memory: Photographs of Colonial Atrocity in Dutch Cultural Remembrance* (2015) about Dutch postcolonial memory and forgetting. In recent years, he has worked on the history of human rights in colonial Indonesia.

Grace V.S. Chin is Senior Lecturer in English Language Studies at Universiti Sains Malaysia. Much of her research examines the intersections between postcolonial and Southeast Asian literatures, with emphasis on race and gender in contemporary societies and diasporas. She has received several grants for her work, and was awarded senior fellowship in 2016 by the Royal Netherlands Institute of Southeast Asian and Caribbean Studies (KITLV) in Leiden. She has published articles in peer-reviewed journals, including *Kemanusiaan: The Asian Journal of Humanities, Journal of International Women's Studies, World Englishes* and *The Journal of Commonwealth Literature*. Her latest publication is an edited volume titled *The Southeast Asian Woman Writes Back: Gender, Identity and Nation in the Literatures of Brunei Darussalam, Malaysia, Singapore, Indonesia and the Philippines* (2018).

Joost Coté is Senior Research Fellow at Monash University, Australia. He has been writing on the significance of R.A. Kartini since 1992 with the publication of the annotated English translation of new letters that had been made public (*Letters from Kartini: An Indonesian Feminist, 1900–1904*). Since then he has published a number of articles on her writing and the colonial context in which she wrote. This includes three further annotated

English translations of her letters, *On Feminism and Nationalism: Kartini's Letters to Stella Zeehandelaar* (2005), *Realizing the Dream of RA Kartini: Her Sisters' Letters from Colonial Java* (2008) and most recently, *Kartini: The Complete Writings* (2014); this latest includes also her published fiction and political writings. As well, he has published critical examinations of various aspects of Dutch colonial policy, practice, and discourse, focusing on questions of colonial modernity, and more recently, colonial urban reform. The latter includes *Cars, Conduits and Kampongs: Modernising the Indonesian City* (co-edited, 2014) and *The Life and Times of Thomas Karsten* (co-author, 2017).

As an Australian feminist, **Kathryn Robinson** has always been attentive to Indonesian gender relations and matters of gender equity since she began her career as an anthropologist of Indonesia in the 1970s. Her principal research has focused on the mining town of Sorowako in South Sulawesi (*Stepchildren of Progress: The Political Economy of Development in an Indonesian Mining Town*, 1986) but she has also researched land-related issues, including land law/rights (*Land and Development in Indonesia: Searching for the People's Sovereignty*, co-editor, 2016); and Indonesian youth and their futures (*Youth Identities and Social Transformations in Modern Indonesia*, 2016). Engagement with issues of gender relations over many years, through academic research and supervision; consulting in aid and development; and friendships with Indonesian women activists resulted in the publication of *Gender Islam and Democracy in Indonesia* (2009). Currently, she is working on publications on Indonesian Islam, and is Emeritus Professor in Anthropology in the College of Asia and the Pacific at the Australian National University.

Danilyn Rutherford is President of the Wenner-Gren Foundation, which is dedicated to the advancement of anthropology throughout the world. She has taught anthropology at the University of Chicago and the University of California, Santa Cruz, and is the author of three books on West Papua: *Raiding the Land of the Foreigners: The Limits of the Nation on an Indonesian Frontier* (2003), *Laughing at Leviathan: Sovereignty and Audience in West Papua* (2012), and *Living in the Stone Age: Reflections on the Origins of a Colonial Fantasy* (2018). She has published essays and articles on kinship, Christian conversion, nationalism, sovereignty, missionary language ideology, Franz Kafka's "In the Penal Colony", affect, money, technology, climate change, and the empirical nature of anthropological work. In 2016, she received a National Science Foundation Scholar's Award to begin a new project on belief and communication in the social worlds of adolescents with severe and profound intellectual disabilities.

Jean Gelman Taylor is Honorary Associate Professor of History, University of New South Wales. She earned a PhD from the University of Wisconsin-Madison. Her research focuses on Southeast Asian history, including Indonesian social histories, modernity, Islamic identity, and the role of women. She is the author of several ground-breaking studies on Indonesia, including *The Social World of Batavia: Europeans and Eurasians in Colonial Indonesia* (1983), *Indonesia: Peoples and Histories* (2003), and *Global Indonesia* (2013). A prolific writer on Kartini, she has also published on the historiography of Indonesia, colonial film and photography and women's history, among other subjects.

1

Introduction

Paul Bijl and Grace V.S. Chin

This volume offers the first book-length study of the circulation and appropriation of Raden Ajeng Kartini (1879–1904, henceforth Kartini), a young Javanese woman whose influential writings emerged during the colonial Dutch East Indies, and who is now recognized as an iconic feminist and nationalist figure in Indonesia and, after Anne Frank, the most well-known Dutch-language author in the world. Spanning across the twentieth and early twenty-first centuries in both Asian and Western contexts, this volume maps and interprets how varying state, social and cultural actors and institutions have appropriated her thoughts to articulate their views on the position of women, race, class, civil rights, nationalism and other subjects in (post)colonial and global Indonesia, Europe and North America.

The world has known Kartini since the publication of a selection of her famous letters in 1911 titled *Door duisternis tot licht* (Through darkness into light) (Kartini 1911). Before that, she was mainly known in Dutch colonial circles, as can be glimpsed from almost one hundred newspaper articles during her lifetime and in response to her death in 1904.[1] Since 1911, she has been translated into numerous languages, including Arabic, Sundanese, Javanese, Japanese, Russian and French, but most influentially into English as *Letters of a Javanese Princess* in 1920

(Kartini 1920) and into Indonesian as *Habis gelap terbitlah terang* (When darkness ends, light appears) for the first time in 1922 (Kartini 1922, 1938). Between 1911 and Indonesian independence in 1945, Indonesian and Dutch newspapers devoted thousands of articles to her and to the "Kartini schools" named after her. Since then, hundreds of books, theses and scholarly articles analysing her life and letters have been produced (Delpher). In the 1960s, she was taken up by the UNESCO Collection of Representative Works, with a foreword for the English edition by Eleanor Roosevelt and by Orientalist Louis Massignon for the French edition (Kartini 1960, 1964; see also Bijl in this volume, Chapter 3). In Indonesia, President Sukarno established Kartini's birthdate, 21 April, as Kartini Day (*Hari Kartini*) in 1946 and made her a national hero in 1964, while under the New Order of President Suharto, Kartini Day was transformed into an annual event that is still celebrated across the archipelago (Sears 1996; Rutherford's Chapter 5 in this volume; Robinson's Chapter 6 in this volume).

Kartini is the most well-known figure in Indonesian history: all school children in Indonesia encounter her at a young age on Kartini Day and every cab driver in Indonesia's capital, Jakarta, can sing the "Kartini song" entitled *Ibu kita Kartini* (Our mother Kartini). The internet and social media are full of creative remediations of Kartini's texts and imagery, including the admonishing meme of *Pergi gelap pulang terang* (Going out in darkness, coming home at dawn), which shows the supposed decline in the morals of Indonesian women doing all-nighters. Women's groups and feminist movements have broadly embraced her, including Poetri Mardika in the 1910s, the communist women of Gerwani in the 1950s with their journal *Api Kartini* (Kartini's flame), and the current transnational gender research network "Kartini Asia" (Blackburn 2004; Martyn 2005; Robinson 2009; Wieringa 2002; Chin's Chapter 4 in this volume). Several films have been made about her life, including the New Order movie *R.A. Kartini* (1983) and, more recently, *Surat cinta untuk Kartini* (Love letters for Kartini, 2016), and *Kartini* (2017). In Indonesian literature, she inspired biographies, including Pramoedya Ananta Toer's *Panggil aku Kartini sadja* (Just call me Kartini, 1962) and Sitisoemandari Soeroto's *Kartini: Sebuah biografi* (Kartini: A biography, 1977; see also Rutherford 1993, reprinted in this volume, Chapter 5) and is a role model for one of the main characters in Y.B. Mangunwijaya's *Burung-burung manyar* (The weaverbirds, 1981). Kartini has even been picked up by Indonesian advertising companies to both attract female customers and celebrate nationalist culture. The 2015 billboard "Come Celebrate Kartini Day with Mitsubishi", for instance, not only displayed a portrait of Kartini but also the Indonesian flag to suggest that buying a Mitsubishi on the birthday of a national hero also meant contributing to the nation. In the Netherlands, the memory of Kartini remains fairly strong in particular corners, evinced by the annual Kartini prize, awarded to those working for the emancipation of migrants and women in the city of The Hague, and the Kartini Wing of the Museum of the Tropics in Amsterdam, which opened in 2004 (Bijl 2015, reprinted in this volume, Chapter 7).

Looking at the history of Kartini as an appropriated figure, we are struck by the rich diversity of appropriative acts as well as by the significance of the roles played by actors and institutions in producing and claiming their "versions" of Kartini. Not only were they involved in the reconstruction of Kartini as a historical figure in cultural memory but they also engaged in contestations and debates that involved the polemics of—broadly speaking—modernity and tradition, religion (particularly Islam) and secularism, colonialism and anti-colonialism, writing and fighting, feminism and sexism, elitism and popularism, Java-centrism and regionalisation, national and regional history, racism and multiculturalism. This list is by no means exhaustive, but it does provide us an insight into the apparent ease with which Kartini has been troped in the past century, and how her life and ideas have lent themselves to multiple, differing interpretations, contestations, and appropriations. It is this very multiplicity or plurality of Kartini as a "floating signifier" (Robinson's Chapter 6 in this volume) that has given rise to this volume, which seeks to show how her symbolism has been used by varying actors and institutions across the twentieth and twenty-first century colonial and postcolonial world.

Despite the multiplicity of Kartini as a cultural, national and feminist discourse, research on her rich afterlife remains lacking, nor has there been an attempt to place her on a transnational scale. As a historical figure, Kartini has been thoroughly examined by one of our authors here, Joost Coté, who has published translations of her letters, notably *Letters from Kartini: An Indonesian Feminist, 1900–1904* (Kartini 1992), *On Feminism and Nationalism: Kartini's Letters to Stella Zeehandelaar 1899–1903* (Kartini 2005), and *Kartini: The Complete Writings, 1898–1904* (Kartini 2014) as well as the letters of Kartini's sisters, *Realizing the Dream of R.A. Kartini: Her Sisters' Letters from Colonial Java* (Coté 2008). Apart from translations, studies on Kartini—both local and international—also focus on her historical or colonial context (Hawkins 2007; Taylor 1976, 1989, 1993, 2010; Watson 2000) and her advocacy of rights and justice especially in relation to women's equality, marriage and education (Blackburn 2004; Muttaqin 2015). Other studies examine the relevance of Kartini as a national figure (Mahy 2012; Rutherford 1993, reprinted in this volume, Chapter 5) as well as her silences (Bijl 2015, reprinted in this volume, Chapter 7; Woodward 2015). However, the majority of essays or books mention Kartini only in relation to their research into other areas of Indonesian life; this particular trend manifests strongly in studies on Indonesian women or on gender and sexuality in Indonesia, and includes Wieringa's *Sexual Politics in Indonesia* (2002), Siapno's *Gender, Islam, Nationalism and the State in Aceh* (2002), Martyn's *The Women's Movement in Postcolonial Indonesia: Gender and Nation in a New Democracy* (2005), Robinson's *Gender, Islam and Democracy in Indonesia* (2009), and Nurmila's *Women, Islam and Everyday Life: Renegotiating Polygamy in Indonesia* (2009), among others. As a result, actual studies on Kartini alone are, in fact, limited. Our volume aims to fill these gaps in the research field and to offer, for the first time, a focused volume of essays on Kartini.

Mapping more than a century's worth of appropriative acts of Kartini's life and writings, this volume explores their influence across varying temporal, spatial, and linguistic contexts, from Dutch colonial imaginaries, postcolonial Indonesian nationalism and the cultural policies of UNESCO in the 1960s to twenty-first century European multiculturalism and contemporary Indonesian labour relations. Significantly, this volume interrogates the discursive underpinnings of the multiple appropriations of Kartini by exploring the ways in which the ideologies and practices of power, both formal and informal, shape how she is remembered by Indonesia and the world. The memory of Kartini has been strategically deployed to cement as well as to undermine existing power structures. Furthermore, appropriations of Kartini tap into underlying political, social, and cultural investments and agendas which can be viewed as responses to the needs or anxieties of those constructing her. Thus, the study of these varying appropriations will provide necessary insights into the complexities of remembrance and representation as well as the intersectional dynamics of gender, race, class, sexuality, religion and (trans)nationality that enter the discursive constructions of Kartini as an icon, a point that is instructive in the study of (post)colonial Southeast Asia, national and cultural memory as well as world literature.

Kartini's Life and Writings

The daughter of Raden Mas Adipati Ario Samingun Sosroningrat, the Regent (*bupati*) of Jepara, and Ngasirah, Sosroningrat's secondary wife,[2] Kartini was born on 21 April 1879 into the *priyayi* or native ruling administrative class in Java. As the fifth child and second oldest daughter among eleven children, Kartini owed her early exposure to Dutch education to her father, a relatively progressive man of his time. Sosroningrat received Dutch education while growing up, and was one of the few regents fluent in Dutch at the turn of the century. Like his own father, he decided that his five sons should receive European education but took it one step further when he allowed his six daughters, among them Kartini, to attend the local free primary school reserved for Dutch and Eurasian children. It was in this manner that Kartini learned how to speak and write fluently in Dutch.

After six years of schooling, Kartini was taken out of school by her family. Having reached puberty, she was expected to, in her words, "enter the 'box'" (Kartini 2014, p. 70), a practice also known as *pingitan* (seclusion). In her letters to Stella Zeehandelaar, her Dutch pen pal, Kartini railed against *pingitan*, revealing how *priyayi* girls were taught to conform to their place in the private domestic realm, and subjected to corporeal forms of training that encouraged bodily and vocal restraint, comportment and etiquette[3] while speech took place in high Javanese. These historically entrenched ritual customs rigidly observed the strict hierarchies, boundaries and privileges accorded to age, gender and rank within the family and wider *priyayi* community. Arranged marriage and polygamy—two feudal practices criticized by Kartini—were a prescribed way of life according to *adat* (customary law), and cloistered *priyayi* daughters, titled Raden Ajeng, had one sole purpose in life, that is to become, as Kartini lamented, a Raden Ayu. Although Kartini was taught by *adat* to prepare for married life as a wife and mother, she resisted and begged instead for her father to allow her to continue her education. But she was refused; it was too big a break from tradition. Moreover, what initially seemed like support from the side of the Dutch also fell apart in the end. For four years, Kartini stayed within the confines of her home while her brothers continued with their education in high school at Semarang. Her letters revealed this period to be a difficult one, marked by frustration, anger and resistance as well as a passionate yearning for freedom and autonomy. When her period of seclusion ended,

Kartini and her sisters were allowed to attend celebrations held outside her home; however, this uncharacteristic breach with gender traditions drew criticism from within the *priyayi* circles.

It was also during this time when Kartini met several important Dutch figures, notably the Abendanons, Jacques—the Dutch colonial equivalent to a Minister of Education—and his wife, Rosa Abendanon-Mandri, Marie Ovink-Soer, the wife of Jepara's Assistant Resident from 1891 to 1899, as well as Nellie van Kol, the wife of Henri van Kol, a parliamentarian and leader of the Social Democratic Workers' Party. These encounters proved fruitful to Kartini whose own feminist thoughts and articulations of ambition and independence found sympathy and encouragement in these colonial friendships. In 1899, Kartini met another like-minded spirit in Stella Zeehandelaar, a young Dutch progressive woman who replied to Kartini's request for a pen pal in a Dutch feminist magazine.

Through Kartini's correspondences with her Dutch friends, we have been offered rare insights not only into the restricted, private world of *priyayi* women but also the ongoing class- and race-related politics of colonial society. The *priyayi* occupied an ambivalent position as the subordinate allies of the Dutch (Pemberton 1994; Sutherland 1979) and as upper-class rulers among the native Javanese. Kartini's letters thus reveal how she straddled the two worlds of European modernity and colonial Javanese society, a hybrid space that helped shape her unique voice and perspective on her identity and position as a woman of colour in the Dutch Indies (Hawkins 2007): on the one hand, she boldly appropriated European feminist ideas in her fight for women's rights to education and freedom but on the other hand, she also criticized its feminist orientalism by exposing the plight of "brown women" who were doubly colonized by both Dutch and Javanese patriarchal, sociopolitical institutions (Bijl 2017). Kartini's embrace of European ideals of emancipation while rejecting its racist discourse, as well as her later "rediscovery" of Java, sometimes read in terms of (Javanese) nationalism (Coté 2014), should be seen as radical and transformative, for they have opened up discursive spaces for the contestations and appropriative acts by many, a phenomenon that is still ongoing.

Rich and multifaceted, Kartini's invaluable legacy of writings reveals a keen mind at work and an intuitive grasp on how to wield the pen to her advantage. She produced writings in different genres such as personal letters, short stories, ethnographic writing and educative memoranda, and was influenced by a variety of styles and genres that she encountered in her broad range of readings which included newspapers and journals, socialist, feminist and pacifist novels, feminist polemics, Orientalist writings, Dutch colonial scholarship as well as modern and religious poetry. Furthermore, she addressed her writings to a variety of readers and addressees, including friends of her own age, much older mentor figures, people working in colonial government or engaged in politics and scholarship (ethnography, linguistics, politics) as well as activists for women's rights, socialist causes and temperance movements. Indeed, the richness of Kartini's writings can best be approached by remembering the etymology of the word "text", which is derived from the Latin *texere*, or weaving. A brilliant author, Kartini wove together strands from countless discourses, genres, styles and social spheres, including such seemingly diverse practices as Islam, law and literature. She also changed and developed her perspectives in many ways, perhaps most famously in her gradual yet incomplete turn from European modernity as she increasingly looked towards Java. This coming together of differing viewpoints, discourses, genres, styles and addressees was, although unstable and contradictory, also productive, generating new ideas, viewpoints, and tropes that helped enrich the field of debates and contestations surrounding Kartini.

At the same time, however, her legacy has also been complicated by censorship, selective editing, and inaccurate translations in the past. The 1911 Dutch edition was, for instance, heavily edited with the excision of many details from her family life, while *Letters of a Javanese Princess* excluded dozens of letters from the 1911 edition and was even criticized for the quality of its translation. As a result, scholars working on Kartini's writings had to rely on incomplete data for several decades. As Taylor points out, the fact that Kartini was "raised in a polygamous household ... was not known to western scholars until the 1960s" (1993, p. 159). Scholarly efforts to reclaim Kartini's "lost" letters began in 1987, when a large portion of her letters emerged into public space (Kartini 1987); this was followed by the publication of updated translations (Kartini 1992, 2005). In 2014, Kartini's collection of complete writings, painstakingly curated and translated by Joost Coté, was published. With these new additions to the scholarship on Kartini, both readers and scholars have also had the opportunity to reassess her life in light of the new revelations that have emerged, including her confession to Rosa Abendanon-Mandri about her birth mother, Ngasirah, as well as her emotional distress at the news of her marriage.

At the end of the day, Kartini's writings can only carry us so far in the analysis of her rich afterlife. We also have to consider the significant role played by the actors and institutions involved in the construction and reproduction of Kartini as a discourse, and its attendant representations and meanings. Most actors, including scholars, pulled out specific threads from her texts and recombined them with their own concerns and needs as well as with the discourses that had shaped them. They looked to what others before them had made of her and borrowed, adapted, or rejected earlier representations; in so doing, they also made Kartini a point of social encounter and a site to battle out points of contestation that went well beyond the confines of her own writings. As the section below shows, acts of appropriation—and the ensuing contestations and debates—do take on a life of their own, feeding on and responding to each other even as they shape and reshape Kartini's legacy and memory.

Contestations and Debates

Mentioning the name "Kartini" often evokes strong emotions. During informal conversations for this volume in Indonesia and the Netherlands, we have had many encounters in which Kartini was both vilified and lovingly embraced. A few examples will show how she is a highly contested figure. An Acehnese soccer team with members in their late teens who were visiting Jakarta in 2015 strongly rejected the project on Kartini which eventually resulted in the current edited volume. Why not investigate Cut Nyak Dhien or Cut Meutia, two Acehnese women who had become Indonesian national heroes in the same year as Kartini (see also Siapno 2002)? More surprisingly, several Indonesian feminists we spoke to over the years also rejected Kartini as soon as we mentioned her. It turned out they were critical of the Kartini who had been shaped by patriarchal state discourses, particularly Suharto's New Order regime; however, they embraced what they saw as the historical, feminist Kartini who stood up for women's rights. On numerous occasions, Kartini's status was questioned by many Indonesian women who had set her up in competition with other historical female figures. What about other women like Dewi Sartika (1884–1947), also a pioneer for education, but who is felt to have undeservedly stood in Kartini's shadow? What about Marsinah (1969–1993), a labour activist and not an elite *priyayi* like Kartini? What about, again, Cut Nyak Dhien (1848–1908) who took up arms against the Dutch instead of sitting behind a desk writing letters? In the Netherlands, Kartini has had a long history as an object of "ethical" care and as a hero for Indonesian women (Vreede-de Stuers 1960), but some Dutch scholars of Indonesia, though acknowledging her importance as a historical figure, had nevertheless whispered in our ears that she was basically a "colonial suck-up". This sentiment was echoed by one of the authors who declined to write for our volume as she felt Kartini sounded like "a Dutch bureaucrat". In the Netherlands, response to Kartini in general can be divided into two categories: 1) people who know little to nothing about Kartini are surprised and interested to hear about a Dutch-language author who is common knowledge to all Indonesians and published by UNESCO, but who nevertheless has almost been forgotten in the Netherlands, and 2) Indonesianists who feel that the subject of Kartini has been endlessly published on and does not need further exploration. Indeed, if there is one figure in Indonesian history who is over-exposed, over-mediated and over-analysed, it would be Kartini. Nevertheless, the range as well as the highly contradictory and contested ways in which she is remembered are what make her a thoroughly unique figure through which the central tensions in colonial and postcolonial Indonesia and Europe can be read and understood.

This volume comes at a timely moment in Indonesia where, as Mary Zurbuchen writes, the fall of the Suharto regime in 1998 has brought with it the decline of its "military-backed monopoly over the production and interpretation of the nation's history" and new possibilities for "[d]ivergent perspectives, controversial events, and critical voices [that] were not allowed to compete alongside the official record" (2005, pp. 4–5). According to Yatun Sastramidjaja, "[i]n Indonesian official history the colonial past has long been stifled as a humiliating episode which had to be un-remembered from the landscape of national memory" (2014, p. 446). However, "the omitting of historical facts [also] creates an opening" (Sastramidjaja 2014, p. 446) for alternative memories to arise. Since 1998, there has been an explosion of appropriative acts, both critical and playful, when it comes to Kartini's symbolism and representation; such acts have been fuelled by the internet and social media, and can be seen interacting with an older albeit strong image of Kartini that had been shaped by Suharto's New Order government. As a result, Kartini has emerged as a flash point in the last two decades, one that reflects how Indonesians are taking issue with, in particular, New Order ideas on the role of the state, gender identities and relations, relations between different regions, and many more issues. A case in point is the cultural

centre *Rumah Kartini* in Jepara, formed by a group of scholars and artists
as a contrast to the state-established R.A. Kartini Museum (based on the
unreconstructed New Order narrative), which seeks to open up Kartini's
image through art works, meticulous reproductions of artisan objects
from Kartini's time (such as a gong and specific batik cloths) as well
as guided tours to the many historical sites from Kartini's life in and
around the town. A crucial part of the group's endeavours is to build
an elaborate research library replete with primary source materials and
scholarly studies on Kartini and other aspects of Jepara's history that
have been either skipped over or selectively interpreted by official history.

The Chapters

The chapters in this volume are multidisciplinary in their approach to
the appropriations of Kartini, with experienced historians of Indonesian
and European (post)colonial history, cultural anthropologists as well
as scholars of literary, gender and memory studies who offer unique
insights and analyses that attest to the multifacetedness of Kartini as a
discourse. Of the eight chapters here, six provide new analyses while
two are reprints of older publications. We have decided to include the
latter here as their perspectives help develop the scope of our study
and enrich the debates contained within this volume. We have also
broadly arranged the chapters along the colonial-postcolonial trajectory
in order to provide a better sense of not just the different kinds of
appropriations that take place within specific temporal settings, but
also how, very often, these different settings speak to and engage with
each other in the discursive revisions and reproductions of Kartini's
legacy and memory.

    We begin after this Introduction with Joost Coté's "Crafting Reform:
Kartini and the Imperial Imagination, 1898–1911" in Chapter 2,
which investigates colonial reforms and attitudes towards the Native
("*Inlandsche*") arts and crafts from 1898 to 1904, and how Kartini was
appropriated by progressive elements of contemporary metropolitan
and colonial Dutch society who wished to showcase her as the face
of "Native arts and crafts" for a Dutch readership. Documenting
Kartini's place in the interconnection between the turn-of-the-
twentieth century Dutch arts and crafts (*Nieuwe Kunst*) movement,
with its discourses on *nijverheid* (industry) and *kunstnijverheid* (arts
and crafts), and the contemporary agenda for colonial reform as

well as the activities of the Dutch feminist movement, this chapter argues that this moment in colonial history has relevance for our understanding of how Kartini "had straddled two primary themes in this early articulation of a new imperial discourse: an emerging curiosity about the Native other, and the need to give expression to a new sense of Dutch nationalism" (p. 38).

Chapter 3, Paul Bijl's "Hierarchies of Humanity: Kartini in America and at UNESCO", offers a different perspective on colonial discourse by analysing critical Western appropriations of Kartini in the ideological articulation of modern "human equality and human inequality" (pp. 57, 69), with examples drawn from key publications of Kartini's letters in America and Europe, including her selected letters in *Atlantic Monthly*—an influential American journal—in 1919 and 1920, the 1920 publication of Symmers' translation titled *Letters of a Javanese Princess* by Alfred A. Knopf, the American publishing house, and the inclusion of her letters in French (1960) and in English (1964) in the UNESCO Collection of Representative Works. Examining the paradoxes and contradictions presented by the people involved in the (re)publications, ranging from translators (Symmers) to publishers (*Atlantic Monthly*, Alfred A. Knopf) and writers who wrote the Introduction (Couperus) or Preface (Massignon, Roosevelt), Bijl argues that their liberal views and attitudes towards peoples of colour are invariably undermined by prevailing concepts of race and cultural hierarchies that are reflective of human inequality.

The next few chapters situate the study of how Kartini has been appropriated in Indonesia by exploring colonial and postcolonial contexts, often by straddling the two. In Chapter 4, Grace V.S. Chin's "Ambivalent Narration: Kartini's Silence and the Other Woman" critiques Kartini's silence about lower-class women—represented by the *selir* (secondary wife) and peasant women during the colonial era—and how it reflects a class entitlement that is seldom touched on in Indonesian feminist scholarship. Chin argues that Kartini's silence about the Other woman reveals class-related complicity and conformity that can be traced into the postcolonial patriarchal contexts of the Old Order and New Order, during which the elite women continued to be empowered while subaltern femininities, such as the unskilled female labourers, remained silenced and disenfranchised. Calling this Kartini's "ambivalent legacy of progress and subjection" (p. 76), Chin analyses the twists and turns it has taken in both colonial and postcolonial discourses, and how it is reflected in Indonesian women's politics through the hierarchical relationships and divisions among women.

We then move to Danilyn Rutherford's "Unpacking a National Heroine: Two Kartinis and Their People" in Chapter 5. First published in 1993, Rutherford's analysis of Kartini—referred to multiple times in the volume by different authors—still bears much relevance for our understanding of the historical ways in which Kartini has been appropriated and revised to fit the state narrative of its time. Referring to two Indonesian biographies on Kartini, namely Pramoedya Ananta Toer's *Panggil aku Kartini sadja* (1962) and Sitisoemandari Soeroto's *Kartini: Sebuah biografi* (1977), Rutherford reflects on how Kartini was used to legitimize the state ideologies and national narratives of the time: whereas Pramoedya locates Kartini and her people in a history of struggle of post-independence Old Order Indonesia, Soeroto places her within the "naturalized categories and boundaries" (p. 105) of the New Order state, thereby revealing the ideological difference between Old Order and New Order Kartini. In so doing, Rutherford also shows how both biographers attempted to construct their version of the "real Kartini behind the myth" (p. 106) for the Indonesian public.

Chapter 6 presents Kathryn Robinson's "Call me Kartini? Kartini as a Floating Signifier in Indonesian History", which explores Kartini's multifaceted symbolism as a "floating signifier" in Indonesian history, with particular focus on *Hari Kartini* in the post-New Order era through the social media movement known as "Kartini *jaman now*". Drawing on a range of representations of Kartini as a symbolic icon, Robinson provides fresh insights into the appropriations and restatements of Kartini's ideas in a varied range of mediums, including newspaper accounts, academic and artistic works, social media sources as well as interviews with feminists and university students. The rich variety of appropriations, celebrations and even repudiations of Kartini by different generations of Indonesians, including contemporary youth, reflect how "Kartini" as a floating signifier absorbs these fluctuating and often competing meanings.

The following Chapter 7, Paul Bijl's "Kartini and the Politics of European Multiculturalism", moves back to the Western world by showing how the transnational Kartini connections that had been developed during Dutch imperialism still "echo" in postcolonial Netherlands. The second republished article in our volume, this chapter examines colonial and postcolonial silences related to Kartini's memory in the Netherlands, notably within the context of European discourses on multiculturalism. Bijl investigates the ways in which Kartini—the representation of a colonized voice—is rarely heard of in the Netherlands. Calling for a different way of looking at Kartini, Bijl points out that Kartini has (unexpectedly) popped-up in particular spaces such as the Amsterdam Museum of the Tropics, and whose name has been invoked to promote multiculturalism, notably seen in the establishment of the Kartini prize in The Hague in 2000, also known as "foreign women prize" (p. 165) since it focuses on Dutch migrant women of different colour. Providing an analysis of the discourses surrounding the Kartini prize, Bijl unpacks the complex race, cultural and (post)colonial politics that have been perpetuated in Kartini's name, and how these discourses continue to be reflected in contemporary struggles faced by Dutch women of colour.

We wrap up the volume with the Afterword—a fitting finale to our volume—from Jean Gelman Taylor, which reflects on the volume and its place in Indonesian historiography and Western/European (post) colonial discourse. In illuminating the finer points of each chapter and how they are linked to a broader history, Taylor observes that the act of appropriation is in fact deeply psychological; it is "about us, whether we are Europeans or Indonesians. It is a fascination with ourselves" (p. 184). She also reminds us that appropriation works to detach "individuals from their family, society and times" (p. 184) and that behind Kartini the icon lies a real person with a rich emotional life composed of relationships and correspondences that have continued to develop long after her death. Taylor asks us, as scholars and historians, to go beyond the textual Kartini and contemplate the contextual factors that had shaped her as a pioneer, as well as the women—such as her maternal grandmother, a *Hajjah*, and other historical women like Aceh's Cut Nyak Dhien and sultanahs—who continue to represent the subaltern, silenced voice in history. All in all, Taylor's Afterword is a timely reminder that there is much more work to be done in order for us to have a fuller understanding of how Kartini has played a vital role in the shaping of modern Indonesia and Indonesian women.

NOTES

1. We base this number on the Dutch digital text database called Delpher: www.delpher.nl (Delpher).
2. Chronologically-speaking, Ngasirah was Sosroningrat's first wife but was considered a "secondary" wife due to her non-*priyayi* status. See Chin's

Chapter 4 and Taylor's Afterword for more information on women's positions during Kartini's time.
3. For details, see Kartini's letter to Stella Zeehandelaar dated 18 August 1899 (Kartini 2014, pp. 75–78).

REFERENCES

Bijl, Paul. 2015. "Colonial and Postcolonial Silence: Listening to Kartini in the Netherlands". In *Beyond Memory: Silence and the Aesthetics of Remembrance*, edited by Alexandre Dessingué and Jay M. Winter. London: Routledge. Reprinted in this volume as Chapter 7: "Kartini and the Politics of European Multiculturalism".

———. 2017. "Legal Self-fashioning in Colonial Indonesia: Human Rights in the Letters of Kartini". *Indonesia* 103: 51–71.

Blackburn, Susan. 2004. *Women and the State in Modern Indonesia*. Cambridge: Cambridge University Press.

Coté, Joost, ed. and trans. 2008. *Realizing the Dream of R.A. Kartini: Her Sisters' Letters from Colonial Java*. Ohio: Ohio University Press; Leiden: KITLV Press.

———. 2014. "Reading Kartini: A Historical Introduction". In *Kartini: The Complete Writings, 1898–1904*, by Kartini. Edited and translated by Joost Coté. Clayton, Victoria: Monash University.

Delpher. Online text base. https://www.delpher.nl/ (accessed 1 April 2018).

Hawkins, Michael. 2007. "Exploring Colonial Boundaries: An Examination of the Kartini-Zeehandelaar Correspondence". *Asia-Pacific Social Science Review* 7, no. 1: 1–14.

Kartini, R.A. 1911. *Door duisternis tot licht: Gedachten over en voor het Javaansche volk*. Edited by J.H. Abendanon. Semarang: Van Dorp.

———. 1920. *Letters of a Javanese Princess*. Translated by Agnes Louise Symmers. New York: Knopf.

———. 1922. *Habis gelap terbitlah terang: Boeah pikiran*. Weltevreden: Balai-Poestaka.

———. 1938. *Habis gelap terbitlah terang*. Translated by Armijn Pane. Jakarta: Balai Pustaka.

———. 1960. *Lettres de Raden Adjeng Kartini: Java en 1900*. Edited and translated by Louis Charles Damais. Paris: Mouton.

———. 1964. *Letters of a Javanese Princess*. Translated by Agnes Louise Symmers. New York: W.W. Norton.

———. 1987. *Brieven aan mevrouw R.M. Adendanon-Mandri en haar echtgenoot*. Edited by F.G.P. Jaquet. Dordrecht: Foris.

———. 1992. *Letters from Kartini: An Indonesian Feminist, 1900–1904*. Edited and translated by Joost Coté. Clayton, Victoria: Monash Asia Institute, Monash University.

———. 2005. *On Feminism and Nationalism: Kartini's Letters to Stella Zeehandelaar, 1899–1903*. Edited and translated by Joost Coté. 2nd ed. Clayton, Victoria: Monash Asia Institute, Monash University.

———. 2014. *Kartini: The Complete Writings, 1898–1904*. Edited and translated by Joost Coté. Clayton, Victoria: Monash University.

Mahy, Petra. 2012. "Being Kartini: Ceremony and Print Media in the Commemoration of Indonesia's First Feminist". *Intersections: Gender and Sexuality in Asia and the Pacific* 28. http://intersections.anu.edu.au/issue28/mahy.htm (accessed 10 September 2017).

Martyn, Elizabeth. 2005. *The Women's Movement in Postcolonial Indonesia: Gender and Nation in a New Democracy*. London: RoutledgeCurzon.

Muttaqin, Farid. 2015. "Early Feminist Consciousness and Idea Among Muslim Women in 1920s Indonesia". *Jurnal Ilmiah Peuradeun/The International Journal of Social Sciences* 3, no. 1: 19–38.

Nurmila, Nina. 2009. *Women, Islam and Everyday Life: Renegotiating Polygamy in Indonesia*. London: Routledge.

Pemberton, John. 1994. *On the Subject of "Java"*. Ithaca, NY: Cornell University Press.

Robinson, Kathryn. 2009. *Gender, Islam and Democracy in Indonesia*. London: Routledge.

Rutherford, Danilyn. 1993. "Unpacking a National Heroine: Two Kartinis and Their People". *Indonesia* 56: 23–40. Reprinted in this volume as Chapter 5.

Sastramidjaja, Yatun. 2014. "'This is Not a Trivialization of the Past': Youthful Re-Mediations of Colonial Memory in Jakarta". *Bijdragen tot de taal-, land- en volkenkunde* 170: 443–72.

Sears, Laurie J., ed. 1996. *Fantasizing the Feminine in Indonesia*. Durham: Duke University Press.

Siapno, Jacqueline Aquino. 2002. *Gender, Islam, Nationalism and the State in Aceh: The Paradox of Power, Co-Optation and Resistance*. London: RoutledgeCurzon.

Sutherland, Heather. 1979. *The Making of a Bureaucratic Elite: The Colonial Transformation of the Javanese Priyayi*. Southeast Asia Publication Series 2. Singapore: Heinemann.

Taylor, Jean Gelman. 1976. "Raden Ajeng Kartini". *Signs: Journal of Women in Culture and Society* 1, no. 3: 639–61.

———. 1989. "Kartini in Her Historical Context". *Bijdragen tot de taal-, land- en volkenkunde* 145, no. 2–3: 295–307.

———. 1993. "Once More Kartini". In *Autonomous Histories, Particular Truths: Essays in Honor of John R.W. Smail*, edited by Laurie J. Sears. Madison, WI: University of Wisconsin; Center for Southeast Asian Studies.

———. 2010. "Een gedeelde mentale wereld: Multatuli en Kartini". In *De minotaurus onzer zeden: Multatuli als heraut van het feminisme*, edited by Myriam Everard and Ulla Jansz. Amsterdam: Aksant.

Vreede-de Stuers, Cora. 1960. *The Indonesian Woman: Struggles and Achievements*. The Hague: Mouton.

Watson, C.W. 2000. *Of Self and Nation: Autobiography and the Representation of Modern Indonesia*. Honolulu: University of Hawaii Press.

Wieringa, Saskia. 2002. *Sexual Politics in Indonesia*. Houndmills: Palgrave Macmillan; The Hague: Institute of Social Studies.

Woodward, Amber. 2015. "Historical Perspectives on a National Heroine: R.A. Kartini and the Politics of Memory". Independent Study Project (ISP) Collection (Fall). Paper 2189. https://digitalcollections.sit.edu/isp_collection/2189 (accessed 10 August 2016).

Zurbuchen, Mary S., ed. 2005. *Beginning to Remember: The Past in the Indonesian Present*. Singapore: Singapore University Press.

2

Crafting Reform: Kartini and the Imperial Imagination, 1898–1911

Joost Coté*

In the decade before the 1911 publication of a selection of her letters unleashed a century of Kartini image-making, there was a "real" Kartini. A few Dutch men and women maintained a correspondence with her; even fewer had met her in person. And even while this "historical Kartini" was writing long private letters projecting images of herself as a "modern girl", she was already being imagined by others in the colonial capital and abroad. Her name was beginning to circulate in contemporary media in the Netherlands and its East Indies colony to conjure up a new vision of an imperial mission.

In exploring the ways in which Kartini was variously imagined by Europeans in the few years of her adult public life, this chapter reads back from the extant correspondence and archival record to examine the discursive contexts that first framed the now century-old image of Kartini.

* I am grateful to the National Library of Australia for the award of a study grant that enabled me to examine their relevant Dutch archival holdings at length. This chapter was stimulated by the work of the members of Rumah Kartini, the enthusiastic Japara-based craft revival association dedicated to the memory of Kartini.

It focuses on elucidating the contemporary (in Kartini's lifetime) Dutch "cultural imaginary" in terms of the ways in which, it is here argued, an awareness of Kartini was being processed, as well as the ways in which Kartini attempted to present herself.

The notion of a "cultural imaginary", Dawson (1994) argues, is a useful way of giving recognition to the

> fluid imaginative connection between patterns of linked associations [that] can be traced across cultural representations both in textual form and as these have been institutionalised into the practical arrangements that govern activities and social relations within the social world. (Dawson 1994, p. 50)[1]

In brief, the concept alerts us to the importance of taking account of the variety of intertwined influences and cultural institutions that need to be adduced in constructing historical explanations. Here, it suggests that any attempt to unravel the contemporary Dutch reception of "the idea of Kartini" needs to be located in recognition of the complex set of interrelated politico-cultural perceptions, practices and policies present at a particular moment in Dutch cultural, political, social and imperial history. In this, the chapter argues, the contemporary "imagined Kartini" performed a highly pertinent function. Her "discovery" fed into a range of interrelated discourses and sensibilities that implicated new dimensions in the Netherlands' imperialist project. For their advocates, seeking political and popular support in both metropolitan and colonial circuits of influence, Kartini provided a useful emblem. At the same time, her "discovery" and its discursive value were dependent upon Kartini herself being consciously and actively engaged in this process.[2]

The aim of this chapter, then, is to investigate the interaction between the "historical Kartini" and this Kartini persona, as it initially emerged in the particular context of Native arts and crafts discourse between 1898 and 1904 (the years of her "public" life), until the posthumous publication of her correspondence in 1911. In keeping with the personal nature of the Kartini archive, this chapter proceeds by tracing the web of personal contacts and various discursive and policy orientations to which her correspondence alludes. After briefly sketching Kartini's personal association with the "Native arts and crafts" phenomenon, the chapter follows these networks outwards to identify, firstly, their relevant colonial references, before following these to their metropolitan Netherlands connections. It demonstrates how, in the few years of Kartini's public adult life (between 1898 and 1904), Kartini provided an ideal symbol in the early articulations of a "new imperialism" (Locher-Scholten 2012; Touwen 2013) that heralded what has been generally alluded to as the era of "ethical policy". At the same time, this "imagined Kartini" was reflective of a new aesthetic and political culture in the Netherlands in which, as V. Kuitenbrouwer (2011) has argued, "empire" was centrally implicated. In this new era of colonial governance, Kartini came to epitomise "the Native" who would become the recipient of imperial beneficence.

Kartini and Dutch Discursive Agendas

It is possible to begin to reconstruct this contemporaneous Dutch utilization of an imagined Kartini by examining the evidence available in the extant Kartini correspondence. From this perspective, her writing can be seen to reflect several sets of specific discursive preoccupations that were emerging in the Netherlands and colonial Java at the time. Most clearly, as I have discussed in detail elsewhere (Coté 2014a), Kartini was referenced by, and herself referenced, an emerging reformist imperial discourse advocating "Native education". Here, perhaps most obviously, the image of Kartini was used by the colonial director of Native Education, Jacques Abendanon (1900–5), in the pursuit of his progressive agenda for expanding Javanese access to Dutch language education (see further below). This indeed later motivated his publication of Kartini's correspondence in 1911 (Coté 2014a; Miert 1991, pp. 61–66). Explicit also in Abendanon's policy initiatives, and clearly framing Kartini's correspondence, was the contemporary social and political impact of feminism (Grever and Waaldijk 2004, pp. 163–64; Miert 1991, pp. 66–67). In its colonial reference, this was largely reflected in a critique of the colonial moral order and a rationalization for the conquest of "backward" feudal states and the reform of "primitive" Native society (Coté 2004, 2009). From this perspective, a contemporary metropolitan Dutch reading of Kartini referenced her—as she did herself—in terms of being both a victim of feudal tradition and an object of imperial Dutch benevolence.

But the image of Kartini also participated in another, related, theme of "new imperialism" in which Abendanon, as director of Native

Industry, was also directly implicated. When Kartini participated in the high-profile Dutch feminist National Exhibition of Women's Work in The Hague in 1898—encouraged to do so by her colonial Dutch mentor, the amateur writer and feminist Marie Ovink-Soer—it was not education, or indeed the condition of Native women that attracted attention, but the impetus it provided for promoting a metropolitan Dutch interest in Native arts and crafts. In the correspondence that directly followed on from this event, it is evident that the matter of arts and crafts was of more direct interest than her classroom experiment with which, in the end, Kartini herself had little direct involvement (Coté 2014a). Within her own correspondence also, beyond the initial reference to a new fashionable colonial interest in decorative Native hand-crafted, European-styled furniture, a more important theme is also implicated: a discourse on Native arts and crafts. It is a theme that came to occupy an important place within what became known as the "ethical policy", and one in which, it is here argued, Kartini willingly positioned herself.

Two distinct inflections can be observed in its articulation, reflecting the ambiguities of the welfarist orientation of that policy. For some, it reflected an intrinsic artistic or "scientific" (ethnographic) interest in the culture of the Native, whose revival (as a result of ethical colonial policies) would represent a major contribution to the supposed cultural decline of the Javanese. For others, interest in Native arts and crafts focused on its economic contribution to Native welfare. It imagined the possibility of village craftwork constituting a "Native industry". These two strands were linked by a common assumption that the revival of Javanese society (whose unfortunate condition was admitted by some progressives as the result of previous colonial policies) was now dependent upon wise European intervention.

In this bi-focal colonial reformist agenda, the articulate, Dutch-speaking, socially well-positioned daughter of a highly respected (and apparently pro-Dutch) dynasty of Javanese regents provided—as she did for Abendanon's failed education initiative—a symbol as well as a practical avenue for implementing progressive intentions. Kartini's response to these approaches and expressions of interest, as documented in her extant correspondence, reveals her awareness of these interests and her attempt to exploit them in what can be represented as a nascent articulation of a Javanese cultural nationalism (Coté 2014e).

Kartini and Craftwork

Already mentioned in the first extant letters exchanged in 1899 with Stella Zeehandelaar soon after the Dutch Exhibition of Women's Work, references to Jepara woodcraft soon dominated the correspondence Kartini conducted with the Abendanon family, whom she first met in August 1900. As well as woodcraft, in response to their questions and requests, the correspondence refers to pearl, gold and silver craft, and ornamental deer heads and feathers while revealing Kartini's own interest in batik and gamelan music. Encouraged by the Abendanons, and responding to an increasing number of orders from the colonial elite in Batavia this connection facilitated, Kartini in 1901 was directly enrolled into the operations of the Netherlands-based *Vereeniging Oost en West* (East and West Association). Her role, shared by (and later—after her death—taken over by) her sister Roekmini, was to deliver craft products, initially directly to European consumers and later to the organization's Native craft exhibitions and shop. By 1902, Kartini was reportedly overwhelmed by orders; she was therefore much relieved when the *Vereeniging* took over the task of managing in-coming orders for her to then pass on to the Jepara woodworkers.

In responding to this role, Kartini saw herself not only as promoting European awareness of Javanese aspirations by exploiting their new interest in Javanese craft, but also as generating work opportunities for local Jepara craftsmen. Crucially, in response to requests from her European customers, she encouraged the craftsmen to adapt traditional designs and decorative features, and develop new skills to manufacture new products for this expanding European market. Obtaining design ideas from the European homes she visited, and from items she noticed in the houses of "*Inlanders*" (Natives) and from Chinese models, Kartini also invented new designs and decorations that would later place her in some dilemma. Inasmuch as she was congratulated for these innovations by her European customers, she was also criticized (by anonymous European and Javanese critics) for corrupting the traditional craft. In one notable account, she faced opposition from artisans who feared the consequences of reproducing *wayang* (puppet) figures as decorative features.

Possibly the most dramatic response by Kartini to this new European fascination with Native craftwork came in August 1903 when, in the midst of preparing for her impending marriage less than three months later, she outlined plans for a woodcraft factory in Rembang once she was installed there as Raden Ayu. Earlier that year she had contributed items for an exhibition held in Semarang which she hoped would lead to the establishment of a permanent outlet for Jepara craftwork. Now, counting on her future husband's cooperation, she outlined plans for a large craft workshop for which

> many workmen need to be employed and apprentices trained and made to work under regular supervision…. As long as money is there—it would need several thousands to build a workplace, to buy materials, to maintain workmen and to train apprentices. Singo [head artisan in Jepara] would be in charge of this. I believe that within a year, at most two, the capital that was invested would have been retrieved. (Letter, 25 August 1903; Kartini 2014, pp. 664–65)[3]

Kartini was too ill for much of 1904 to be able to carry out this plan, but there are—amongst the last surviving letters she wrote in 1904—several references to ongoing visits and enquiries from European arts and crafts aficionados.[4]

Native Arts and Crafts and the Implementation of an "Ethical" Colonial Policy

Colonial interest in and the subsequent promotion of Native arts and crafts represent a key theme in the discursive as well as practical engagement with Java's "declining welfare" in the progressive colonial agenda of the first years of the twentieth century. While in Europe the exhibition and museumization of arts and crafts from the East Indies had a long history, it was only at the end of the century that a broader interest in the practices and sociocultural conditions of its production became evident. In part, this coincided with and can be explained by the expansion of colonial authority both within Java and the wider archipelago since the latter decades of the nineteenth century, which facilitated and promoted ethnographic research and the collection of a greater quantity and range of cultural objects.

This is particularly evident when one traces the activities of the *Bataviaasch Genootschap van Kunsten en Wetenschappen* (Batavian Society of Arts and Sciences) in the last decade of the nineteenth century. Its annual *notulen* (minutes of meetings) in the course of the 1890s not only indicate the extraordinary inflow of "ethnographic objects"—and increasingly photographs—from the recently conquered states to its museum, but also an intensification of cultural research, particularly in relation to antiquities, in Java. While much of its efforts were focused on expert scholarship which, in particular, found expression in the establishment of the *Oudheidkundige Commissie* (Antiquities Commission) in 1901 to study and safeguard classical Hindu-era monuments, the drive to expand public display facilities to inform a colonial public also became more evident in the final years of the century. This colonial interest supported, as well as was stimulated by, the emergence of a parallel popular interest in "oriental arts" in the Netherlands.

The development of what might then be called an embryonic "colonial arts and crafts movement" is clearly evident in the Kartini correspondence in which each of its key proponents can be identified. All but one were regular visitors to the Jepara *kabupaten* (the official residence of a regent) and represented both the colonial administration and private enterprise; all were members of the *Bataviaasch Genootschap* as well as of the colonial branch of the *Vereeniging Oost en West*, the newly established organization devoted to the popularization of Native arts and crafts in the Netherlands. They were J.H. Abendanon, Director of Native Education, Religion and Industry, H.J.W. van Lawick van Pabst and J.E. Jasper (two officials Abendanon had appointed to assess possibilities for the Native crafts industries), and two businessmen, M.C. Brandes and Victor Zimmermann.

Van Lawick van Pabst, head government inspector of (rice and sugar) cultures as well as a founding member of the *Vereeniging* when it was formed in 1899 (*Voorloopige notulen* 1899), became the president of its Indies branch on his return to the colony. He had probably already been made aware of Kartini in the Netherlands by her brother, Sosrokartono. One of the earliest of a growing stream of young Indonesians sent to study in Holland, Kartono played an important role in advising the earliest Dutch associations in promoting greater popular involvement in the colonies (Coté 2008, p. 31; Poeze 1986, pp. 29–32). Returning to Java, Van Lawick van Pabst worked closely with Kartini in her role as the *Vereeniging*'s local "agent", assisting her to organize an efficient system for dealing with "supply and demand".[5]

Jasper, although not directly mentioned in Kartini's correspondence, appeared in the background as organizer and curator of the first Native arts and craft exhibitions in Batavia and Semarang to which Kartini had contributed items of Jepara woodcraft. Although a junior colonial official, a *controleur*, he had already come to be recognized as the colonial expert on Javanese arts and crafts. Indies born, and later to become Governor of

Yogyakarta, he had by 1902 already published several articles on Javanese crafts (pottery, metal work, gold, silver and bronze work), *"volkenkunde"* (ethnography and geography) and other cultural topics as well as some light fiction in the colonial media (Doorn 1998). While none of his articles appeared in the established "scientific" journals of the day (so that in this regard he remained an exponent of a nineteenth-century amateur ethnographer tradition), his more popular publications and his practical engagement in their promotion revealed that he played a key role in this early manifestation of the imperial concern for the survival of Javanese arts and crafts.[6] After Kartini's death, he worked closely with her sister, Roekmini, before her marriage in efforts to establish a craft centre in Surabaya (Coté 2008, pp. 122–24, 132)[7] and subsequently also with her brother Boesono, Regent of Ngawi, to develop a *"huisvlijt"* school, an indigenous institution for training Javanese craftsmen (Doorn 1998).

The two other regular visitors to the Jepara *kabupaten* cited by Kartini in her correspondence, Brandes and Zimmermann, also encouraged her to expand the work of the Jepara woodcraftsmen as an economic enterprise. The former was chief agent of the *Cultuur Maatschappij der Vorstenlanden* (Principalities Agricultural Company) who, as the brother of the archaeologist Dr J.L. Brandes, could be expected to have developed a deeper awareness of Javanese culture; the latter was a Batavia businessman, also a keen supporter of Kartini's work, who no doubt had an eye on its commercial viability. More importantly, both men were active members of the local branch of the *Vereeniging Oost en West*, and the *Batviaasch Genootschap*. As the *notulen* (minutes) of that institution reveal, both became increasingly prominent in their efforts to exhibit and disseminate information on the arts and crafts of the archipelago. Their attention to Jepara craft and interaction with Kartini were manifestations of this involvement.

As the colonial official charged with overseeing the development of "Native Industry", Jacques Abendanon occupied a key position in an emerging colonial arts and crafts movement. A long-time member and previous secretary of the *Bataviaasch Genootschap* before becoming director of Native Education, Religion and Industry, he was already— as the *Genootschap*'s minutes reveal—actively promoting a new policy for that institution to expand the public exhibition of its ethnographic collections. In 1903, Abendanon was responsible for launching Kartini in the metropolitan Netherlands as "the face" of Javanese woodcraft, by then an increasingly fashionable commodity within the elite circles of

Dutch society. In this he was undoubtedly encouraged by his wife, Rosa, through whom—it would appear from the correspondence—Kartini's role as craft agent for Batavia's social set had initially evolved. Abendanon encouraged Kartini to write an account of the Jepara craft workplace for publication in an influential metropolitan cultural journal, *Eigen Haard*.[8] Its dramatic impact was to provide interested Dutch readers with a virtual connection to Jepara artisans who were providing many of the craft products they were ordering. Accompanied by photographs of their work, this publication, and its accompanying introduction by the influential feminist Nellie van Kol together with the enthusiastic editorial comment, arguably launched Kartini's popular image in the Netherlands.[9] By then, as noted above, she had already become familiar to a more intimate metropolitan circle through her link with the *Vereeniging Oost en West*, as will be further elaborated later.

But Abendanon's most important and direct involvement in the development of a Native arts and crafts "industry" policy framework, apart from his earlier appointment of the two colonial officials to "survey the field", was his own inquiry the following year into the potential of *Inlandsche nijverheid* (Native industry). The report of that survey, to which his two "agents" contributed, was hurriedly undertaken at the request of then Minister of Colonies, A.W.F. Idenburg. It coincided with a ministerial inquiry being undertaken in the Netherlands on ways to implement the 1901 colonial "ethical policy", discussed later in this chapter. Abendanon's remit was to investigate "Measures that could be taken in the interests of [promoting] Native industry" (Abendanon 1904, p. 1). Subsequently dismissed by "colonial experts" in the Netherlands (Miert 1991, p. 77), the negative reception of Abendanon's report points to the significant divide in the "ethical" reform movement between the "idealists" and the "realists" within the emerging "Native arts and crafts" movement through which the image of Kartini was being constructed.

Abendanon's report, completed in record time, had attempted to balance a realistic assessment of the economic potential of Native crafts for improving the actual material condition of the Javanese population, with an appreciation of their aesthetic value. His conclusions contrasted starkly with the general opinion of local colonial officials at the time—largely shared in the Netherlands—whose views were reported in appended accounts of regional meetings held in the course of this inquiry. Most expressed the view that support for Native industries, let alone for greater indigenous involvement in European enterprises, would be fruitless. Reporting on one such meeting held in Semarang to consider the possibility of a "Native run" craft factory as envisaged by Kartini, Abendanon wrote:

> Many at the gathering were of the opinion that it would not be possible to appoint an *Inlander* to run what would possibly be a quite complex factory, or that it was likely that this could be the case for the foreseeable future. (Abendanon 1904, p. 153)

In his report, Abendanon openly criticized the colonial practice of encouraging large-scale European importation of imitation batik (rather than sourcing local productions) as well as lamented what he described as the oppressive and unfair dominance of Chinese entrepreneurs in this sector. He nominated eighteen existing economic activities that could be defined as Native craft industries, and advocated sixteen measures to foster economic activity, including the provision of vocational art and craft training facilities, and the establishment of exhibitions and markets.

The contributions of Van Lawick van Pabst and Jasper to Abendanon's report defined more clearly the fracture within Dutch circles interested in the promotion of Javanese arts and crafts. Van Lawick van Pabst's ten-page addendum to the report was contributed in his capacity as the official representative of the *Vereeniging Oost en West* and reflected the aims of that association. He argued that if Native arts and crafts were to contribute to the improvement of the Native economy, then craftsmen would have to cater to European tastes to ensure export potential to Europe and America. He also amplified Abendanon's recommendation for vocational training, advocating the need for technical schools—*ambachtsscholen*—to train Javanese in efficient work methods since "the *Inlander* works in such a sloppy and rough way" (Lawick van Pabst 1904, p. 267).

While Jasper's lengthy 32-page submission to the Abendanon inquiry also sought a practical outcome to rescue Javanese arts and crafts "which are at the point of as good as disappearing forever" (Jasper 1904, p. 348), it nonetheless reflected a more intimate appreciation of Native society than that evidenced by Van Lawick van Pabst. Like Abendanon, he saw as one of the major causes of impoverishment in Java the competition of cheap imported imitation batik, which he claimed discouraged skilled practitioners from producing fine detailed work. However, he questioned whether the provision of colonial technical institutions would be effective. Attempts to upgrade methods of production or introduce equipment to enable artisans to participate in a modern industrial economy would be "like attempting to bring a dead person to life" (p. 336). Instead, Jasper urged that, in order to make a realistic assessment of a craft's value to the domestic and European markets, a clear distinction had to be first made between Native crafts and Native arts (p. 338). With regard to the former, if these involved the production of "goods for daily use by other nationalities", these should be clearly distinguished from efforts to ensure that "original forms" preserved their "Native character" (p. 347).

The key issue for Jasper, which he stated in language reflective of the contemporary European arts and crafts movement, was that

> nothing should be allowed to affect what is actually the essence of the art, and if, through necessity, one is yet necessitated to [adopt a policy of modernizing the crafts industry] it should be forcefully insisted that the modern industry should always remain focused on the beauty of the art, produced by their ancestors, which must remain unchanged as the people's art [*volkskunst*]. (Jasper 1904, p. 342)

To ensure this, he proposed a system of craft museums in key centres where the respective crafts were still being undertaken. These would exhibit models of artistic excellence to be collected by specially appointed Native inspectors who would also need to approve any new articles or designs (p. 359).

A third contribution to Abendanon's report came from the *Nederlandsch-Indische Kunstkring* (Netherlands Indies Arts Society). Established in Batavia in 1902, with similar societies soon established in other cities, its aim was to raise the cultural standards of European settlers and strengthen their cultural ties with the motherland. The "Native art" (*Inlandsche kunst*) and "Native craft industries" (*Inlandsche kunst-industrieën*) had, however, also come to be "a particular focus of attention" (*Gedenkboek* 1927, p. 4). In its response to the Abendanon inquiry, the *Kunstkring* declared support for the principle enunciated by Jasper, that

> both the aesthetic and economic development must be shaped by the thought that the Native arts, even within its industrial application, must ensure that it remains true to itself; that the national traditions, still alive in many areas of the archipelago, must be maintained and elsewhere revived; that it was only then that it would be possible for Native arts and crafts industries to retain their place in the European market. (*Gedenkboek* 1927, p. 4)

These colonial respondents to the metropolitan-initiated inquiry regarding the economic relevance of Native arts and crafts were key representatives of an emerging discourse promulgated within colonial cultural elite circles. Distancing themselves from a nineteenth-century creole *Indisch* planter society, and representative of both administrative and civil society communities, their interest in the culture of "the other" formed part of a new sense of "being Dutch" (cf. Bosma and Raben 2008).[10] Increasingly influenced by sociocultural changes in, as well as migration from, Europe, this new consciousness brought with it a sense of separation from, but also a sense of responsibility for, the social and cultural forms of the Native subject. For these individuals, the articulate Kartini provided a doorway into a world they were now interested in exploring as well as a channel of communication via which she might be able to "educate" her Dutch contacts and also realize her own aspirations. These colonial developments were symptomatic of similar cultural and policy orientations emerging in the distant metropole. There too, the image of a Dutch-speaking Javanese woman was to provide a focus to justify, substantiate and promote new directions in colonial policymaking. What precisely these would be, of course, would become the subject of further political debate.

Native Arts and Crafts in the Netherlands

Towards the end of the nineteenth century, academic and artistic interest in oriental arts had emerged in Europe as part of a wider cultural phenomenon that challenged "the existing hierarchy of the arts" (Greenhalgh 2000, p. 20). In the Netherlands where this came to be known as the *Nieuwe Kunst* (New Arts), it overlapped with a growing public awareness of an expanding imperial presence in Asia. The recognition of Native arts and crafts from the colonies contributed to the energizing of the European arts and crafts movement in the metropole (Waaldijk and Legêne 2003). In particular, it participated in a renewed interest in the applied arts as both traditional European craft and new industrial occupation (Groot 2007) which, in turn, shaped colonial attitudes to Native arts and crafts.

Influential in this development was the first *Nieuwe Kunst* craft exhibition mounted in 1888. Echoing the aims of the English arts and crafts movement, it was pointedly titled *Kunst toegepast op Nijverheid* (Art applied to industry; Eliëns 1997, p. 13). Subsequently leading to the establishment of a training school and museum to develop and showcase traditional Dutch crafts, it stimulated new interest in the design and crafting of house furniture (Eliëns 1997). Amongst other activities, practitioners such as C.A.

Lion Cachet and J. Thorn Prikker experimented with batik. Drawn by its aesthetic and technical—rather than its ethnographic—characteristics, and using newly invented chemicals, they developed batik style materials for interior decoration and in other applications, such as for book binding. At the same time, Dutch and other European cloth manufacturers were developing batik-styled decorative cloth for both the internal European and colonial export market (Brommer 1989; Lintsen 1994).

A batik exhibition held in Brussels in 1898 and, more significantly, an exhibition of Dutch batik mounted by the Dutch arts and crafts group in The Hague in 1899 by Thorn Prikker, confirmed the popularity batik had gained not only within these circles but also within the commercial sector (Joosten 1972). Concurrently, "extensive [ethnological] collections from the colonies"—often the product of military conquest (Budiarti 2007; Ernawati 2007; Stevens 2007) that were sometimes "too much to handle" and which had previously been poorly curated (Keurs 2007, p. 4)—were now also beginning to be better managed and exhibited. They provided a resource for the sequence of colonial exhibits and international trade fairs that in turn promoted wider public interest. At the same time, there was a discernable improvement in the way knowledge of the colony was processed and presented within academic and colonial service training institutions (Buskens and Kommers 2007).

While the exhibits or scholarly articles did not translate into an empathetic or any "real" understanding of the colonial subject, what they did contribute to, Bloembergen argues, was a growing sense that "the Dutch East Indies [was] unquestionably Dutch, in the eyes of a far larger domestic public and in those of the visitors from abroad" (Bloembergen 2006, p. 105; Lith 1883; Mattie 1998, pp. 59–65).[11] They added to the impact of more regular international travel, better international communications, more frequent accounts of colonial life in popular media and a new genre of "realistic" colonial literature (Bell 1993) by giving focus to a new sense of national pride at the centre of a global empire. Arguably more effective than elite scholarly writing in stimulating public interest, the growing popularity of Native arts and crafts, despite (or because of) their trivialization of Indies cultures, enabled scholarly and popular interest to increasingly coincide with and reinforce each other in what Bloembergen suggests might be described as "popular anthropology" (2006, pp. 162–63). In this context, Kartini became one more element in assisting a "colonial vanguard to gain a better grip on the unknown world of the Dutch East Indies ... and to familiarise the Dutch general public with this world" (Bloembergen 2006, p. 38).

An interest in craftwork was also stimulated through activities of the women's movement in the Netherlands. The exhibition of women's needlecraft work by the *Arbeid Adelt* (Labour Ennobles) and *Tesselschade* committee of the *Algemeen Nederlandsche Vrouwenvereeniging* (United Dutch Women's Association) in 1883 (Grever and Waaldijk 2004, pp. 183–85) was one indicator of a wider interest in craftwork within a growing sense of nationalism within which the women's movement played an important role (Groot 2007). By the time it mounted the *Nationale Tentoonstelling van Vrouwenarbeid* (National Exhibition of Women's Work) in the Dutch capital in 1898, the women's movement was able to bring together "the[se] diverse traditions of colonial awareness under a new denominator" (Grever and Waaldijk 2004, p. 164). It was precisely the success of this exhibition in engaging with the sociocultural inflections of a new imperial consciousness that provided the fertile context for the emergence of an imagined Kartini—a context which Kartini in turn sought to harness.[12]

Although the event had not reflected any particular interest in Native women or Indonesian people as such—as Kartini had lamented—and although, typical of its time, the art and craft objects that constituted the *Inlandsche Afdeeling* (Native Section) had consisted largely of private local donations and items from Dutch museum collections (Grever and Waaldijk 2004, p. 158), the positive response received by the exhibition led to a proposal to establish an organization to promote greater interest in the colonies. The aim of what was to become the *Vereeniging Oost en West*[13] was to

> [d]isseminate popularised knowledge of our Indies among the entire nation and the promotion of prosperity in those regions, and by these means as well as by providing mutual assistance, to cultivate sincere interest and affection between the Netherlands here and there. (Cited in Bloembergen 2006, p. 400n93).

As the minutes of its earliest meetings make clear, the *Vereeniging*'s primary focus was on developing a sense of "*verbroedering*" (brotherhood), a greater sense of intimacy and awareness, between metropolitan and colonial settler Dutch by strengthening the metropole's links with its Dutch colonial diaspora.[14] This would be achieved, in the first place, by providing assistance to the increasing numbers of "*Indiers*" (i.e. colonial

Europeans) who were coming to the Netherlands to educate their children and, by implication, improve themselves.[15] Secondly, it aimed to generate popular interest and knowledge in the Netherlands about the Dutch empire by promoting an interest in "Native arts and crafts".

This objective of developing a greater awareness of empire and of the Dutch diaspora it had spawned, was also shared by the *Algemeen-Nederlandsch Verbond* (ANV, General Dutch Union) founded two years earlier. The two organizations shared the aim of unifying "northern" and "tropical" Netherlands. This could be achieved, as Nellie van Zuylen-Tromp, the *Vereeniging* president, put it, by "bring[ing] to all Netherlanders in Europe a knowledge of our [two] Indies and thus, inevitably, also a desire in them to bring them up to a higher level" (1900, p. 25). For the ANV, the key to achieving this was through the promotion of Dutch language which, as well as cementing the links between Dutch colonists abroad and the motherland, would "increase the general standard of civilisation of our nation, ... promote the manifestations of its art, ... maintain its independence and improve its material welfare" (Zuylen-Tromp 1900, p. 25).

At the founding conference of Leiden University *Indologie* (Indies-related studies) in 1897, Professor H. Kern declared that the ability "to exert a beneficial influence over our overseas territories" lay in "our Dutch, our European character" through, in particular, the dissemination of the Dutch language. It was in line with this principle that Kartini's brother, Sosrokartono, was invited to address the ANV members at its conference held in Ghent two years later. The first Indonesian to address a European audience on the aspirations of the Javanese (Groeneboer 1993), Kartono spoke of the importance for the Javanese to have greater access to Dutch language education (Poeze 1986, pp. 30–32). In 1900, Kartini and her sisters became the first "Native" members in the colony of this organization,[16] encouraging the director of Native Education, when he first met Kartini that year, to believe he had found a suitable candidate to head his proposed first Dutch language school for Javanese girls. Kartini (and Kartono), however, had a different objective in mind to that of their European promoters (Coté 2014b; Kartini 2014, pp. 93–99).

Like the *Vereeniging*, the AVN had quickly established itself in the colony, and both organizations soon found in the Dutch-literate Kartini an indigenous anchor for their policies in both exemplifying and contributing to the objectives they had set for themselves. For the *Vereeniging*, as noted above, Kartini became its agent for sourcing Native arts and crafts; for the ANV, it was hoped that she might become a regular contributor of articles to its journal, *Neerlandia*. While Javanese etiquette prevented Kartini from responding to this request (the response to her "launch" in the *Eigen Haard* article was indicative of the conservative backlash that might follow), similar requests continued to arrive. Prominent feminist writer, Nellie van Kol, wanted Kartini to do research on, and provide her with, Javanese "fairy tales" while the editors of the journals *De Hollandsche Lelie* (The Dutch lily) and *Belang en Recht* (Interest and justice) as well as of the colonial women's journal *De Echo* (The echo) approached her to "write about" Java more generally, believing this would now find an enthusiastic European readership (Coté 2014c).

At the same time, as an examination of the membership of the *Vereeniging*'s committee reveals, supporters of these initiatives included leading progressive educationists, academics, writers, politicians and prominent public figures of the day.[17] The social prominence of this membership provided the organization with the necessary social, political and cultural status to engage with an informed public in the Netherlands, and ensure it had a voice within elite policymaking circles in both the Netherlands and its colonies to advance a broader progressive discourse for change.

A major target of the *Vereeniging*'s education committee was to enable young readers to "get to know about life in the Indies and the Indies nations in a pleasant way" (*Voorloopige notulen* 1900) in order to gain a favourable impression of "*land en volk*" (the land and its people). This reflected the by then well-established Dutch academic discipline of *volkenkunde* (literally, knowledge of people) (Josselin de Jong and Vermeulen 1989, p. 287). Explaining the kinds of things it intended, the committee suggested that young readers would be interested to read about

> their [the Native's] struggle with wild animals in their district, their cultivation of plants and minerals, how they prepared food, clothing, housing, weapons, transport, their customs and their relations with other inhabitants as well as white people. (*Voorloopige notulen* 1900)[18]

The Association's key "arts and crafts" committee, which counted amongst its members W.P. Quartero (later to feature prominently in Kartini's correspondence) and H.J.W. van Lawick van Pabst (as already noted), also included Leiden museum curator, G.P. Rouffaer, then an emerging informed writer on the Indies arts (without having yet been to the Indies!).[19] The committee's expressed aims neatly defined the then commonly held view on Native crafts amongst progressive circles by investigating how to:

> give new life to disappearing forms of crafts (*nijverheid*) and arts (*kunst*), to attempt to establish and introduce new industries, and raise the quality of arts (*kunstnijverheid*), the traditional ones, which in many respects are showing signs of decline, as well as those that have emerged more recently, which have not yet established their own character. (*Voorloopige notulen* 1900)

To do so, it declared it would

> do everything in its power to advance the interest of arts and crafts, such as arrange lectures, small exhibitions and attempt to win over the [indigenous] manufacturers who work for the Indies-based market to modify their authentic Indies arts and style. (*Voorloopige notulen* 1900)

In the first years of the century, paralleling the activities of its representatives in Java, the *Vereeniging* successfully arranged its first international exhibition of arts and crafts from both the West and East Indies at the 1900 Paris Exhibition. Following its first local exhibition in The Hague that same year, it mounted a series of regional local exhibitions of Native arts and crafts throughout the Netherlands. By 1902, with the establishment of a company, NV Boeatan, and with the assistance of its colonial agents, including Kartini, it had succeeded in initiating a reliable "supply chain" of Native products suitable for the European market.

Implementing a "Native Crafts" Policy

Translated into the political domain as the rhetorical centrepiece of the Dutch government's new "ethical" colonial policy, the distinction between *Inlandsche nijverheid* (native industry) and *Inlandsche kunstnijverheid* (native arts) hardened. As is evident in Abendanon's 1904 report and Kartini's responses to contemporary European interest, the dominant question in the implementation of the so-called ethical policy with regard to arts and crafts had become whether or not it had any potential economic significance in addressing the declining welfare of the Javanese. This was the issue being pursued by the Dutch government in establishing a range of inquiries in both the colony and the Netherlands. Coinciding with the 1904 Abendanon inquiry, it also instituted a more detailed,

long-term multi-focused colonial inquiry into the causes of, and solutions
to, the declining welfare of the Native population of Java and Madura
(*Onderzoek naar de mindere welvaart der Inlandsche bevolking van Java
en Madoera*). Amongst its 11 major and 32 separate reports published
between 1905 and 1914 were a series of inconclusive recommendations
on the category of Native non-agricultural, craft and trade occupations
(*Handel en nijverheid* 1906–1907). Commenting in 1904 on media reports
on the proposed *Onderzoek* (research), Kartini's husband, Djojo Adiningrat,
described it as "a set of confused guidelines … creating a great deal of
work for officials, particularly Native officials, as a result of which people
will remain as hungry as before". In his view, this contrasted markedly
with what he described as the "clear vision" of Abendanon's inquiry
(Letter, 10 August 1904; Kartini 2014, p. 680).

Meanwhile, in Europe, a team of "colonial experts" led by a
prominent advocate of colonial policy reform, Conrad van Deventer,
was commissioned to advise the imperial government as to the best way
forward in implementing the key objective of its new colonial policy. In
his overview of its findings,[20] Van Deventer returned to the main theme of
his influential 1899 article *"Een Eereschuld"* (A debt of honour), which had
provided a major impetus for colonial policy reform. He emphasized not
so much the past failings of colonial economic policies but the past colonial
neglect of the spiritual and intellectual development of the Javanese that
had now left them incapable of "withstand[ing] the increasingly sharper
struggle of existence" as a result of colonialism (Deventer 1904, p. 255).
Having denied the Javanese middle and upper classes the possibility of
engaging in colonial European economic development, and given that,
in his view, the lower classes of Native society were "too inclined to
lack concern for the future, and to sacrifice the future for the present"
(Deventer 1904, p. 256), the only practical solution to improve the Native
economy now, he argued, was to provide more effective support for
the occupations to which the *Inlanders'* abilities were best suited. These,
in Van Deventer's view, were limited to agriculture. Beyond that, he
recommended more effective training to enable them to be incorporated
into a European-directed colonial economy. His final recommendations
therefore emphasized expenditure on colonial infrastructure development,
such as irrigation, the provision of agricultural credit and population
redistribution (emigration) and training. These were to constitute the
key ingredients of the ethical policy.

Authors of two separate volumes of the report, Dirk Fock and E.B. Kielstra, indicated a more cultural perspective. Fock, a lawyer, had been an active member of the *Vereeniging Oost en West* as a regional representative prior to his elevation in the ministry in 1905 as Minister of Colonies (Anrooij 2013; *Voorloopige notulen* 1900). Kielstra, a former long-serving colonial army engineer (1863–84) and subsequently a member of parliament (1884–94), represented, like Fock, the *Liberale Unie* (Liberal Union), a moderate liberal political party; he is now perhaps better known in his capacity as honorary president of the *Indisch Genootschap* (Indian Society) and director of KITLV (Royal Institute for Linguistics, Geography, and Ethnology). He was an acknowledged "authoritative colonial expert in the Netherlands", and a regular contributor of articles on colonial policy, geography and history (M. Kuitenbrouwer 2001, p. 53). Both men were able to reference examples of *"Inlandsche nijverheid"* which had the potential to be developed as productive Native industries. Fock explicitly reflected the views of the *Vereeniging* in his suggestion that their viability would depend on the introduction of more efficient methods to "rescue [such activities] from the oppressive, restrictive bonds of archaic practices" (Fock 1904, p. 110) through vocational training, but only if their product was adapted to European tastes and uses. He specifically cited Jepara woodcraft along with batik and weaving, as well as other skills—such as housebuilding, stone work, lime works, carpentry, coach building, and tin making—that could be developed as sources of income. In line with the image Kartini provided of the Jepara woodcraft centre, he emphasized the importance of village cooperatives and, like Abendanon, drew attention to the need to rescue Native artisans from the clutches of unscrupulous Chinese moneylenders (Fock 1904, pp. 107–9).

But it was an accompanying report (effectively ignored in Van Deventer's overview) by Gerret Pieter Rouffaer that provided the most optimistic prognosis on the potential of *Inlandsche Nijverheid*. A subordinate of Kielstra at the KITLV, Rouffaer, the institution's secretary and curator, was already a noted batik scholar and an authority on colonial ethnography.[21] He was also the editor of two leading journals of colonial ethnography and geography, *Bijdragen tot de taal-, land-, en volkenkunde* (Contributions to linguistics, geography and ethnology) and *Tijdschrift van het Koninklijk Nederlandsch Aardrijkskundig Genootschap* (Journal of the Royal Dutch Geographical Society).[22] Drawing on his own extensive archival research, Rouffaer provided a comprehensive overview of "the main industries of the Native populations of Java and Madura"

(Rouffaer 1904). It covered Javanese weaving and batik, and other textile crafts, woodwork, house and shipbuilding, rattan weaving, stone and ceramic pot baking, stone carving, and metal and leather work. This account, arguably, was to form the basis of later accounts of Native arts and crafts, including those of J.E. Jasper. Although, like Jasper, Rouffaer was contemptuous of the contemporary popular European interest in, particularly, batik because of the deleterious impact this was having on its artistic quality, he believed batik did present

> an industrial and artistic opportunity for Java [which] strong and secure in itself, and as it were, of interest to the entire population, can be singled out for further, more varied and more general development. (Rouffaer 1904, p. 30)

But this would only develop if it was protected from *"Europeesche bestweterij"* (European know-all-ness), *"Europeesche waansmaak"* (European bad taste), and *"Europeesche regelementeerzucht"* (the European drive for regimentation).[23]

In formulating a new imperial vision, colonial "realists" and policymakers like Van Deventer saw their mission as preparing the Native for the modernity that European colonialism would engender in regions still gripped by archaic practices. They had no time for the particularities and nuances of everyday life of their Native subjects, seeking instead the implementation of broad practical policies which later practice would gradually modify (see for instance Moon 2007). The small but influential group of individuals and organizations directly engaged with Native arts and crafts at the turn of the century, for whom the figure of Raden Ajeng Kartini briefly provided a focal point, shared this vision, viewing it more narrowly through the prism of Europe's arts and crafts movement and the popular cultural fashions this had generated. The concern expressed for Native welfare, however, hinged on an assumption of the superiority of European civilization and its ability to guide Native society along the material and cultural paths towards modernity.

It was only at the end of the first decade of the twentieth century—by which time a concern for Native arts and crafts (particularly in relation to the newly colonized Bali) (Schulte Nordholt 2000) had become more general in cultural and academic as well as administrative circles—that Van Deventer publicly expressed any real interest in "Native arts and crafts". Although reporting positively on what he saw at the Dutch pavilion at the 1910 Brussels Exhibition, he saw—as asserted earlier in

1904—no possibility of their economic viability as "Native industries". Instead, he mused on the possibility of establishing a colonial government programme to improve the quality of Native arts. This would institute an inquiry, headed by an "expert" which would "as far as possible" take account of "the feelings and insights of the best amongst the people" (Deventer 1910, p. 256).[24]

In the following year, he "discovered" Kartini. Having commented in 1910 on what he considered a notable improvement in the demeanour of the "Inlanders" at the Brussels exhibition, he found—in reviewing Abendanon's 1911 publication of an edited selection of Kartini's letters—further confirmation of this "improvement". He saw in Kartini—as revealed in Abendanon's publication—evidence of the results of the new colonial policy that he had advocated. What had most impressed Van Deventer in 1910 was how "the people show some more daring [*durf*] and a greater sense of self-confidence [*vrijmoedigheid*]" (Deventer 1910, p. 241) compared to when he lived in Java. This he also found in reading Kartini's letters: a willingness and ability to "speak". At last, he implied, the Javanese were beginning to express themselves like European people, in Dutch, and on subjects that he could agree with. For Kartini specifically, he noted this self-expression had only become possible because of her "love of our language" (Deventer 1911, p. 494). Her writing, despite the little mistakes (*foutjes*) he had noticed, provided evidence of what a Native "without the knowledge of any other Western language but our own, can achieve in terms of cultural refinement and the expression of deepest feelings" (Deventer 1911, p. 506). This was because "[k]nowledge of the Dutch language is *the* key which unlocks the treasure chambers of Western culture [and] sciences" (1911, p. 500, original emphasis).

Praising Abendanon's efforts in bringing Kartini's writing to public attention, and for envisaging a school carrying Kartini's name for the education of young Javanese ladies in like fashion,[25] Van Deventer concluded:

> It would be difficult for a colonial power, which had aimed to bring the people it ruled to a higher level and to tie them with lasting bonds to the motherland, to find more encouraging evidence than Kartini's thoughts about and for her people. (Deventer 1911, p. 505)

The publication of her correspondence, he continued, also provided readers in the Netherlands with a means to "understand" the Native subject.[26] This included becoming aware of an emerging sense of nationalism evident in Kartini's writing which was, he noted, *"nationaal-Javaansch gezind"* (nationalist-Javanese minded) (1911, p. 494). However, this was not a matter for concern since the carefully selected and edited letters evinced a clear sense of commitment of a modernizing, nationally conscious Java to the Dutch nation. In this, he believed, they echoed the ideal of "association"—of the colonial subjects with the goals of their European guides and advisers—as defined by the influential Leiden professor and Islamist, Snouck Hurgronje (1911, p. 497).[27]

Times had indeed changed since Kartini had written these letters. The close relations between metropole and colony that the supporters of colonial reform had envisaged at the beginning of the century, was becoming a reality. The aims of the *Vereeniging* and the ANV were being realized, and the image of Kartini that had been filtering into the Dutch metropole a decade earlier was now entrenched as part of a progressive colonial vision.

Conclusion

In the course of little over a decade, 1898–1911, the cultural imaginaries underpinning a new Dutch imperial discourse had solidified into a more clearly definable and more broadly accepted message. The fleeting, turn-of-the-century images of a distant, living, Javanese Kartini had now emerged, after her death, as fully formed documentary evidence. Initially grounded in the fascination with the material heritage of Javanese culture, and largely driven by changing social and cultural preoccupations in Europe, the Dutch reception of Kartini's overtures had gained credence from their perceived alignment with evolving political and economic interests. This Kartini persona had straddled two primary themes in this early articulation of a new imperial discourse: an emerging curiosity about the Native other, and the need to give expression to a new sense of Dutch nationalism. This was made possible by Kartini herself during the short period of her public life, as she undertook an astutely perceived and well-informed strategy of enabling her European audience to have access to their imagined Native other. By the end of the decade, the policy directions giving expression to these themes had become clear. In the intervening years the archipelago had been conquered, the colonial administration was centralized, and a modern economic structure put in place. The Kartini initially known only to a select few had metamorphosed into a monument of self-congratulatory imperialism. By then, however, another Kartini was already emerging in its shadow. There was already a hint that the East Indies was on the cusp of further change, and for which Kartini would represent a bulwark against the emergence of an Indonesian nationalism. Although citing Van Deventer (Djajadiningrat-Nieuwenhuis 1993, pp. 46–47) in reviewing Abendanon's publication in 1911, Noto Soeroto, the chair of a newly reconstituted, Netherlands-based Indonesian students' association, heard instead a subtly different voice in Kartini's correspondence: the emerging voice of an autonomous individual outlining a trajectory for an Indonesian future (Karels 2008, pp. 39–40).

NOTES

1. Frank (2017) recently deployed this concept in the broader discussion of contemporary public discourse.
2. For a detailed discussion of Kartini's personal interaction with these cultural discourses and their adherents and literary exemplars, see Coté (2014a, 2014e). In brief, her appropriation of this European "cultural imagery" as "a Native" can be identified in terms of what Homi Bhabha (1984) defines as "mimicry".
3. She reports that she was assured funding would be available for this project.
4. This is amplified in a collection of recently uncovered but as yet unpublished Kartini letters from 1904.
5. In a letter to Stella Zeehandelaar (11 October 1901), Kartini reveals her awareness of "a movement [that] has begun to revive the arts of the Indies which have fallen into neglect" (Kartini 2014, pp. 252–53).
6. The seriousness of Jasper's interest is highlighted by his criticism of the interest that had emerged in fashionable circles in the decorative value of Native arts and crafts (Jasper 1902). Between 1912 and 1928, Jasper, with Javanese co-writer Pirngadie, published a series of highly regarded volumes on Javanese material culture. The first volume, on batik, appeared just before the more "scientific" work on batik by the Dutch-based Gerret Pieter Rouffaer, published in 1914, which included Kartini's 1898 article on batik (Coté 2014d).
7. Roekmini's correspondence in 1906 reveals her active engagement with the *Vereeniging Oost en West*, including arranging for the supply of Jepara woodcraft for its craft shop, Boetan, as well as assisting Jasper with his craft exhibitions in Java (Coté 2008, pp. 122–34).
8. Abendanon's involvement is mentioned in letters dated 11 October and 21 November 1902. Kartini's article was titled "Van een vergeten uithoekje" (From a forgotten little corner) and appeared in *Eigen Haard* on 3 January

1903. See Kartini (2014), pp. 772–81. The title *Eigen Haard* refers to the Dutch proverb *"Eigen haard is goud waard"* which literally means "One's own hearth is worth gold." An English equivalent is "There's no place like home."

9. In a letter to Mrs Abendanon, Kartini details her links with the *Vereeniging* by stating that "[m]uch has befallen me as a consequence of its publication but it has not failed to achieve its aim" (Letter, 9 March 1903; Kartini 2014, p. 579).

10. The phrase echoes the title of Bosma and Raben's examination of the changing nature of colonial society but is not intended to imply concurrence with their analysis.

11. Van Lith's review of the exhibition points to the growing and merging of academic and popular interests.

12. By contrast, the Dutch exhibit at the 1889 *Exposition Universelle* in Paris, which featured a very popular "native *kampong*" (village) including "a *gamelan* with dancing girls", was criticized as a trivialization of the ethnographic exhibit and had failed to attract Dutch government support or interest from scientific or cultural institutions while the *Maatschappij ter Bevordering van Nijverheid* (Dutch Society for the Promotion of Industry) made no mention of Asian *"nijverheid"* in its 1889 report (Bloembergen 2006, pp. 131–32).

13. The name was decided upon at an initial meeting of interested supporters who met in May 1899 in order to emphasize the importance of both the Netherlands' East and West Indies colonies.

14. This sentiment was to play out significantly in Dutch responses to events during the Boer War.

15. Later the *Vereeniging* was active in supporting Indonesian students studying in the Netherlands, including the offer to assist Kartini. Kartini's brother, Sosrokartono, amongst the first wave of Indonesian students to enter the Netherlands for study, was a key adviser in the association's founding years with regard to Javanese affairs.

16. The ANV announced their membership in a brief notice in *Neerlandia* in 1900 entitled "Voor Nederlandsche vrouwen een voorbeeld" (An example to Dutch women) ("Voor Nederlandsche vrouwen" 1900).

17. Space does not allow further exposition of the committee members and their own circles of influence. Also of significance is the attendance at public meetings and regional branch membership recorded in *Vereeniging* minutes, which indicates the interest of a broad range of recognizable proponents of sociocultural and colonial reform, including Henry van Kol, Dirk Fock, and representatives of the *Anti-Revolutionaire Partij* (Anti-Revolutionary Party) which introduced the "ethical policy".

18. The meeting of the *Vereeniging Oost en West* was attended, apart from the executive, by 50 donators and members. Total membership was recorded as 400.

19. Rouffaer's first publication on batik in 1899, *De batik-kunst in Nederlandsch-Indië en haar geschiedenis* (The art of batik in the Netherlands Indies and its history), carried the subtitle "Based on material present in the state ethnographical museum and other public and private collections in the Netherlands".

20. The report for which Van Deventer provided the overview came in three volumes with an additional subreport by G.P. Rouffaer.

21. By 1898, Rouffaer had written extensively on Native arts and crafts in a massive three-volume text that remained unpublished, as well as a five-volume history of the Indies.

22. See Jaquet (2014). In 1901, Rouffaer was appointed secretary of the *Commissie van Bijstand der Oudheidkundige Commissie* (Committee of Support for the Antiquity Society) which undertook preparation for the restoration of Borobudur before undertaking a tour of the archipelago between 1909 and 1911.

23. In commenting on batik and on Kartini's 1898 article on the batik process in the 1914 edition of his work, Rouffaer emphasized the importance of the Native informant in providing insight into the cultural as well as technical details of the craft (Coté 2014d, pp. 789–90).

24. See also Bloembergen's extensive discussion of the significance of the 1910 Brussels exhibition as a review of the Netherlands debate on Native arts and crafts (Bloembergen 2006, Chapter 5).

25. In the proposed Kartini school, "Dutch language and literature would take a central place alongside a Native language or languages" (Deventer 1911, p. 506).

26. The first Javanese language edition of the publication did not appear until 1939, a year after the Indonesian translation, *Habis gelap terbitlah terang* (From darkness into light) was published by Indonesian writer, Armijn Pane. This version superseded an earlier 1922 translation. International readers, in particular supporters of the international women's movement, had access to the thoughts of R.A. Kartini with the publication of Agnes Symmers' "enthusiastic" English translation in 1920, *Letters of a Javanese Princess*.

27. Professor Snouck Hurgronje, the key exponent of a colonial "association policy", had published a major article *Nederland en de Islam* (The Netherlands and Islam) in support of this policy that same year.

REFERENCES

Abendanon, Jacques H. 1904. *Rapport van den Directeur van Onderwijs, Eeredienst en Nijverheid, betreffende de maatregelen in het belang van de Inlandsche nijverheid op Java en Madoera in verband met de door het moederland voor dit doel beschikbaar te stellen fondsen.* Batavia: Landsdrukkerij.

Anrooij, F. van. 2013. "Fock, Dirk (1858–1941)". In *Biografisch woordenboek van Nederland*, 12 November 2013. http://resources.huygens.knaw.nl/bwn1880-2000/lemmata/bwn1/fock (accessed 16 October 2017).

Bell, Jacqueline. 1993. *Nederlandse literatuur in het Fin de Siècle (1885–1900): Een receptie-historisch overzicht*. Amsterdam: Amsterdam University Press.

Bhabha, H. 1984. "Of Mimicry and Man: The Ambivalence of Colonial Discourse". *October* 28: 125–33.

Bloembergen, Marieke. 2006. *Colonial Spectacles: The Netherlands and the Dutch East Indies at the World Exhibitions, 1880–1931*. Translated by Beverly Jackson. Singapore: Singapore University Press.

Bosma, Ulbe and Remco Raben. 2008. *Being "Dutch" in the Indies: A History of Creolisation and Empire, 1500–1920*. Translated by Wendie Shaffer. Singapore: NUS Press; Athens, OH: Ohio University Press.

Brommer, B. 1989. *Katoendruk in Nederland*. Tilburg: Nederlands Textielmuseum; Helmond: Gemeentemuseum Helmond.

Budiarti, H. 2007. "Taking and Returning Objects in a Colonial Context: Tracing the Collections Acquired During the Bone-Gowa Military Expedition". In *Colonial Collections Revisited*, edited by P. ter Keurs. Leiden: CNWS.

Buskens, L. and J. Kommers. 2007. "Dutch Colonial Anthropology in Indonesia". *Asian Journal of Social Science* 35, no. 3: 352–69.

Coté, Joost. 2004. "'A Conglomeration of [...] Often Conflicting Ideas': Resolving the 'Native Question' in Java and the Outer Islands in the Dutch East Indies, 1900–1925". *Itinerario: Journal on the History of European Expansion and Global Interaction* 27, no. 3–4: 160–88.

————, ed. and trans. 2008. *Realizing the Dream of R.A. Kartini: Her Sisters' Letters from Colonial Java*. Ohio: Ohio University Press; Leiden: KITLV Press.

————. 2009. "'Sins of Their Fathers': Culturally at Risk Children and the Colonial State in Asia". *Paedagogica Historica* 45, no. 1–2: 129–42.

————. 2014a. "Reading Kartini: A Historical Introduction". In *Kartini: The Complete Writings, 1898–1904*, by Kartini. Edited and translated by Joost Coté. Clayton, Victoria: Monash University.

————. 2014b. "Letters 1900: Introduction". In *Kartini: The Complete Writings, 1898–1904*, by Kartini. Edited and translated by Joost Coté. Clayton, Victoria: Monash University.

————. 2014c. "Introduction to the Published Short Stories". In *Kartini: The Complete Writings, 1898–1904*, by Kartini. Edited and translated by Joost Coté. Clayton, Victoria: Monash University.

————. 2014d. "Introduction to the Ethnographic Writing". In *Kartini: The Complete Writings, 1898–1904*, by Kartini. Edited and translated by Joost Coté. Clayton, Victoria: Monash University.

————. 2014e. "Raden Ajeng Kartini and Cultural Nationalism in Java". In *Connecting Histories of Education: Transnational Exchanges and Transfers in (Post) colonial Education*, edited by B. Bagchi, E. Fuchs and K. Rousmaniere. New York: Berghahn.

Dawson, G. 1994. *Soldier Heroes: British Adventure, Empire and the Imagining of Masculinities*. London: Routledge.

Deventer, C. van. 1899. "Een eereschuld". *De Gids* 63: 205–57. http://www.dbnl.org/tekst/_gid001189901_01/_gid001189901_01_0073.php (accessed 22 July 2017).

———. 1904. *Overzicht van den economischen toestand der Inlandsche bevolking van Java en Madoera*. 's-Gravenhage: Martinus Nijhoff.

———. 1910. "Insulinde te Brussel". *De Gids* 74: 240–56. http://www.dbnl.org/tekst/_gid001191001_01/_gid001191001_01_0151.php (accessed 22 July 2017).

———. 1911. "Kartini". *De Gids* 75: 479–507. http://www.dbnl.org/tekst/_gid001191101_01/_gid001191101_01_0099.php (accessed 22 July 2017).

Djajadiningrat-Nieuwenhuis, M. 1993. "Noto Soeroto: His Ideas and the Late Colonial Intellectual Climate". *Indonesia* 55: 41–72.

Doorn, S. van. 1998. *Johan Ernst Jasper: Indisch ambtenaar, leven en werk, 1874–1945*. Master's thesis, Leiden University.

Eliëns, T. 1997. "*Nieuwe Kunst*: Dutch Decorative Arts from 1880–1910". In *Avant-garde Design: Dutch Decorative Arts 1880–1940*, edited by T. Eliëns, M. Groot and F. Leidelmeijer. London: Phillip Wilson.

Ernawati, W. 2007. "The Lombok Treasures". In *Colonial Collections Revisited*, edited by P. ter Keurs. Leiden: CNWS.

Fock, D. 1904. *Beschouwingen en voorstellen ter verbetering van den economischen toestand der Inlandsche bevolking van Java en Madoera*. 's-Gravenhage: Martinus Nijhoff.

Frank, M. 2017. *Cultural Imaginary of Terrorism in Public Discourse, Literature and Film: Narrating Terror*. London: Routledge.

Gedenkboek uitgegeven bij gelegenheid van het 25-jarig bestaan van de Vereeniging de Nederlandsch-Indische Kunstkring te Batavia, 1902–1927. 1927. Batavia: Kolff.

Greenhalgh, P. 2000. "The Style and the Age". In *Art Nouveau, 1890–1914*, edited by P. Greenhalgh. London: V&A.

Grever, M. and B. Waaldijk. 2004. *Transforming the Public Sphere: The Dutch National Exhibition of Women's Labour in 1898*. Durham: Duke University Press.

Groeneboer, K. 1993. "Nederlands in den vreemde: Het Algemeen-Nederlands Verbond in Nederlands-Indië 1899–1949". *Neerlandia* 97: 140–44. http://www.dbnl.org/tekst/_nee003199301_01/_nee003199301_01_0106.php (accessed 14 April 2017).

Groot, M. 2007. *Vrouwen in de vormgeving, 1880–1940*. Rotterdam: Uitgeverij 010.

Handel en nijverheid: Samentrekking van de afdeelingsverslagen over de uitkomsten der onderzoekingen naar handel en nijverheid. 1906–7. Vol. VI of *Onderzoek naar de oorzaken van de mindere welvaart der Inlandsche bevolking op Java en Madoera*. Batavia: Van Dorp.

Jaquet, F.G.P. 2014. "Rouffaer, Gerret Pieter (1860–1928)". In *Biografisch woordenboek van Nederland*, 17 November 2014. http://resources.huygens.knaw.nl/bwn1880-2000/lemmata/bwn1/rouffaer (accessed 16 October 2017).

Jasper, J.E. 1902. "Hollandsche leken over Indische kunst". *Tijdschrift voor het Binnenlands Bestuur* 23: 419–21.

———. 1904. "Nota van den Controleur bij het Binnenlands Bestuur, J.E. Jasper, over het opbeuren van Inlandsche nijverheid". In *Rapport van den Directeur van Onderwijs, Eeredienst en Nijverheid, betreffende de maatregelen in het belang van de Inlandsche nijverheid op Java en Madoera in verband met de door het moederland voor dit doel beschikbaar te stellen fondsen*, edited by J.H. Abendanon. Appendix 7. Batavia: Landsdrukkerij.

Joosten, J.M. 1972. "De batik en de vernieuwing van de nijverheidskunst in Nederland 1892–1905". *Nederlands Kunsthistorisch Jaarboek (NKJ)/Netherlands Yearbook for History of Art* 23: 407–29.

Josselin de Jong, P.E. and H.F. Vermeulen. 1989. "Cultural Anthropology at Leiden University: From Encyclopedism to Structuralism". In *Leiden Oriental Connections 1850–1940*, edited by Willem Otterspeer. Leiden: Brill.

Karels, R.B. 2008. "Mijn aardse leven vol moeite en strijd: Raden Mas Noto Soeroto, Javaan, dichter, politicus, 1888–1951". PhD thesis, Leiden University.

Kartini. 2014. *Kartini: The Complete Writings, 1898–1904*. Edited and translated by Joost Coté. Clayton, Victoria: Monash University.

Keurs, P. ter. 2007. "Introduction: Theory and Practice of Collecting". In *Colonial Collections Revisited*, edited by P. ter Keurs. Leiden: CNWS.

Kuitenbrouwer, M. 2001. *Tussen oriëntalisme en wetenschap: Het Koninklijk Instituut voor Taal-, Land-, en Volkenkunde in historisch verband*. Leiden: KITLV Press.

Kuitenbrouwer, V. 2011. "Songs of an Imperial Underdog: Imperialism and Popular Culture in the Netherlands, 1870–1960". In *European Empires and the People: Popular Responses to Imperialism in France, Britain, the Netherlands, Belgium, Germany and Italy*, edited by J. MacKenzie. Manchester: Manchester University Press.

Lawick van Pabst, H.J.W. van. 1904. "Bijlage 111, Van Lawick, Nederlandsch-Indische Vereeniging *Oost en West*, 4 February 1904". In *Rapport van den Directeur van Onderwijs, Eeredienst en Nijverheid, betreffende de maatregelen in het belang van de Inlandsche nijverheid op Java en Madoera in verband met de door het moederland voor dit doel beschikbaar te stellen fondsen*, edited by J.H. Abendanon. Batavia: Landsdrukkerij.

Lintsen, H. 1994. *Techniek, beroep en praktijk*. Vol. 5 of *Geschiedenis van de techniek in Nederland: De wording van een moderne samenleving 1800–1890*. 's-Gravenhage: Stichting Historie der Techniek; Zutphen: Walburg Pers. http://www.dbnl.org/titels/titel.php?id=lint011gesc05 (accessed 15 July 2017).

Lith, P.A. van. 1883. "Catalogus der afdeeling Nederlandsche Koloniën van de Internationale Koloniale en Uitvoerhandel Tentoonsteling te Amsterdam,

1883". *De Gids* 47: 157–65. http://www.dbnl.org/tekst/_gid001188301_01/_gid001188301_01_0078.php (accessed 15 July 2017).

Locher-Scholten, E. 2012. "Imperialism and the Great Wave: The Dutch Case in the Netherlands East Indies, 1860–1914". In *Liberal Imperialism in Europe*, edited by M. Fitzpatrick. London: Palgrave Macmillan.

Mattie, E. 1998. *World's Fairs*. New York: Princeton Architectural Press.

Miert, H. van. 1991. *Bevlogenheid en onvermogen: Mr. J.H. Abendanon (1852–1925) en de ethische richting in het Nederlandse kolonialisme*. Leiden: KITLV Press.

Moon, S. 2007. *Technology and Ethical Idealism: A History of Development in the Dutch East Indies*. Leiden: CNWS.

Poeze, H. 1986. *Indonesiërs in Nederland 1600–1950*. Vol. I of *In het land van de overheerser*, edited by H. Poeze. Dordrecht: Foris.

Rouffaer, G.P. 1904. "De voornaamste industrieën der Inlandsche bevolking op Java en Madoera". In *Overzicht van den economischen toestand der Inlandsche bevolking van Java en Madoera*, edited by C. van Deventer. 's-Gravenhage: Martinus Nijhoff.

Schulte Nordholt, Henk. 2000. "The Making of Traditional Bali". In *Colonial Subjects: Essays on the Practical History of Anthropology*, edited by P. Pels and O. Salemink. Michigan: University of Michigan Press.

Stevens, H. 2007. "G.C.E. van Daalen: Military Officer and Ethnological Field Agent: The Ethnological Exploration of Gayo and Alas, 1900–1905". In *Colonial Collections Revisited*, edited by P. ter Keurs. Leiden: CNWS.

Touwen, J. 2013. "Paternalisme en protest: Ethische politiek en nationalisme in Nederlands-Indië, 1900–1942". *Leidschrift* 15, no. 3: 67–93. http://www.leidschrift.nl/nl/archief/file/357-04_touwen (accessed 14 April 2017).

Voorloopige notulen algemeene vergaderingen der Vereeniging Oost en West. 1899–1912. Archive *Koninklijke Vereeniging Oost en West*. Shelfmark ubl300. Special Collections, Leiden University.

"Voor Nederlandsche vrouwen een voorbeeld". 1900. *Neerlandia* 4: 118. http://www.dbnl.org/tekst/_nee003190001_01/_nee003190001_01_0133.php (accessed 20 July 2015).

Waaldijk, B. and S. Legêne. 2003. "Vernieuwing van de beeldende kunsten in een koloniale context". In *Kunsten en beweging 1900–1980*, edited by R. Buikema and M. Meijer. Den Haag: Sdu Uitgevers.

Zuylen-Tromp, N. van. 1900. "Oost en West". *Neederlandia* 4: 25. https://www.dbnl.org/tekst/_nee003190001_01/_nee003190001_01_0026.php (accessed 20 July 2015).

3

Hierarchies of Humanity:
Kartini in America and at UNESCO

Paul Bijl *

Introduction

In her book on the invention of human rights in the course of the eighteenth century, Lynn Hunt offers an analysis of the type of person that is considered "human" in European modernity. She discusses the crucial relationship between autonomy, empathy and human rights by stating that "[t]o have human rights, people had to be perceived as separate individuals who were capable of exercising independent moral judgment" and as "able to empathize with others" (Hunt 2007, p. 29). However, Hunt writes, not everybody was deemed to have such a moral autonomy and deep inner life: children, slaves, servants, the propertyless, women and, we can add, colonized peoples were seen as lacking the right qualities to be deemed (fully) human. Kartini was well aware of the privileges of being identified as human. Her connections with Dutch feminists and socialists were complex, for whereas these two groups primarily fought their battles in terms of gender and class, race

* I want to thank Adele Torrance and her colleagues of the UNESCO Archives for their help.

was a different category altogether as it was largely unacknowledged by the international women's movement of the late nineteenth and early twentieth centuries (Rupp 1997). Unfazed by this extra challenge, Kartini engaged proactively with international discourses on humanity, human equality, human inequality and rights by constructing in her letters an empathetic, wilful inner life that made her part of what was at the time considered "humanity" (Bijl 2017). On 20 May 1901, she wrote to her socialist-feminist pen pal, Stella Zeehandelaar, in her characteristically ambiguous tone which hovers somewhere between admiration, irony and anger:

> Seeing that in enlightened Europe, the centre of civilization, the source of Light, the struggle for the right of women is still being fought so fiercely and furiously, can we expect that the Indies, which has been in deep slumber for centuries and which is still asleep, would accept, would permit, that women, who throughout the centuries have been looked upon as inferior beings and have been treated as such, see themselves as *humans* who have the *right* to an *independent conscience*? (Kartini 1911, p. 154; Kartini 2014, p. 196. original emphasis)[1]

Hunt's emphasis on empathy, autonomy and human rights was perfectly captured by Kartini when six months later on 20 November 1901 she wrote to Mrs Abendanon-Mandri: "I learned three things from the Europeans. Love, pity, and the concept of right—I want to live according to them" (Kartini 1987, p. 98; Kartini 2014, p. 226). Here speaks a human being who knows what she wants: to feel for others and have rights. Seen in the light of Hunt's work, the sentimentality of many of Kartini's letters should not only be interpreted as imitating the style of the times, for instance, of certain Dutch poets she had read, but also as asserting a deep inner life of empathy and compassion.

One of the tragic ironies is that while Kartini fully acknowledged the workings of both overt and more benign forms of racism in her life, most Western commentators have skipped over these obstacles in the appropriation of her ideas and symbolism. Kartini had a keen eye for the ways in which she was treated as a lesser human or not as a human at all because of the ways in which she was racialized. In 1900, she wrote to Zeehandelaar: "The Dutch laugh and ridicule our ignorance, but when we try to develop ourselves, they adopt a defiant attitude toward us!" (Kartini 1911, p. 32; Kartini 2014, p. 101). In remarks like these, Kartini traces white racializations that posit essential or gradual differences between Javanese and Dutch as well as white anxieties that the Javanese might be able to "catch up" with the Dutch in terms of "development". Irony is a strong weapon in her hands, seen, for instance, in her response to a group of Dutch women eager to help her and her sisters prepare for a colonial exhibition: "The relations with these cultured and highly-educated pure-blood Dutch ladies had a beneficial influence on the brownies [*bruintjes*]" (Kartini 1911, p. 20; Kartini 2014, p. 86). By taking over the derogatory vocabulary of these ladies, which she critically discusses elsewhere in her letters, she effectively subverts it.

This same quote, moreover, allows me to point out another structure of signification that, time and again, is visible in Western appropriations of Kartini: cosmopolitan distinction. The pure-blooded Dutch ladies from this quote, Kartini implies, were not a little proud to have been of help to what they considered their younger, brown "sisters". On top of that, the context of the exhibition provided them with a perfect opportunity to put their benign acts on display before other Westerners. According to Sandra Ponzanesi, building on the work of Pierre Bourdieu, cosmopolitan distinction creates a double hierarchy, namely, between "provincials" and "cosmopolitans" in the West and between, in this case, the white "discoverer" and the Asian woman, who is seen as being brought from the local to the global (Ponzanesi 2014). Kartini has been presented by many of her Western appropriators as a rare find (for instance, her first editor J.H. Abendanon), a trend that can be seen also within the Dutch women's movement. However, because of the structural hierarchies of power between Kartini and Westerners (who had, for instance, the kind of access to publishing and other industries which she lacked), the act of placing Kartini on a global stage inevitably reproduced structures of inequality. At the same time, Kartini's letters have remained a source of critique of these inequalities, as they keep on speaking back to their later editors and publishers. What Kartini's work—like the writings of several other Indonesian writers during the colonial period such as Soewardi Soerjaningrat, Soewarsih Djojopoespito and Sutan Sjahrir—indicated and exploited was the gap between the discourses on modern equality and those on modern inequality. Like Kartini, they did so through, on the one hand, protest and critique and, on the other hand, tropes such as irony and paradox that indicated contradictions and tensions in Western racialized discourse. As we will see, the cosmopolitan distinction with which Kartini's American publisher afforded himself in using the epithet

"Javanese Princess" was quickly (and, of course, posthumously) ridiculed by Kartini herself in one of her letters.

This chapter analyses the different Western conceptions of human equality and inequality that can be glimpsed from the ways in which American, French and other Western actors and institutions appropriated Kartini as they selected, edited, translated and published her works. It builds on the history of discourses on human equality and inequality (Hunt 2007; Stuurman 2017) to argue that Kartini was, on the one hand, presented as equal with her Western audiences in terms of their shared humanity, but on the other hand, the ways in which she was framed also showed conceptions of racialization and hierarchies of culture, or modern inequality. Modern Western conceptions of human equality and inequality, as becomes apparent from both Stuurman's and Hunt's work, were full of tensions. Although the late eighteenth century developed powerful ideas about human equality, the rise in the nineteenth and twentieth centuries of abolitionism, workers' movements, women's movements, coalitions against child labour, anti-racism (particularly in the United States) and human rights-inspired anti-colonialism proved that these ideas were far from universally accepted and implemented. Many contradictions remained, often linked to issues of temporality and anatomization. In terms of temporality, nineteenth-century ideas about progress and modernity especially placed the people of the world on a developmental timeline in which Asians and Africans were seen as lagging behind Europeans. This conception was the driving force behind many justifications for colonialism: governing people of colour—after conquering them—was presented as a way to bring them into modernity from, for instance, Antiquity or the Middle Ages. Whereas in such conceptions human equality was presented as a possible achievement in the (far) future, in conceptions of anatomization the adagio was "anatomy is destiny". Both scientific racism and biological sexism positioned people of colour and women, and women of colour in a double sense, as essentially different from the white men who formed the top of the colonial and metropolitan hierarchies. Tensions in modern Western discourses on human equality and inequality often become visible if we, in specific instances, critically investigate the ways in which this equality is imagined, and the kinds of conditions in which it might be denied. For instance, the conception of psychological equality—in which people of colour were deemed to have the same mental and emotional capacities as white people—was often not translated into political or legal equality; an example is the capacity for self-government, which was often presented as being "still" underdeveloped. Acknowledging Kartini's capacity to write a "human document", as her first English translator Agnes Louise Symmers (1882–1941) characterized her letters, did not automatically imply her entitlement to equal rights as she was part of a racialized group ("the Javanese" or even "Orientals") that still needed to be guided into European modernity (Symmers 1920, p. xi). Western discourses on human equality, in other words, often remained entrenched within structures of racial inequality.

Based on the work of Michel Foucault, I see the figure of the human as a discursive construction that produces identities within hierarchical power structures. Being identified as human is often a coveted status, as it brings with it many privileges. At the same time, being seen as and actually treated as human does not mean an escape from the processes of discipline and biopolitics. Additionally, the figure of the human is unstable: in different contexts, "being human" has different and often contradictory meanings. The ways in which Kartini was humanized, though almost consistently to a lesser degree than her appropriators saw themselves, vary greatly. "Humanity", moreover, can serve as a blanket term which hides inequalities, such as when somebody is seen as equal in terms of race, but not in terms of gender, or vice versa. Throughout the history of appropriating Kartini, class, race and gender continuously played important roles with regard to the privileges she was offered or denied.

In *The Invention of Humanity* (2017), Siep Stuurman maps the world-historical polyphony of discourses of common humanity and equality from ancient history to the present day, tracing their many shapes in religion, philosophy, history and ethnography. Throughout most centuries, he writes, it was in fact inequality that "was the habitual and reasonable standard, while equality stood in light of justification, if it was considered at all" (2017, p. 2). For the contexts that will be discussed in this chapter, what Stuurman calls the idea of "modern equality" as it was invented during the European Enlightenment, is important. In both Kartini's writings and those of the authors who wrote about her, modern equality's potential to critique inequality in terms of gender and race, among other anthropological categories, is immediately apparent (on the issue of class, see Chin's Chapter 4 in this volume). However, drawing on the same European Enlightenment as their ultimate source, the editors, publishers and introducers of Kartini discussed here were also strongly influenced by conceptions of modern *in*equality, which Stuurman sees as trickling down from eighteenth-century Europe in four variants, two of which are of special interest here: 1) racial classification, and 2) often overlapping with the former, the authority of the enlightened few over the not (yet) enlightened many (Stuurman 2017, p. 24).[2] Racial classification came in several variants: while some Enlightenment thinkers did not essentialize race and saw all people as possessing the capacity for development, others viewed race according to "coloured" rankings within a rigid hierarchy (Bijl 2009). In these latter systems, white was the "default setting of humanity" (Stuurman 2017, p. 344), while people of colour represented various degrees of degeneration. The coexistence and tensions between ideas of modern equality and modern inequality, as we will see, led to questions among the white actors who appropriated Kartini on whether she could *become* like a white person, or whether she was *like* a white person at all.

Now that in the twenty-first century we are able to read Kartini through the lenses of postcolonial and critical race studies, and more specifically African-American studies, one of the findings of this chapter is the painful recognition of how little Western actors and institutions engaged with her critiques of European discourses of racial equality and inequality. Of importance in this respect is the special status in the hierarchy of humanity accorded to Kartini by several of her appropriators in relation to other Javanese, who were regularly presented as "under the sway of tradition" (Symmers 1920, p. xii). In contrast to her fellow Javanese, Kartini had in important ways been discursively humanized, and had also humanized herself, through a process of individuation which allowed her to make the transition from "being culture" (being bogged down by tradition) to "having culture" (being a modern, self-made individual). The epithet "pioneer of her people" which has so often been accorded to her, is ambiguous, for while it indicates that people of colour could "become" modern humans, it also suggests that until they did so, they were not fully human. At the same time, parading this young woman often had a clear function for those organizing the parade. By positioning themselves as explorers, or even "older sisters", who found in Kartini the kind of proof they were looking for (in that all of humanity was equally gifted), several of those who appropriated her in fact reified structures of racialization *and* subverted the idea of human equality.

This chapter discusses the most important Western appropriations of Kartini outside the Netherlands, focusing on the ways in which she was positioned in Euro-American conceptions of human equality and inequality.[3] It will address two sets of texts from two different periods: 1919–20 and 1960–64 (between these two periods, Kartini did not register in the West outside the Netherlands). In 1919 and 1920, a number of Kartini's letters were translated for the American magazine *Atlantic Monthly*, while in the latter year, the famous *Letters of a Javanese Princess* was published (from here onward *Javanese Princess*). In the first half of the 1960s, UNESCO initiated the publication of a French (Kartini 1960) and an English (Kartini 1964) version of Kartini's letters as part of the UNESCO Collection of Representative Works (henceforth 1960 UNESCO edition and 1964 UNESCO edition).

In all these cases, the institutions and actors involved—from journal editors to selection committees and publishers—mapped the relations between themselves and Kartini within the contexts of changing colonial, postcolonial and other global relations. Of particular interest to those who produced the figure of Kartini in these contexts was the question of her humanity. According to the editor and translator of *Javanese Princess*, Agnes Louise Symmers, the "chief interest" of Kartini's letters—as stated earlier—"lies in their value as a human document" (1920, p. xi). For UNESCO, books like the collection of Kartini's letters were the media through which different cultures could be seen as sharing in a universal oneness, a collective humanity (Lembrecht 2013, p. 104). The way in which Kartini's humanity is so often emphasized, however, raises questions precisely about her status as a human being in Western eyes, questions that she herself had already addressed in her letters. Crucially, the different members of humanity were not always portrayed as equal; this is apparent in Eleanor Roosevelt's (1884–1962) preface to the 1964 UNESCO edition, in which she writes: "[i]n many ways [these letters] will help us understand what we of the Western world must understand if we are to be helpful to nations emerging from old customs into new" (Roosevelt 1964, p. 5).

Kartini in America (1919–20)

Atlantic Monthly

Kartini's American debut was in November 1919 (Kartini 1919a) in the journal *Atlantic Monthly* (henceforth *Atlantic*). Texts written by her also appeared in the magazine in December 1919 and January 1920 (Kartini 1919b, 1920a). Besides a very short introduction and afterword by the editors (both of around fifty words), and a handful of footnotes by the translator, Symmers, who would later on go to publish *Javanese Princess*, Kartini's texts were presented as if "[t]hese letters tell their own story" (Kartini 1919a, p. 591). Both the selections and translations that were made, however, as well as the brief introduction and titles given by the editors or translator offer clues as to how these letters were to speak for themselves. The title of the first, "The Old Life and the New Spirit", sets up the central tension for the three articles developed in later pieces titled "A Javanese Wedding"—clearly a description of the "Old Life" and "The New Woman in Java"—to announce the "New Spirit". Immediately, we can recognize one of the discourses of modern inequality, namely, the one on the enlightened few and the unenlightened many.

Atlantic's Kartini in some important ways differs markedly from the one we have inherited through Abendanon's book *Door duisternis tot licht* (Through darkness into light, Kartini 1911), on which Symmers' translations were based, though we can also recognize many similarities. She embraces modernity and Europe while (initially) rejecting the laws and customs of "India" and, more broadly, of "the Orient" and "the East", especially when it comes to arranged marriage and the position of women. She nevertheless stays true to her family and people, and finally finds "[a] noble man" who will help her realize her cause, which—in the words of the unnamed editors in the introduction—was "to educate her people ... not to make of them pseudo-Europeans, but better Javanese" (Kartini 1919a, p. 591). Although all of these elements could also be found in Abendanon's edition, the selection made in *Atlantic* leaves out many passages that make Kartini's letters such a complex and multidirectional whole; it also suggests, more strongly than the 1911 book, that Kartini embraced marriage, slowly but certainly (Coté 2014, p. 297). Although this Kartini is in some ways familiar to many who have read all of her work, this selection nevertheless silences Kartini's criticism of European racism, sexism, exoticism as well as her ridicule of Dutch paternalism. Kartini's wishes and plans to go to Europe to continue her education and how in the end her European contacts did not help her are only visible in passing. In *Atlantic*, European colonialism is off the hook, while Kartini's gradual embrace of Javanese modernity is essentially presented as a step forward. At first sight, this implicit endorsement of embracing one's own culture may appear as a form of cultural relativism and therefore of human equality: cultures are different but reside on a level playing field. As I will show, however, seen within the broader context of *Atlantic*, Kartini's positioning as essentially Javanese placed her in a hierarchy of race and culture in which the editors and readers of *Atlantic*, not this Javanese author, took pride of place.

Atlantic was founded in 1857 with roots in the American anti-slavery movement and had, throughout the nineteenth and early twentieth centuries, developed perspectives on America as a nation and the role of the United States internationally. The *Atlantic*, in the words of Susan Goodman, who wrote the magazine's history up to 1925, "served the cause of freedom through literature" (Goodman 2011, p. ix) and had a wide range of famous authors publishing in its pages, including Harriet Beecher Stowe, Frederick Douglass, W.E.B. Du Bois and Ralph Waldo Emerson. The cover of the *Atlantic*'s first issue has an image of John Winthrop (1587–1649), whose famous phrase "We shall be as a city upon a hill. The eyes of all people are upon us" cast the United States as a model for the world. By 1919, *Atlantic*'s editor, Ellery Sedgwick (1872–1960), a social progressive with strong political interests who was also the owner of the magazine, saw it as offering "intelligent American opinion" (Goodman 2011, pp. 224–25). The publication of Kartini's work fitted the *Atlantic*'s mission of crafting an American national consciousness concerning the United States itself as well as its relation to the rest of the world, especially when seen in the light of contemporary American debates on both migration and race. Kartini's position in terms of human equality and inequality was ambiguous in the magazine. On the one hand, she was offered a welcoming stage, just like several African-American, Asian and migrant authors had been, yet on the other hand, the ways in which her writings were framed suggest the superiority of the United States as a country built on Anglo-Saxon (white) principles.

With respect to immigration, key to understanding Kartini's relation to American debates on this subject is the editors' phrase that Kartini wanted to educate her people to become not "pseudo-Europeans, but better Javanese", later repeated by Symmers in her introduction to *Javanese Princess*. It was also crucial for Sedgwick that through the reading of *Atlantic*, its readers, including immigrants, would start sharing in a collective American way of life; in other words, they would not remain pseudo-immigrants but become better Americans. One example of this attitude during his long tenure as editor (1909–38) can be found in his response to the Russian-American immigrant, Mary Antin, who published parts of her autobiography *The Promised Land* (1912) in the magazine's pages after Sedgwick praised its "strength, sincerity, faith" and saw it fitting his journal's aims "to be the exponent of American ideals" (cited in Goodman 2011, p. 226). Yet, while Antin received his praise for her embrace of what he saw as American culture, Sedgwick did not agree with Randolph Bourne's 1916 essay "Trans-National America", in which the latter had argued against the idea of a melting pot in which all immigrant cultures would come together while defending a cosmopolitanism that nurtured cultural diversity. Sedgwick wrote to Bourne that the United States was "created by English instinct and dedicated to the Anglo-Saxon ideal" (cited in Bender 1987, p. 247) and considered Bourne's paper radical and unpatriotic. As can be seen from these examples, Sedgwick had essentialist ideas concerning national cultures, and hierarchical ones with respect to these cultures' relations.

By being selectively inspired by new developments coming from abroad while at the same time embracing what was considered her own culture, *Atlantic*'s Kartini can be connected to several changes in the magazine that had been propelled by World War I and which, paradoxically, spelled both the magazine's more outward and inward gaze (Goodman 2011). The outward gaze concerned its growing wish to signify what was going on in the world at large, while the inward gaze was a response to an enhanced focus on the domestic fears that the global turmoil had been causing. On the one hand, Kartini was part of the increase in foreign contributors, especially on Europe and the Pacific, in the wake of growing international tensions. On the other hand, the editors' remark that Kartini wanted to make her people not "pseudo-Europeans, but better Javanese" can be read in light of the "Americanisation movement" which aimed to integrate groups of immigrants, especially from Europe, into a single "core" national identity (Goodman 2011, pp. 233–35). In order to foster this national consciousness, many Americans at that time saw a crucial role for education, not coincidentally also an important theme in Kartini's letters in *Atlantic*. Kartini, as a foreign correspondent of sorts, therefore not only had a story to tell about "the Orient", but implicitly also about America and the ways in which it was both exceptional and could retain its exceptionality. Kartini's letters in two ways shored up what has been called "American exceptionalism", an ideology which has been developed since the early nineteenth century and of which Winthrop's phrase of "a city upon a hill" has been seen as an early expression. While these letters presented at the time what the editors called "Western freedom" as its main source of inspiration (and what country and magazine represented "liberty" better than the United States and *Atlantic*?), they also showed that nations needed to stick to some core identity and be great in their own way ("better Javanese") without reverting to any pseudo-identities that would undermine their integrity. Paradoxically, therefore, a non-American author like Kartini was cast as the ideal expression of the "American idea" in the sense that she not only showed the importance of Western influence in the world (with Europe as good and America as best), but also emphasized the importance that all nations had a core to which they should stick—the core of America being simply "the best". What made American exceptionalism, and therefore the *Atlantic*, so extraordinary was not only its ability to collect the best of American writing, but also its capacity to recognize "American" brilliance the world over, even if it was written by a Javanese woman. The paradox is that Kartini's exceptionality has been translated into America's and the *Atlantic*'s exceptionality, for where else but in the pages of this magazine, published in the United States, that city upon a hill, could you find a brilliant Javanese woman like her? Taking up Kartini's letters in the pages of *Atlantic* offered both those who made and read the magazine a good dose of cosmopolitan distinction as well as self-esteem.

According to Goodman, *Atlantic*, "like the nation itself, reflected polarities of opinion" (Goodman 2011, p. 236). This is not only visible with respect to immigration (despite his objections to Bourne's essay, Sedgwick did publish it), but also in the case of a strongly related topic which brought Kartini closer to certain African-American as well as other anti-colonial writers like herself: race. In this, she joined the ranks of Du Bois, who in *Atlantic* had written critically about European colonialism in Africa (Du Bois 1915), and Rabindranath Tagore, who, also in *Atlantic*, had argued against nationalism which, he wrote, should be opposed "for the sake of humanity" (Tagore 1917, p. 291). Yet while Du Bois and Tagore were working within the discourses of modern equality, the magazine also published Theodore Lothrop Stoddard's theory of the superiority of the "Nordic race", further developed in his classic scientific and racist book *The Rising Tide of Color Against White World-Supremacy* (1920); Stoddard was obviously an exponent of modern inequality. As many Americans saw race as intimately tied up with nationality, stating that Kartini wanted to make her people better Javanese instead of pseudo-Europeans can also be read as a backhand compliment which actually meant that a Javanese woman simply cannot be European because she is not white. This is a far cry from Du Bois' wish for "a new peace and a new democracy: a great humanity of equal men" (Du Bois 1915, p. 714).

In the meantime, readership of *Atlantic* had grown enormously, from 38,000 in 1915 to 100,000 in 1918. Goodman writes that "[r]eaders thought that literature expressed not only the heart of their respective nations, but also the strivings of humanity" (2011, p. 242). This is precisely the ambiguity visible in the case of *Atlantic*'s Kartini, whom the editors seemed to have questioned in terms of how she was the same, or how she was different from they themselves with regards to culture, race and humanity. On the one hand, Kartini´s letters in the magazine can be read (by the Americans) as contributions from a less well-known branch of "the family of man", which would then suggest the equality of Kartini as a human being and of Java as a culture. On the other hand, the space provided in *Atlantic* for American exceptionalism, Americanization and scientific racism clearly also indicates the presence of ideas of modern inequality; in this light becoming "better Javanese" gained racial overtones.

Letters of a Javanese Princess

Tensions between notions of human equality and human inequality continued in the edited translation of Kartini's letters which appeared in 1920, the famous *Letters of a Javanese Princess*. In her introduction, Symmers interprets Kartini's letters' "chief interest ... as a human document" and reads them as a manifestation of "the old truth of the oneness of humanity" (1920b, p. xi). However, she also holds that before "[t]he principles for which Kartini struggled" had, she believes, become "more or less universally accepted by her fellow countrymen" (Symmers 1920, pp. xii, xvii), Java had formed "an ancient and outworn civilization" (Symmers 1920, p. xi). Symmers is juggling here with different modern discourses on human equality and inequality. Humanity is one, but some are more human than others, and Kartini's individuation, followed by the rest of Java, is presented as a step forward on the path that had long ago been taken by Enlightened Westerners. Crucially, moreover, the human equality suggested by Symmers for Kartini and the Javanese remains on the level of the individual conscience and does not translate into legal equality and rights. Symmers praises Kartini's "self-searching" and wish for "greater freedom of the mind and of the spirit", but contrasts these endeavours negatively with "the material freedom" for which "the Javanese of the past had sometimes waged a bloody warfare" (Symmers

1920, pp. xi–xii). In Symmers' view, Javanese self-analysis is good but the struggle for Javanese self-rule is bad; this perception again shows the trickiness of the concept of human equality, which in this case pertained to psychological, but not political, equality.

Javanese Princess was published by the publishing house, Alfred A. Knopf, in a book series called Borzoi, named after the Russian wolfhound. Anyone who knows anything about Kartini's thought, including attentive readers of *Javanese Princess*, will be somewhat stunned by the book's title. Already in the first two letters translated in it, Kartini posthumously, as it were, corrects her portrayal on the book's cover not only through her famous "Call me simply Kartini" (Kartini 1920b, p. 9), but also by ridiculing a Dutch guest in their house who had imagined her and her sisters as princesses in "glittering garments, fantastic Oriental splendor" (Kartini 1920b, p. 12). When called "Princesses of Java", Kartini writes, she and her sisters are "embarrassed" (Kartini 1920b, p. 12). When we look at the policies of Knopf, however, the title makes much more sense because of their emphasis on luxury and splendour, which can be seen, for instance, in an advertisement from 1923: "Borzoi books are books de luxe! In the refinement of the format—in the stability of the binding—in fact, in all those things that make a book worthwhile—its intellectual appeal, its ornamental appeal, and its appeal as a desirable permanent possession, Borzoi Books are Books de Luxe, equally a delight to the mind and an addition to the home" (cited in Clements 2013, p. 1). Kartini, cast as an "Oriental princess", has been pulled into a semantic field from which she had attempted to distance herself. According to Amy Root Clements, Knopf (1892–1984) and his wife, Blanche Knopf (1894–1966), who together started the publishing company, were masters at branding the beauty of their books and selling a higher standard of book production and content (Clements 2013, p. 2). One of their tactics was "to confer prestige (a manufactured value) on the authors who were chosen to be associated with Borzoi Books" (Clements 2013, p. 3). In Kartini's case, this seems to have meant giving her a noble title as well as a foreword by one of the most well-known Dutch authors at the time, Louis Couperus (1863–1923), whose reputation was cemented by 1920 due to the publication of ten English translated novels. Just how important Couperus was to Alfred Knopf became apparent that same year, when in a published self-congratulatory anthology called *The Borzoi 1920: Being a Sort of Record of Five Year's Publishing*, we find Couperus' introduction to *Javanese Princess* but not a single letter written by Kartini herself. According to Clements, "the impression that the Borzoi roster was elite … was enhanced by the company's emphasis on European works" (Clements 2013, p. 52). In most of the company's first fifteen years, the majority of Borzoi authors were born in Europe, and Couperus—"the great Dutch novelist" as Alfred Knopf had cast him (Knopf 1920, p. 136)—fitted the Knopfs' agenda of "prestigious literature" (Clements 2013, p. 52).

In the same anthology, Alfred Knopf offers other clues as to why Kartini was selected in the first place. He had discovered her through the publications in *Atlantic*, writing that this magazine "occupies a unique position among our magazines, and most publishers, I think, realize the recommendation that serialization in it carries to readers of books" (Knopf 1920, pp. 135–36). In other words: the prestige already conferred upon her by *Atlantic* was reason enough to consider her for publication as a Borzoi. Alfred Knopf calls Kartini "by the way … the youngest daughter of a Javanese regent and probably the first feminist of the Orient" (Knopf 1920, p. 136). Finally saying something about Kartini herself, as well as the content of her writings, Alfred Knopf does this in a strikingly casual aside, giving the impression that she, compared to his other valued authors, is more of a *bijoux*.

This tendency to see the publishing of the work of authors of colour, as well as of novels featuring characters of colour, as a means to achieve cosmopolitan distinction, is also visible in other instances in the case of the Knopfs. Clements writes that for the Knopfs, the republication in 1916 of W.H. Hudson's 1904 novel *Green Mansions*, set in Guyana and Venezuela, was important because "the book's praise of the noble native gave it a progressive air" (Clements 2013, p. 60). Blanche Knopf's biographer, Laura Claridge, writes that "[u]nlike many middle-class white women of her generation, Blanche felt no hesitation mingling with people of various races and sexual orientations, this was part of the very definition of being modern"; this suggests that hanging out with black people was for Blanche a way to fashion a modern self (Claridge 2016, p. 100). However, Claridge also writes that Blanche Knopf was shocked and dismayed by Wallace Stevens' racism (he once called Gwendolyn Brooks "a coon"). The Knopfs, moreover, are widely credited because they were the first to publish Harlem Renaissance authors, Langston Hughes and Nella Larsen. George Hutchinson writes in *The Harlem Renaissance in Black and White*: "There is just not much evidence that [Alfred] Knopf was guilty of the sort of exploitative mentality that supposedly typified the white publishers' approach to black authors' work" (Hutchinson 1995, p. 365). John Young, however, argues in *Black Writers, White Publishers: Marketplace Politics in Twentieth-Century African American Literature* that in the case of the Knopfs, "the underlying social power reinforcing racial systems is also an inescapable presence, one which operates either benignly or malignantly, but unavoidably" (Young 1998, p. 14). The exoticizing and cursory way in which Alfred Knopf treated Kartini seems to confirm Young's point. Due to structural power differences between this Javanese author and her American publishers, as well as persistent, racialized discourses on human inequality, attempts at achieving human equality were inevitably tainted.

Javanese Princess is prefaced by texts of Symmers and Couperus, and starts with a brief passage from Marco Polo (1254–1324). No comment is provided on the reason for opening with his description of Java (excerpted from the 1871 translation, *The Book of Ser Marco Polo*, by the British Orientalist, Henry Yule). Polo praises the island as "great", with a "great King", and as the source of "surpassing wealth", predominantly spices. Its people, he claims, are idolaters. Standing iconically at the beginning of *Javanese Princess*, American readers were introduced to unknown lands by a relatively well-known thirteenth-century Italian merchant who functioned as a middle man, just as Polo's writings had done for European audiences for many ages (Akbari and Iannucci 2008). By opening with Polo's words, the collection gained prominence as a Borzoi book; after all, Polo was one of the European authors through whom the Knopfs attempted to accumulate symbolic capital for their book series and publishing house. But the use of Polo's words also held other meanings that are significant to the present analysis. Since the late nineteenth century, the United States had itself become an imperial power, just like many European countries, with colonies in the Philippines, the Pacific and the Caribbean. Goodman writes that many *Atlantic* writers "supported imperialism when it advanced the interests of their home country" (Goodman 2011, p. 234). In 1909, the British historian, C. Raymond Beazley, had in an article in *Atlantic* directly connected Polo to the "European expansion" and placed him at the beginning of "[t]he history of the growth of Christian civilization into a practically universal predominance" (Beazley 1909, p. 493). Those were indeed the days when, as Stuurman writes, "white global hegemony attained its all-time high" (Stuurman 2017, p. 415) and American audiences were well aware of this fact and often not a little proud of it.

Couperus, whose foreword immediately followed the passage from Polo, initially pulls Kartini into the semantic field of his novel *The Hidden Force* (*De stille kracht*, literally: The silent force, 1900) when it was published as an English translation by Dodd, Mead and Company in New York in 1921. He describes Kartini and her family in the terminology of the late nineteenth-century European decadent movement: they lived in "sombre obscurity" and lead "often melancholy lives" (Couperus 1920, p. vii). He describes Java as an oriental spectacle, full of "weird mystery", adding that while his family had for generations been in the service of the colonial government, the Dutch had yet to "penetrate its mystery": "there was a quiet strength, *'Een Stille Kracht'* [A Silent Force] unperceived by our cold, business-like gaze" (Couperus 1920, pp. vii–viii). Just like in his famous novel, the heart of the matter in the separation between "East" and "West" was for Couperus "[t]he difference of race" which "forms an abyss so deep that though they may stand face to face and look into each other's eyes, it is as though they saw nothing" (Couperus 1920, p. viii). The novel carries the paradox of "racist anti-colonialism": on the one hand, its anti-colonialism is apparent from the downfall of its main protagonist, a Dutch civil servant named Otto van Oudijck who succumbs to mysterious Indonesian counterforces and his own non-comprehension; on the other hand, its racism is visible from the reason of his downfall as given by the novel, namely that white and brown people should not live together in the same polity as they are fundamentally incompatible. One of the main tropes of the novel is the drama of miscegenation, for mixing races, it holds, will inevitably lead to disaster. In both the novel and Couperus' foreword to *Javanese Princess*, we find modern inequality in terms of a rigid racism.

Yet Couperus' introduction to *Javanese Princess*, written twenty years after his novel, also departs from the latter in a remarkable sense. Near the end of his brief four-page text, Couperus portrays Kartini as raising her voice and bringing "[t]he mysterious 'Quiet Strength' … into the light", where it shows itself to be "tender, human and full of love" (Couperus 1920, p. x). Kartini's is a lonely voice in an "unknown" land otherwise characterized by "subjection and concealment". Against this background, Couperus first calls her a "little bird" and finally "a woman" who "had dared to fight for feminism" (Couperus 1920, pp. viii–ix). In terms of human equality and inequality, the essay makes a remarkable turnaround, from a claim that race is an abyss separating the Dutch from the Java and its "Quiet Strength" to the individuation of Kartini and the humanization of the Javanese. We recognize the two legacies of modern equality and modern inequality, as well as the striking ease with which an author like Couperus was able to switch between these two discourses, showing the prominence of both. Of relevance is what Murat Aydemir has called "the modern sex/culture split", in which "[m]odern individuation hinges on sexuality, based on the exercise of desire in defiance of the shaming constrictions that are imposed by family, religion, community, and tradition" (Aydemir 2011, p. 14). This split can be directly mapped on the racialized distinction between "modernity" (represented by the era of Europe) and "tradition" (where European colonials positioned Asians and Africans). In Couperus' portrait of Kartini, it is through becoming a woman that Kartini moves from "being culture" to "having culture". Yet this production of Kartini as a modern individual, possibly in some or all ways equal to Westerners like Couperus, comes at the price of placing the rest of the Javanese in the past since they, along one of the conceptions of modern inequality discussed above, are positioned as the unenlightened many who need to be brought into modernity by the enlightened few.

Kartini at UNESCO (1957–64)

Between the 1920s and the 1960s, Kartini dropped from the international radar outside Indonesia and the Netherlands. In the early 1960s, she resurfaced internationally through the publication of her translated writings in French (1960) and in English (1964) under the UNESCO Collection of Representative Works. In the final section of this chapter, I will analyse the politics behind the two publications of Kartini in the UNESCO Collection as well as the roles played by two towering figures who wrote forewords to the 1960 and 1964 editions respectively: the French Orientalist, Louis Massignon (1883–1962), and the American diplomat and activist, Eleanor Roosevelt (1884–1962). Although the early 1960s showed important continuities with the 1920s in terms of Western conceptions of human equality and inequality, these two appropriators of Kartini also worked within very different political and institutional contexts than the ones discussed above. Much more explicitly concerned with questions of human equality and inequality, especially through their work for the United Nations and UNESCO, both Massignon and Roosevelt felt the figure of the human was of central importance. Nevertheless, religious—in Massignon's case—and political considerations—for Roosevelt—produced ambiguities in their presentation of Kartini, who was seen as an exceptional figure from an otherwise backward Muslim world and Indonesian nation.

According to Christina Lembrecht, who wrote a history of UNESCO's book politics between 1948 and 1982, the UNESCO Collection of Representative Works embodies the broader perspective developed at UNESCO after World War II in which literature was seen as having the potential to bring cultures together. Although all literature was seen as marked by nationality, great literature was also conceptualized as universal and as transcending national borders. Translation, however, was essential. Already in 1948, UNESCO initiated a programme called "Translation of Great Works" which would later morph into the Collection project. An explicit goal was to move beyond the dominant languages of English and French to include works from the global south as well as from smaller European nations, though translations in English and French still formed the lion's share of published books. Next to Kartini's work, one other text written by an Indonesian was translated—Achdiat Karta Mihardja's 1949 novel *Atheis*—whereas no works have been translated into Indonesian in this series. Of all the translated works, more than 50 per cent came from Asia, while African, Arabic and Latin-American literature combined together amounted to 22 per cent of the published works. In 1951, the first translations, from Arabic, were published; the programme ended in 2005, yielding a total of 1,060 titles. To select titles, UNESCO asked for lists from its national committees as well as from scholars, publishers and translators. UNESCO did not publish these works itself, but cooperated with a wide variety of publishers. Although the variety of texts selected for the Collection is wide and unfocused, this diversity is precisely what was needed then to show that all these works "belonged to a universal unity", a "global unity" (Lembrecht 2013, p. 128). UNESCO's Collection project shows both the loftiness and drawbacks of twentieth-century Western conceptions of world literature, for on the one hand, it engendered the (re)publication of Kartini and Mihardja, yet on the other hand, it masked striking inequalities under the banner of universal humanity.

Kartini was first mentioned in the UNESCO archives in 1957, surprisingly in the Subcommittee for Translations from Arab and Persian. Earlier, she had not appeared on the lists that had been handed in by the various national committees, in particular those of the Netherlands and Indonesia. This was probably due to her liminal position: a Javanese woman writing in Dutch. It was in fact Massignon who mentioned Kartini in the Subcommittee for Arab and Persian; he held that this particular committee on Arab literature had a "right of inspection" concerning the literature of Islam and proposed to have Louis Damais of École française d'Extrême Orient (EFEO) translate the letters of "princess" Kartini, erroneously characterized in the notes as "written in Javanese" (*Sous-Comité* 1957, p. 2).

Louis Massignon and Kartini's Place in Human History

In Massignon's preface to *Lettres de Raden Adjeng Kartini: Java en 1900*, published in 1960, we enter his unique Orientalist universe, which, as Edward Said writes, was much in line with the ideas of other French Orientalists and therefore also part of the larger European grid of intelligibility (Said 2003, p. 271). According to Massignon, Kartini can best be interpreted as the "resurgence of an old archetype of humanity: the isolated apparition of an exceptional, 'sublimated' person, of a woman 'masculinized into a hero', for the initiation of other women into a Knowledge normally reserved for men" (Massignon 1960, p. 6, original emphasis). We can start making sense of this view of Kartini within the context of Massignon's vision of human history, in which heroic individuals who transcend cultural limits play a crucial role. According to Jerrold Seigel, these heroes, also called "saints" by Massignon, "gave symbolic expression to what lay at the core of the group's history ... [they] bear within themselves the genuine meaning of the collective experience that binds a group together [and knit] the particular features of their lives into a whole whose meaning transcends its local and temporal determinants" (Seigel 2016, pp. 146–47). Crucial to my discussion on the place of Kartini in the Western discourse of humanity is that according to Massignon, "heroes" like Kartini, as their life and work become part of their people's self-awareness, were vital in his progressive conception of human history in which he saw a "curve" in time through which not only all people would return to their original ground, but eventually also humanity as a whole. Heroes therefore not only advance the "curve" of their group, but also of the human race. Kartini's contribution, Massignon suggests, lies in "the intellectual advancement of Muslim women in her country" (Massignon 1960, p. 6). His emphasis on Kartini's faith is important. According to Christian Krokus, Massignon "imagined and worked toward a revolution in the relationship between Muslims and Christians, from one poisoned by fear and rivalry to one rooted in mutual understanding" (Krokus 2017, p. 1). This search is also what Said appreciates in Massignon: the latter was always looking for "the human spirit across space and time" by emphasizing the "vital forces" in Eastern cultures (Said 2003, p. 264). Massignon, Said holds, avoided static interpretations of Islamic texts, as he always included as much of the context of a text as possible and emphasized the need for complex readings: "one would be foolish not to respect the sheer genius and novelty of Massignon's mind" (Said 2003, p. 269).

This emphasis on context and complexity is both apparent and absent from Massignon's introduction to Kartini. He delves into the history of the Indonesian archipelago in search of women who can be interpreted as Kartini's predecessors and compares her to similar figures in the Middle East and Europe: Qurratu l-'Ayn from Persia (1814/17–52, better known as Táhirih), the French hero and Catholic saint, Joan of Arc (15th century), and the Dutch mystic, Lidwina (14th–15th century). He also discusses the role of women in *Serat Centhini*, a Javanese collection of tales published in the nineteenth century. However, this construction of an elaborate context does not lead to a complex reading as Massignon makes no attempt to connect it to Kartini's texts: she is not even quoted once and is effectively silenced in the introduction to her own letters.

Massignon's ambiguity with respect to human equality and inequality becomes visible when he introduces one of his co-workers in this Kartini translation, the ethnologist Jeanne Cuisinier, to show "the friendship of an older sister who adopted and co-opted her younger sisters from Indonesia" (Massignon 1960, p. 13). How can we explain this simultaneity of Kartini as both a saint and a younger sister who is never quoted? What becomes apparent here is that not all saints work on the same curve of human history, or, to put it differently, that human history is made up of several hierarchically positioned curves. For Massignon, no other religion equalled Roman Catholicism and the best that could happen to Islam was that "the particular 'curve' of Islamic history would eventually join up with the universal one traced out by Christianity" (Seigel 2016, p. 146). He saw Muslims as the "'doubly excluded,' first from the religious truth of Christianity and second from social well-being" (Seigel 2016, p. 129). According to Said, Massignon followed mainstream (French) Orientalism by seeing the difference between East and West as one between tradition and modernity. His interest in Islam would stem from "the entire nineteenth-century tradition of the Orient as therapeutic for the West" (Said 2003, p. 271). In Massignon's view, human equality lies on the horizon at the end of human history. In historical time, his conception of different curves, however, produced hierarchies of humanity in which the Roman Catholic curve was leading while the Islamic curve was, at most, a supplementary one. Kartini is his foreword has become a saint of the lower order.

Eleanor Roosevelt and the Hierarchy of Humanity

In 1964, W.W. Norton in New York republished Symmers' translation of *Letters of a Javanese Princess*, albeit with the introductions by Indonesianist Hildred Geertz and by Eleanor Roosevelt. Geertz offers a rich reading of Kartini's life in which she discusses her letters in a universalizing framework of the crossing of adolescents "between innocent childhood and self-reliant maturity" (Geertz 1964, p. 7). In her preface, Roosevelt shows a comparable ambiguity vis-a-vis Kartini's equality as a human being that we have already encountered in earlier analyses of other actors and institutions. Modern equality is voiced in the following phrase: "If we are to become cognizant of the oneness of humanity, regardless of race or creed or color, this book will be one of the ways that we will learn" (Roosevelt 1964, p. 5). Modern inequality, however, is phrased as such: "In many ways [these letters] will help us to understand what we of the Western world must understand if we are to be helpful to nations emerging from old customs into new" (Roosevelt 1964, p. 5). It is a rather complicated and ambiguous move Roosevelt is suggesting here, for Kartini is both produced as a guide and an object of care. "The Western world" is placed ahead on a developmental timeline, with both Indonesians and Americans being part of humanity, somehow, but also in different stages. The same seems to be true for the relation Roosevelt imagines between herself and Kartini.

When reviewing the literature on Roosevelt, it is not easy to place these comments as she has been heralded mostly as a champion of human rights, equality and anti-racism. Roosevelt, who was the chair of, and the United States representative to, the United Nations Commission on Human Rights between 1946 and 1953, had played a role in drafting the Universal Declaration of Human Rights (UDHR). M. Glen Johnson places her in what he sees as the historical United States' "leadership role in the quest for a standard of human rights with global applicability", noting that she played a "key role" in drafting the UDHR (Johnson 1987, pp. 19–20). Johnson presents Roosevelt as going against mainstream post-war US politics, in which "human rights have not had a high place" (Johnson 1987, p. 30). Susan Waltz writes that "without her the entire project might have been lost" (2002, p. 442). In Waltz's account, Roosevelt, though endowed the title of "First Lady of the World" by President Harry S. Truman (in office 1945–53), bravely faced a coalition of the US State Department, the right-wing opponents known as the Old Guard and "racists working under the banner of 'state' rights'" (Waltz 2002, p. 443). She has also received laudatory evaluations with respect to African-American history. In *Encyclopedia of African American History*, for instance, she is described as pushing for "racial equality" for African American citizens, and standing up for her beliefs "both in the public spotlight and, often more effectively, behind the scenes" (Finkelman 2009, vol. 4, p. 245). The entry describes Roosevelt's efforts against the lynching of African Americans, for their appointment in higher positions in government, and to be photographed together with black US citizens. It has been suggested that only "[t]he political realities of her day sometimes limited what she was able to do" (Finkelman 2009, vol. 4, p. 245).

A different picture, however, and one closer to the Roosevelt we saw in her preface to Kartini, starts emerging when we look at her *My Day* newspaper columns. She wrote these between 1935 and 1962, but the ones closest to her preface, written in 1961, are the most relevant here, especially when we focus on her views on colonialism. On 30 November 1960, for instance, Roosevelt discussed attempts by the Soviet Union as well as by a coalition of African and Asian states to abolish colonialism. According to Roosevelt, however, the Afro-Asian resolution has one weakness, namely, its demand that the "'inadequacy of political, economic, social or cultural preparedness' shall not serve as a pretext for denying independence" (Roosevelt 2017b). Initially, Roosevelt writes that she finds this demand "quite natural", as this idea of a lack of preparedness has often been used to prevent decolonization. Next, however, she asks what "self-determination" actually means, claiming that it was never well defined. Then, surprisingly, she comes up with the definition that she has just rejected, claiming that for "most people" self-determination requires "certain abilities or qualities in the people", and finally dismisses the notion that self-determination is "a basic right without any qualifications attached to it". She concludes that "one should ... still set some qualifications that must be met before self-determination is granted" (Roosevelt 2017b).

One year earlier in 1959, after both speaking out principally against colonialism and predicting its demise, she nevertheless writes: "So, it seems to me, the important thing for all who have an opportunity to help develop these areas of the world is to look upon the future as an opportunity to live together and work cooperatively and to prepare the peoples of the new nations for their future responsibilities as well as possible" (Roosevelt 2017a). As in her preface to Kartini, Roosevelt here sees colonized people as those in need of help and, moreover, as unprepared for independence.

This less-than-progressive Roosevelt, as I indicated above, is not often found in the literature. Roosevelt's most recent biographer, Blanche Wiesen Cook, characterizes her response to the 1951 UN petition "We Charge Genocide: The Crime of Government Against the Negro People" as being "[b]lindsided by her Cold War priorities" (Cook 2016, p. 562). Roosevelt had called the petition "perfect nonsense" (Cook 2016, p. 562). In 1947, she was equally displeased with Du Bois' protest to the UN against US racism entitled "An Appeal to the World: A Statement of Denial of Human Rights to Minorities in the Case of Citizens of Negro Descent" (Cook 2016, p. 561). A more explicitly critical approach to Roosevelt can be found in Carol Anderson's *Eyes off the Prize: The United Nations and the African American Struggle for Human Rights*, which notes that Roosevelt, although clearly committed to some level of civil rights, was "both unable and unprepared to fight for a world that embraced full equality for African Americans" (Anderson 2003, p. 2). Like other authors, Anderson points to the importance of the Cold War and to the Southern Democrats who were afraid that international human rights would lead to investigations into as well as alterations of race relations in the American South. Anderson characterizes Roosevelt as "one of the masters of symbolic equality" who had manipulated human rights treaties "to shield the United States from UN scrutiny" and ward off the Soviet Union (Anderson 2003, p. 4). When we read both Roosevelt's preface to Kartini and her remarks on the conditions for self-determination, it becomes clear that her concerns with the realities of national and international politics go hand in hand with the separation of the "already" and the "not yet" enlightened. Although in her preface Kartini is individuated, the latter is presented as only somewhat at the forefront of a people who still "are" culture, unaware of modernity's achievement to "have" culture. The distinction between tradition and modernity that is implied here can also be found in Roosevelt's quoted phrase that Kartini can teach the West what it needs to teach the East. Roosevelt, in other words, showed more than pragmatic, political cunning alone, for she had in her assessment of both Kartini and decolonization, actively deployed the vocabularies of modern inequality.

Conclusion

In many ways, Kartini herself laid the groundwork for several of the appropriations discussed in this chapter. In her letters, she probed the tensions between Western discourses on human equality and human inequality, and presented herself as humanized and individuated, often in contrast to other Javanese, particularly those of different classes or those untouched by the cluster of ideas called modernity. Throughout this chapter, I have presented my own understanding of Kartini, which has been shaped by postcolonial studies, critical race studies as well as African-American studies. By keeping our eyes on Kartini's own critical thought on structural racism, we are confronted with the fact that all emancipatory projects initiated in the West that had in some way involved her work and figure, including the present edited volume, have reproduced structural power differences that are, more often than not, strongly characterized by what Rey Chow calls the "ethnicization of labor" (Chow 2002, p. 34). International work on Kartini, from the early twentieth century until now, is mostly done by white people working in Western institutions. In this sense, this chapter offers no more than an awareness of the pitfalls in employing Kartini in Western contexts. Studying Kartini's Western appropriations offers necessary insights into the ambiguities of the discourses of modern equality and inequality, and of human rights, as is also evidenced by my other chapter (Chapter 7) in this volume. As Kartini argues in her writings on rights, real change demands more than an awareness; it demands an institutional and legal overhaul.

NOTES

1. All translations of Kartini in this chapter are mine. Kartini's original texts in Dutch have not yet been collected in one volume. Therefore, I sometimes refer to a 1911 collection (Kartini 1911) and sometimes to a 1987 collection (Kartini 1987). References to Joost Coté's translation are added so readers can look up the broader context of the quotes (Kartini 2014).

2. The other two forms of modern inequality identified by Stuurman are political economy ("a new science that justified social inequality in terms of utility and productivity") and biological and psychological theories of sexual difference (Stuurman 2017, p. 24).
3. For Kartini in the Netherlands, see in this volume Coté, Chapter 2 (colonial context) and Bijl, Chapter 7 (postcolonial period).

REFERENCES

Akbari, Suzanne Conklin and Amilcare Iannucci, eds. 2008. *Marco Polo and the Encounter of East and West*. Toronto: University of Toronto Press.

Anderson, Carol. 2003. *Eyes off the Prize: The United Nations and the African American Struggle for Human Rights, 1944–1955*. Cambridge: Cambridge University Press.

Aydemir, Murat. 2011. "Introduction: Indiscretions at the Sex/Culture Divide". In *Indiscretions: At the Intersection of Queer and Postcolonial Theory*, edited by Murat Aydemir. Amsterdam: Rodopi.

Beazley, C. Raymond. 1909. "Marco Polo and the European Expansion of the Middle Ages". *Atlantic Monthly* 111, no. 10: 493–500.

Bender, Thomas. 1987. *New York Intellect: A History of Intellectual Life in New York City, from 1750 to the Beginnings of Our Own Time*. New York: Knopf.

Bijl, Paul. 2009. "Old, Eternal and Future Light in the Dutch East Indies: Colonial Photographs and the History of the Globe". In *Mediation, Remediation and the Dynamics of Cultural Memory*, edited by Astrid Erll and Ann Rigney. Berlin: De Gruyter.

————. 2017. "Legal Self-fashioning in Colonial Indonesia: Human Rights in the Letters of Kartini". *Indonesia* 103: 51–71.

Chow, Rey. 2002. *The Protestant Ethnic and the Spirit of Capitalism*. New York: Columbia University Press.

Claridge, Laura. 2016. *The Lady with the Borzoi: Blanche Knopf, Literary Tastemaker Extraordinaire*. New York: Farrar, Straus and Giroux.

Clements, Amy Root. 2013. *The Art of Prestige: The Formative Years at Knopf, 1915–1929*. Amherst: University of Massachusetts Press.

Cook, Blanche Wiesen. 2016. *The War Years and After, 1939–1962*. Vol. 3 of *Eleanor Roosevelt*. New York: Viking.

Coté, Joost. 2014. "Letters 1902: Introduction". In *Kartini: The Complete Writings, 1898–1904*, by Kartini. Edited and translated by Joost Coté. Clayton, Victoria: Monash University.

Couperus, Louis. 1920. Foreword to *Letters of a Javanese Princess*, by Kartini. Translated by Agnes Louise Symmers. New York: Knopf.

Du Bois, W.E.B. 1915. "The African Roots of War". *Atlantic Monthly* 117, no. 5: 707–14.

Finkelman, Paul, ed. 2009. *Encyclopedia of African American History 1896 to the Present*. 5 vols. Oxford: Oxford University Press.

Geertz, Hildred. 1964. "Kartini: An Introduction". In *Letters of a Javanese Princess*, by Kartini. Translated by Agnes Louise Symmers. New York: W.W. Norton.

Goodman, Susan. 2011. *The Republic of Words: The Atlantic Monthly and Its Writers 1857–1925*. Hanover, NH: University of New England Press.

Hunt, Lynn. 2007. *Inventing Human Rights: A History*. New York: W.W. Norton.

Hutchinson, George. 1995. *The Harlem Renaissance in Black and White*. Cambridge, MA: Belknap Press of Harvard University Press.

Johnson, M. Glen. 1987. "The Contributions of Eleanor Roosevelt and Franklin Roosevelt to the Development of International Protection of Human Rights". *Human Rights Quarterly* 9: 19–48.

Kartini, R.A. 1911. *Door duisternis tot licht: Gedachten over en voor het Javaansche volk*. Edited by J.H. Abendanon. Semarang: Van Dorp.

———. 1919a. "A Javanese Wedding: More Letters from Java". *Atlantic Monthly* 121, no. 12: 749–59.

———. 1919b. "Javanese Letters: The Old Life and the New Spirit". *Atlantic Monthly* 121, no. 11: 591–602.

———. 1920a. "The New Woman in Java". *Atlantic Monthly* 122, no. 1: 56–65.

———. 1920b. *Letters of a Javanese Princess*. Translated by Agnes Louise Symmers. New York: Knopf.

———. 1960. *Lettres de Raden Adjeng Kartini: Java en 1900*. Edited and translated by Louis Charles Damais. Paris: Mouton.

———. 1964. *Letters of a Javanese Princess*. Translated by Agnes Louise Symmers. New York: W.W. Norton.

———. 1987. *Brieven aan mevrouw R.M. Adendanon-Mandri en haar echtgenoot*. Edited by F.G.P. Jaquet. Dordrecht: Foris.

———. 2014. *Kartini: The Complete Writings, 1898–1904*. Edited and translated by Joost Coté. Clayton, Victoria: Monash University.

Knopf, Alfred. 1920. *The Borzoi 1920: Being a Sort of Record of Five Year's Publishing*. New York: Knopf.

Krokus, Christian. 2017. *The Theology of Louis Massignon: Islam, Christ and the Church*. Washington: The Catholic University of America Press.

Lembrecht, Christina. 2013. *Bücher für alle: Die UNESCO und die weltweite Förderung des Buches 1946–1982*. Berlin: De Gruyter.

Massignon, Louis. 1960. Preface to *Lettres de Raden Adjeng Kartini: Java en 1900*, by Kartini. Edited and translated by Louis Charles Damais. Paris: Mouton.

Ponzanesi, Sandra. 2014. *The Postcolonial Cultural Industry: Icons, Markets, Mythologies*. Basingstoke: Palgrave.

Roosevelt, Eleanor. 1964. Preface to *Letters of a Javanese Princess*, by Kartini. Translated by Agnes Louise Symmers. New York: W.W. Norton.

————. 2017a. "My Day, December 3, 1959". *The Eleanor Roosevelt Papers Digital Edition*. https://www2.gwu.edu/~erpapers/myday/displaydoc. cfm?_y=1959&_f=md004605 (accessed 14 February 2018).

————. 2017b. "My Day, November 30, 1960". *The Eleanor Roosevelt Papers Digital Edition*. https://www2.gwu.edu/~erpapers/myday/displaydoc. cfm?_y=1960&_f=md004883 (accessed 14 February 2018).

Rupp, Leila. 1997. *Worlds of Women: The Making of an International Women's Movement*. Princeton: Princeton University Press.

Said, Edward. [1978] 2003. *Orientalism*. 25th Edition. London: Vintage.

Seigel, Jerrold. 2016. "The Islamic Catholicism of Louis Massignon". In *Between Cultures: Europe and Its Others in Five Exemplary Lives*, by Jerrold Seigel. Philadelphia: University of Pennsylvania Press.

Sous-Comité Pour les Traductions de l'Arabe et du Perse. 28 October 1957. Typescript. CIPSH/Trad/57/22, UNESCO Archives, Paris.

Stuurman, Siep. 2017. *The Invention of Humanity*. Cambridge, MA: Harvard University Press.

Symmers, Agnes Louise. 1920. Introduction to *Letters of a Javanese Princess*, by Kartini. Translated by Agnes Louise Symmers. New York: Knopf.

Tagore, Rabindranath. 1917. "Nationalism in the West". *Atlantic Monthly* 119, no. 3: 289–301.

Waltz, Susan. 2002. "Reclaiming and Rebuilding the History of the Universal Declaration of Human Rights". *Third World Quarterly* 23, no. 3: 437–48.

Young, John. 1998. *Black Writers, White Publishers: Marketplace Politics in Twentieth-Century African American Literature*. Jackson: University Press of Mississippi.

4

Ambivalent Narration: Kartini's Silence and the Other Woman

Grace V.S. Chin

Introduction

In studies on Kartini, observations have been made about the ironies and contradictions presented by the liberal, modern and feminist persona in her letters. Goenawan Mohammad for instance points out how Kartini would negotiate on "what to say and what is not to be said" (2005, p. vi) in her letters to Stella Zeehandelaar, noting that while she denounced women's suffering in arranged and polygamous marriages as well as their lack of access to education, she was also remarkably reticent when it came to divulging the truth about her own polygamous family background. Despite their shared passion in gender reforms, Zeehandelaar never knew that Kartini was the daughter of a *selir*, a secondary wife named Ngasirah. Kartini, who readily identified herself as a member of the *priyayi*, had omitted the fact that the "mama" she spoke of in relation to "Madura royalty" (Kartini 2005, p. 30; Kartini 2014, p. 75) was in fact her stepmother, Raden Ayu Moerjam, also the consort wife (or *padmi*) to the *bupati* of Jepara, Kartini's father. What I find interesting here, however, is not so much Kartini's attempt to hide her polygamous family background from Zeehandelaar, but rather the way in which her pride as a member of the *priyayi* class comes to the fore. Kartini's silence in fact smacks of complicity that is implicitly class-related. As a member of the privileged class, Kartini—despite her resistance against native patriarchy—had little to say about the lower-class women who occupied the ideological and material fringes of her world, including the *selir* and peasant women (Gouda 1995; Hawkins 2007).[1] As Manderson states, Kartini's "contrary portrait of women imprisoned, literally and metaphorically, seems peculiarly bound by class and region" (1983, p. 2).

This chapter examines how Kartini's silence about the Other woman—represented by the *selir* and female peasant in Kartini's own lifetime, and the lower-class women in the postcolonial context—problematizes the popular narrative of her feminist progressiveness in Indonesian history. Of significance here is the manner in which Kartini's class consciousness has been maintained and reproduced by entrenched attitudes and viewpoints towards women who occupy the bottom rung of the social ladder in post-independence Indonesia. Focusing on Kartini's silence as the disruptive site of ambivalence, I consider how her memory and symbolism—based on stereotyped ideas of her feminist and nationalist consciousness—are in fact rooted in embedded structures of silence as well as erasure, violence and trauma that attend contemporary narratives of feminist struggle in Indonesia. These structures of silence I contend, reveal relational hierarchies of power that intersect social class (elitism), race (Javanese-ness) and gender, through which socially inferior and non-Javanese women have been silenced and marginalized at different points of colonial and postcolonial history. Kartini's silence—defined in relation to Javanese *priyayi* elitism and class consciousness—can thus be used to read against the grain of dominant interpretations of her symbolism in Indonesian history, which have mainly centred on resistance and agency, and linked to nationalism and feminism (see the editors' Introduction, pp. 1–16). Recent studies have begun digging into the silences and gaps related to Kartini's life, notably Woodward (2015), which examines what has been silenced and lost during the processes of appropriation, and Bijl (in this volume, Chapter 7), which associates silence with resistance, truth and protest. As yet, few studies have considered the complexities and contradictions posed by her silence or the ways it has been appropriated and reproduced in the postcolonial narratives of race, class and gender.

Addressing this omission, I contend that Kartini's silence about the Other woman bears significant ramifications for Indonesian women in the postcolonial patriarchal imaginary, seen in the hierarchical relationships and ideological divisions between elite and lower-class women, and the ways in which they obtain, negotiate and use power, even when they are positioned as secondary in the gender binary. By tracing the strange twists and turns that attend the historical appropriations of Kartini's silence, I explore how it reflects the ideological imperatives and hegemonic discourses of the ruling patriarchal elite: upheld by the Dutch who also promoted Kartini as a shining symbol of colonial success, downplayed by Sukarno whose populist Old Order government reconstructed Kartini as a non-elite Indonesian, and, finally, resurrected by Suharto's elitist regime during which Kartini was revised yet again, but this time as an obedient, domesticated *ibu* (mother). It was also during Suharto's repressive rule that the class differences among women were reified by the racializing and gendering strategies deployed as part of the state's neo-colonizing projects of conquest and domination across the archipelago. As a result, the symbolism of Kartini's *priyayi* elitism during this period was burdened by the silencing of not only lower-class women but also of non-Javanese women.

While the impact of patriarchal authority on women's daily lives is undeniable, my aim here is to examine the ways in which generations of Indonesian elite women have participated in the male-centric class system in their attempt to realize their own independence and achieve agency. As a result, elite women have—whether directly or indirectly—contributed to the divisions among women of different social levels in Indonesia. In short, lower-class women who fight for Kartini's ideals have also been subverted by male *and* female elitist attitudes at the top. A Janus-faced ambivalence is thus constructed around Kartini's iconicity, for even as she is upheld at the ideological, national level as the champion of women's causes, Kartini's *priyayi* elitism has remained entrenched within the social and national discourses of Indonesia. This ambivalence can in fact be traced through the two narrative threads that have remained constant despite the different articulations and shifts in meaning that attend Kartini's memory and symbolism. The first is the popular trope of Kartini's feminist progressiveness and national consciousness, but the second is her less visible, quieter legacy of *priyayi* elitism, which has been maintained by the upper echelons of Indonesia's ruling elite, the politically powerful Javanese male rulers and their female consorts, whose feminine authority over non-Javanese, lower-class women reached its peak in the New Order with the rise of Dharma Wanita under the leadership of the First Lady, Raden Ayu Siti Hartinah, also President

Suharto's wife. I describe this second narrative thread as "less visible" because classism is not a characteristic readily associated with Kartini. Kartini's ambivalent legacy thus holds double-edged implications that reflect the ironies and contradictions in Indonesian women's movements and struggles, for it simultaneously promotes the narrative of women's progress, equality and freedom, *and* undermines these ideals through the continued subjection of women according to class and, outside of Java, race.

In using the term "Janus-faced", I adapt Homi K. Bhabha's theory of nation and narration to my reading of Kartini's ambivalent legacy of progress and subjection, mainly, how "a particular ambivalence haunts the idea of the nation, the language of those who write of it and the lives of those who live it" (1990, p. 1). According to Bhabha, the ambivalent narration of the nation reveals the split between ideology and material practice, for while the nation homogenizes all differences under the immutable sign and ideology of the nation (which includes its history and origins), the lived, material experiences of our fast-changing world reveal "a much more transitional social reality" (1990, p. 1) that is based on the constant processes of change, hybridization, and transformation. The term "Janus-face" in fact captures the contradictions and paradoxes of the language employed to narrate the modern nation as it comes into being. Building on Bhabha's argument of the "Janus-faced ambivalence of language itself in the construction of the Janus-faced discourse of the nation" (1990, p. 3), I argue that this linguistic ambivalence is reflected in Kartini's letters as she attempted to fashion a certain personality for her Dutch readers (see also Robinson's Chapter 6 in this volume) by selectively choosing whom to withhold information from and whom to share ideas or private details with.[2] Through Kartini's selective words and silences, the first contradictions, paradoxes and ironies are presented to us; these elements are later complicated and reified by both colonial and postcolonial appropriative acts.

Language—defined not just in terms of words and textuality but also as a system of representation, which includes image and the silence of body language, of performativity—is thus significant to the ambivalent narration of Kartini, for even as her words of defiance and protest—most famously *Habis gelap terbitlah terang* (When darkness ends, light appears)—are celebrated (inter)nationally, the silences embedded within her writings underline the continued dominance of upper-class Javanese elites in Indonesian political life. In this manner,

Kartini, the colonial and national symbol, has come to represent the site of an "ambivalent narration that holds culture at its most productive position, as a force for 'subordination, fracturing, diffusing, reproducing as much as producing, creating, forcing, guiding'" (Bhabha 1990, pp. 3–4). As the site of ambivalent narration that is characterized by, on the one hand, the trope of female progress (spread through her words) and, on the other hand, the trope of female subjection (reproduced through her silence), the memory of Kartini also constitutes the discursive space of contestations through which the "meanings of cultural and political authority are negotiated" (Bhabha 1990, p. 4) and produced.

Javanese Women in Kartini's Letters and Time: *Priyayi* and Other

This section enters Kartini's *priyayi* world to examine the identities and lives of Javanese women at the turn of the twentieth century. This very important juncture in Indonesian history, described as an "age in motion" (Shiraishi 1990), saw changes among the *priyayi* as an administrative class as a result of shifts in Dutch policies as well as the influential forces of Western modernity and rising nationalism. Here, I will consider how women were historically constructed and positioned according to social background within the stratified spaces of the *kabupaten*[3] and the kinds of power accessible to them. This analysis is important in establishing the social differences between *priyayi* women and non-*priyayi* women from the rural villages, and how these differences translate into female ranks, status and power acquisition within the male-centric discourses of Javanese nobility. While we have, thanks to Kartini, been given rare glimpses into the private life of a *priyayi* woman, not very much is historically known about village women, who constitute the female masses at the time. This lack of knowledge points not only to the marginalization and erasure of the Other woman in both colonial and national narratives, but also how this subaltern figure has long been subjected to the historical and discursive forces of silencing and being silenced.

The colonial Javanese social world is a complex feudal system based on colonial and local forms of patronage, space (urban, village), religion and culture, among others. However, certain broad features can be found. Geertz's 1956 study shows three major social formations among the natives in the largely agrarian society prior to 1915: the *priyayi*, traders and rural villagers, who were also peasants.[4] The *priyayi* functioned as the aristocratic ruling class; they symbolized the best of Javanese culture with their higher education, refinement in manners and language, and connection with the spiritual and mystical dimensions of Javanese life.[5] Under Dutch rule however, the *priyayi* occupied an ambivalent space, sandwiched between the colonial government and the native population and, depending on context, were perceived as either "a feared and admired ruling class" or "the subordinate agents of an alien regime" (Sutherland 1979, p. 1). As ambivalent as their position was in the colonial context, the *priyayi* were still looked up to as the ruling class among the native population; they were deferred to and respected as leaders who were responsible for the welfare of the village community. However, the cultured *priyayi* tended to be self-contained and maintained their distance from the other groups. The middle class on the other hand comprised of villagers with landed property or urbanized residents involved in commercial activities, i.e. traders and merchants. Meanwhile, the lowest social stratum was formed by landless peasants and rural villagers. According to Sutherland, it is also the lower-class villagers who had a much more difficult relationship with the *priyayi*, one based on "allegiance and alienation" (1979, p. 30). Generally, the *priyayi* perceived the villagers as "ignorant, labouring men knowing nothing of the refinements which set men apart from beasts" (Sutherland 1979, p. 30), and treated them with an authoritarian and paternalistic hand. Due to limited social interaction, the three groups remained fairly segregated while a clear social divide ran between the *priyayi* and villagers.

To an extent, this divide is reflected in Kartini's writings, which "rarely established a linkage between her own predicament and the somber reality of Javanese women's lives in the *desa* [countryside]" (Gouda 1995, p. 32). As scholars have previously observed, Katini's letters carry her unique perspective as a Dutch-educated, modern Javanese *priyayi* woman; her struggles for women's rights to education as well as her bitter opposition against arranged marriage and polygamy[6] reflect concerns arising from the circumscribed lives led by *priyayi* women within the confined spaces of the *kraton* (royal palace) and *kabupaten* (Gouda 1995; Hawkins 2007; Taylor 1976, 1989, 1993, 1997a). Seen in this light, it becomes clear that Kartini's fight for women's rights to education and equality did not in fact extend to the lower class. Even when she wrote passionately about giving the Javanese people education in her famous memorandum, she did not consider those of the lower class as her social equal: "[P]rovide education, instruction, for the daughters of the nobility; the civilizing influence has to flow from here to the people" (Kartini 2014, p. 811). In her mind, the educated, modern *priyayi* women would be cast in new roles and identities as enlightened wives and mothers who "pass[ed] on their refinement and education to their children" (Kartini 2014, p. 811), who could then "safeguard the welfare of the people" (Kartini 2014, p. 811).[7] Kartini might have railed against the gendered injustices suffered by *priyayi* women, but she still subscribed strongly to "notions of what was due to her class and rank", in that the *priyayi* was "uniquely fitted for improving the lot of Java's peasantry" (Taylor 1989, p. 305). Adhering to the proper flow of civilizing power from top to bottom, and according to concepts of rank, status and class in the Javanese social hierarchy, Kartini's vision, influenced by the Dutch notion of *noblesse oblige* and *priyayi* attitude towards the villagers, suggests an innate belief in mutual obligations and reciprocal relations between the superior elites and their inferiors (Gouda 1995; Hawkins 2007). Such a vision not only underscores the Janus-faced ambivalence of Kartini's attitude towards social progress but also reveals her ingrained sense of class entitlement; this *priyayi* characteristic is made apparent in another letter to Stella: "Were I to choose an occupation it would have to be something which was fitting! Work that we would like to do, and which would not shame my most noble and high-placed family (a string of regents from the Oosthoek[8] to central Java)" (Kartini 2005, p. 35; Kartini 2014, p. 80).[9]

The ambivalence of Kartini's "progressive" vision reflects the pervasive influence of class barriers which could be found even in the *kabupaten*, enacted through the segregated lives led within private, domestic walls. As noted in the editors' Introduction (pp. 1–16), Kartini's letters reveal much about the restrictive lives led by *priyayi* women whose identity, role and position had revolved around the traditional discourses of wifehood and motherhood. Living side by side with *priyayi* women within the *kabupaten* however, were the village women of whom relatively little is known about, having mostly been silenced by history, and even by Kartini herself. These women, according to Taylor, were "taken temporarily or permanently into the *kabupaten* as servants, concubines, and secondary wives" (1993, p. 166) and served their function as shadowy figures who nonetheless facilitated the *bupati*'s control over the villages. *Priyayi* men were not the only ones to take advantage of lower-class women; both European and *Peranakan* Chinese men also used them as their *nyai* (native concubine).[10] The majority of such women led lives of poverty toiling in the rice fields or Dutch-owned plantations of sugar, tea and coffee

(Gouda 1995, p. 32). An estimated 4 per cent of these women worked in European and *priyayi* households and were exploited as poorly-paid servants (Gouda 1995). It was also from among this group of women that a secondary tier of wives was formed in the *kabupaten*: the *selir*. Taylor (1989) provides some insight into their realm:

> In the respectable *priyayi* family, secondary wives had always been kept discreetly in the background, enjoying a status akin to that of a high-class servant. Often they were the daughters of village heads in the territories under the *bupati*'s jurisdiction. Marriage as secondary wife to a *bupati* was regarded as an honour for the woman, and it tended to promote loyalty to the ruling house. (p. 304)

While marriage to a *bupati* represented a move in upward mobility, this "promotion" in status was nonetheless tampered by the reality of the Javanese preoccupation with hierarchy, for a *selir* was still a "servant" albeit a "high-class" one.

Domestic power then was held by the consort wife or *padmi* who oversaw the running of the household; she controlled not just the secondary wives but also had authority over their children. The *padmi* wielded power in another significant way, for she was indispensable to her husband's status and authority among the *priyayi*. As long as a *priyayi* man did not have a consort wife, he was viewed by his community as an unmarried man (*jaka*) regardless of the number of *selir* wives he already had (Kukathas 2009). As her husband's social equal, the *padmi* could more fully participate in his social life; at the same time, she helped facilitate relations between local ruling families and households. At the turn of the twentieth century, this role extended to embracing the concept of Javanese modernity, in which having a Dutch education was an asset that enabled the *padmi* to help build colonial alliances for her husband (Taylor 1993). The distinctions between *padmi* and *selir* were not only based on function and role, but also reflected in ceremony as well as living arrangements and spaces. In general, the *padmi* resided with her husband in the main building while the *selir* lived in the grounds; the latter only entered the main residence when called upon by her husband (Kukathas 2009). Unlike the Raden Ajeng and Raden Ayu of the *kabupaten* whose positions were recognized, the village women who made up the ranks of *selir*, concubine and servant remained invisible within and outside the walls of the *kabupaten*:

> Such women were not sent to Dutch schools. They did not visit European ladies and discuss with them the rights of women. They did not attend

meetings of the Indies Chinese Students Association or study law in Holland. They had no rights to their own children, not even to be addressed as 'mother'. (Taylor 1997a, p. xix)

The life of Ngasirah, the most famous *selir* we know of by virtue of her daughter's achievements and memory, is testament to the kind of invisibility and silence experienced by socially inferior Javanese women at the turn of the twentieth century. As sensitive as Kartini was to women's plight in polygamous and arranged marriages, she had—as noted earlier—concealed the truth of her birth mother from her close Dutch friends, including Zeehandelaar and Marie Ovink-Soer.[11] Only one woman, Rosa Abendanon-Mandri—addressed as "little mother" in Kartini's letters—was privy to this secret. Ngasirah was by all accounts a woman who adhered to the prescriptions of *adat* (customary law; Coté 2014, p. 13). Married to Sosroningrat at the age of fourteen, she led a life of obscurity even though she bore him eight children; all acknowledged RA Moerjam as their "mother" and were accorded the *priyayi* status denied to Ngasirah. As the representation of the lowly commoner or village woman, Ngasirah has been the subject of literary and cinematic revisions, notably in Pramoedya Ananta Toer's *Panggil aku Kartini sadja* (Just call me Kartini, 1962) (see Rutherford's Chapter 5 in this volume) and the recent 2017 film titled *Kartini*. Both works portray Ngasirah as a long-suffering woman; the 2017 film takes it one step further by depicting Ngasirah as a common servant whose socially inferior position is reflected not just in her interactions with her *priyayi* betters in the main house but also in the way she has to live in a hut at the back of the house, completely hidden from public view. While Ngasirah's origins and life have received limited scholarly and literary attention, the same cannot be said about Kartini's co-wives, of whom virtually nothing is known about.

It is now well known that Kartini experienced great emotional suffering prior to her marriage to the Dutch-educated *bupati* of Rembang, Djojo Adiningrat, who already had three *selir* and seven children.[12] In the letters written after her marriage however, Kartini seems to have accepted her new role and responsibilities as *padmi*, including that of motherhood:

And our children! How can I tell you about these treasures? They are such dear, lovable things to which I was immediately attached.... My precious ones do not consider themselves above the humblest member of the household, they consider everyone as equals. I have discovered that here the field has been prepared, I have only to sow. (Kartini 2014, p. 660)

The excerpt above—taken from Kartini's letter dated 12 December 1903 to Rosa Abendanon-Mandri—reflects her possessive pride in calling her stepchildren "my precious ones", as well as her pleasure in her new role as *"Moeder"* (mother): "I am writing at 4 o'clock in the morning. The children are awake and are hanging around my chair. Moeder has to give them bread and milk" (Kartini 2014, p. 661). Another letter to Rosa, dated 8 June 1904, also shows how Kartini has settled into a comfortable routine with her new family and home, having "divide[d] my days between my dear husband, my housework and my children, my own and my adopted" (2014, p. 673). Significantly, an idyllic picture of a close-knit nuclear family is being painted in these letters, one in which all signs of polygamy have been erased: "Father reads the paper and my little ones gather themselves around their mother. I sit in an armchair, the two youngest ones on my lap, a child on each arm of the chair and at my knee the oldest. We play games or tell stories" (2014, p. 673). When read together, these letters in fact reveal a disquieting pattern of silence borne out of Kartini's refusal to address, or even acknowledge, the presence of her husband's secondary wives, also the birth mothers of these "little ones" even as she writes, ironically, of equality. As *selir*, these voiceless mothers were, and still are, rendered invisible and absent in Kartini's married life, erased from sight and sound.[13] Regardless of the reasons behind her refusal to speak about her co-wives, Kartini had "exercised her superior rights ... in speaking of 'my children', and she worked to detach her husband's children from their birth mothers" (Taylor 1997a, p. xviii).

Here then we see working in Kartini's writings—"full of 'never tells'" (Taylor 1993, p. 162)—the exclusion of the *selir*, or, the Other woman. This silenced Otherness that is the non-*priyayi* woman constitutes a problematic site of tension, ambivalence and discomfort that disrupts the authenticity and "truth" of Kartini's self-narration and self-representation as a modern, progressive woman; it is the site of ambivalent narration through which the figure of the Other woman continues to haunt and complicate Kartini's legacy and memory, for even as her vision of women's education was being realized by the colonial government, her sisters, and her Dutch friends in the years after her death, there remained, between the *priyayi* world and the lower order, rigid and inviolable class and language boundaries. These boundaries were reified by the colonial educational system in its support of Kartini's vision (and its own civilizing prerogatives), in which the educated *priyayi* woman would light the path for underprivileged Javanese, including poor and illiterate women in both rural and urban areas (Gouda 1995). Invariably too, the hierarchization of colonial education, evinced by "first-class" Dutch native schools that catered to the children of *priyayi* and affluent families, and "second-class" Malay or vernacular medium native schools aimed at children of families lower on the social scale (Gouda 1995), contributed to the deepening of the rift between *priyayi* and non-*priyayi* women whose differences were not only based on class, but also education and language.

The colonial period also saw the opening of girls' schools that included Dewi Sartika's *Kautamaan Istri* (Virtuous Wife) schools, the Kartini Schools, and Van Deventer boarding schools, all of which were intended for native girls of families who rejected mixed-gender education.[14] These schools held similar goals in elevating the position of the native woman; they aimed to train women in ways that would prepare them for work such as teaching and clerical work. However, many of them were also tuition-paying schools and could only be afforded by families with money and status; hence *priyayi* daughters were the ones who mostly benefitted from these schools (Gouda 1995). At the time, it was also commonly held that education for lower-class girls "[did] not need to be too extensive, because it would not be useful for their way of life" (cited in Blackburn 2004, p. 42). Only an elementary education that consisted of reading and writing in Javanese, knowing basic Latin letters and arithmetic was considered "sufficient" (Blackburn 2004, p. 42).

By the 1930s, the Dutch-educated *priyayi* woman became the success story of her Dutch-integrated *priyayi* world, in line with Kartini's vision. Meanwhile, the underprivileged women of the villages and countryside, the majority of whom were illiterate or only had primary education, continued to suffer exploitation and discrimination in silence (Gouda 1995).[15] Although small steps were made to improve their situation, notably by the first Indonesian Women's Congress in 1928 whose initiatives helped establish, among other goals, a scholarship fund that allowed poor girls to access middle and higher education (Blackburn 2008), the social and educational gulf between *priyayi* and non-*priyayi* women remained and was reflected in the uneven developments in women's positions well into the independent, nation-building years of the 1950s. Due to their lack of access to education and vocational skills training, non-*priyayi* women were pushed towards the unskilled sectors of labour and became low wage-earners (Vreede-de Stuers 1960; Elliot 1997). Meanwhile, it was the privileged *priyayi* women, reconfigured as elite career women in the

1950s, who forged their way ahead in the workplace as they broke into male-oriented careers as journalists, doctors and lawyers.

Ambivalent Narration: Kartini in the Old Order

In 1945, Indonesia entered a new political phase as a young, independent nation-state. For Indonesian women, it was to be a new beginning. Under the Constitution, they were granted full citizenship rights and were ideologically equal to men; they could vote, had access to education and social privileges, and were encouraged to participate in the national economy and development projects. Women's rights were also assured by Sukarno's Old Order government (1945–65) whose populist agenda emphasized equality among all citizens as fellow Indonesians (*rakyat*). As a mark of their commitment to Indonesian women, Sukarno's government inaugurated 21 April as Kartini Day in 1946, a national day to commemorate Indonesian women's patriotic efforts and role in the nationalist battle for freedom. It was also on this day that women's issues could be highlighted, including the importance of their role in the family and access to education and work as well as their obligations to the fledgling nation (Mahy 2012). To promote its populist agenda, Sukarno's government toned down Kartini's *priyayi* background and revised her story as a "fellow Javanese and co-equal victims of Dutch colonial oppression" (Gouda 1995, p. 30). In this narrative, Kartini stands *with* the people and whose birth mother, Ngasirah, shares their common roots. Old Order Kartini is thus committed to the populist aspirations of the nation (see Rutherford's Chapter 5 in this volume); she is for every woman, regardless of ethnicity or class.

On the ground however, the government's promise of equality and freedom did not quite translate to material practice. Although nationalism had fuelled women's movements and organizations in the post-independence age, many of the issues raised by Kartini and the Indonesian Women's Congress remained unresolved, including child marriage, polygamy, women's working conditions, illiteracy and women's education. Women still lived in a man's world and were subjected to age-old patriarchal views and practices. The social chasm between *priyayi* and peasant classes also persisted, for Indonesian politics and national organizations continued to be "the preserve of a small Dutch educated elite" (Martyn 2005, p. 69). Although rendered less visible in the public, social space, Kartini's *priyayi* legacy—redefined as the elite class in the Old Order and New Order Indonesia—has been maintained in the postcolonial era by a small group of educated intellectuals with connections to wealth and positions of power and privilege at the top of the sociopolitical ladder. The social differences among Indonesian women manifested through the occupational hierarchy at the workplace and through women's movements and organizations, many of which were dominated by elite, educated and urbanized women who had the resources, including wealth, time, networks and experience (Martyn 2005, p. 13). Based on fee-paying membership structures, such organizations also had problems in recruiting low-income, uneducated women from the rural areas. At the time too, it was widely held that women's "activism was associated with privileged women's duty to assist those less fortunate" (Martyn 2005, p. 70), a perception that revealed the influential reach of Kartini's *priyayi* vision; it was still a matter of the more privileged, elite woman speaking out for her voiceless, disenfranchised sisters, many of whom felt they had not benefitted from Indonesia's independence and for whom the promise of women's liberty and equality was but a pipe dream.

This section explores the ironies and contradictions that manifested themselves more fully during Sukarno's rule through the two narrative threads mentioned earlier in my introduction: the first is the popular, celebrated narrative of Kartini as the champion of every woman, while the second is the less visible, but no less significant narrative of entrenched classism that reinforced the subordination of lower-class women. Both threads, as explained earlier, underline the Janus-faced ambivalence of language used to narrate Kartini's memory and symbolism in the construction of Indonesian women as postcolonial subjects during the independent years of nation-building. Without doubt, Kartini—the symbol of both nationalism and women's liberation—is pivotal to this active phase of women's development in Indonesian society and politics. Her ideas about woman's position and rights in education, marriage, family and society were not only taken up by women's organizations and movements, but had also provided them "an agenda and checklist for women's progress" (Martyn 2005, p. 32). On the other hand, elite women's complicit silence and participation in the class system—which helped reify the existing structures of hierarchy, privilege, and status—could also be traced back to Kartini's *priyayi* legacy. The ambivalent narration of Kartini during this period therefore highlights the ironies and contradictions that attend her memory and iconicity, and is reflected in the contestations and divisions among women, examples of which can be found in the social gap between the urbanized, educated elite and their less educated (or illiterate), unskilled counterparts in the villages and towns as well as in the conflicts and tensions experienced among women's organizations, notably Perwari (*Persatuan Wanita Republik Indonesia,* or Women's Federation of the Indonesian Republic) and Gerwani (*Gerakan Wanita Indonesia,* or Indonesian Women's Movement), also the two largest and most successful women's groups of the 1950s.

Class boundaries and divisions among Indonesian women in the 1950s have been observed by Vreede-de Stuers (1960, p. 156), who identifies four groups of women in the labour force: 1) professionals (doctors, lawyers, etc.), 2) government servants, 3) small traders and those in home-based industries, and 4) labourers and domestic servants. The first group formed the "elite" tier while the last two groups— incidentally the least protected and most vulnerable—made up the non-elite Other and were mainly rural women with little education. According to Diah, elite career women had "little to complain about" (1955, p. 235) since their families and household chores were taken care of by servants and female relations that included grandmothers and aunts.[16] They also had time to participate more fully in women's organizations and movements. Although elite women were also subjected to patriarchal practices in marriage, family and the workplace, they were, nevertheless, in a better position to fulfil Kartini's feminist dream through education and work. Besides, as members of a small, affluent and Western-educated circle with connections to men in positions of power, elite women were able to "take advantage of opportunities" provided by national development and "consolidate their class position" (Manderson 1983, p. 8) which, at the same time, was being safeguarded by institutionalized systems put into place by the elite class itself (Wong 1979, p. 183).

Elite women could enjoy privileges accorded to their class, but only by conforming to a social system that continued to exploit lower-class women as cheap, unskilled labour in low-income jobs in both rural and urban areas. Due to lack of status and education, lower-class women— discursively constructed as non-elite Other—had limited access to work opportunities, and what jobs they had usually paid little. They received lower wages than men and often only minimum wage while their rights at the workplace were violated (Martyn 2005, p. 97). As a result of these class disparities, the "few highly-educated women who succeed in making inroads into the small world of occupational elites may symbolize social *inequalities* rather than the achievement of sexual equality to the majority of the women in the lower and working classes" (Wong 1979, p. 183). Unlike elite women who concurred with Kartini's view that work was a woman's right, lower-class women experienced work differently as it "was not a right but a necessity" (Martyn 2005, p. 96) for them. Another barrier was the persistence of socially ingrained biases since lower-class women continued to be "constructed by the elite-dominated women's movement as victims in need of assistance" (Martyn 2005, p. 96). This stereotype reveals how lower-class women have been silenced and excluded by elite women, a factor that complicates the accepted trope of female progress attributed to Kartini. In short, working-class women did not benefit from Kartini's dream of female empowerment since they remained, in large part, marginalized and disenfranchised by widespread discriminatory attitudes rooted in feudal and colonial legacies of gender and class.

Entrenched class barriers also influenced women's organizations and movements even as they fought to liberate *all* women from feudal patriarchal traditions. Following Kartini's ideas and articulations, Indonesian women's organizations and movements focused on achieving women's rights and equality in education and the workplace, and by opposing polygamy and agitating for reforms related to marriage and inheritance laws. However, divisive lines were also drawn based on the contestations of ethnicity, religion and other ideological differences, including class. Perwari, for instance, embodied a more "bourgeois" brand of Indonesian feminism. Famous for its fierce opposition against Sukarno's polygamous marriages, Perwari was one of the largest and most active national women's organizations to emerge from the Old Order period. A lesser known fact, however, is that Perwari was also a staunch adherent to class imperatives despite its pursuit of feminist goals. Formed by secular, educated and intellectual women of the elite class who had envisioned for themselves an international role (Martyn 2005, p. 162), Perwari aimed "to improve the fate of women in all areas" (Perwari, cited in Martyn 2005, p. 59). Guided by these principles, Perwari was ideologically open to all Indonesian female citizens regardless of class, race and religion while its commitment to women's issues could be seen in the opening of schools, clinics for women and children, and hostels for female students and women workers (Wieringa 2002, p. 121).

Despite these achievements, Perwari's leadership was criticized for being elite and Java-centric:

> In Java, with its hierarchical structure, women in other women's organizations such as Perwari usually only rose to leadership level if they belonged to the *pamong praja* (village leaders) or if they had received a good education, which meant that they belonged to the *priyayi* elite. (Wieringa 2002, p. 154)

One ex-Perwari member disclosed why she left, stating she was unhappy with "the Perwari membership, all wives of village leaders" (cited in Wieringa 2002, p. 143). There was also the perception that Perwari members were "too much like 'ladies'" (Wieringa 2002, p. 165) and that they had "never defended actively the rights of poor women in the villages" (cited in Wieringa 2002, p. 178). Criticized for its perceived social superiority and corresponding silence where lower-class women were concerned, Perwari had in fact conformed to Kartini's *priyayi* notion of the proper flow of class power, from top to bottom.

Still, Perwari's lack of egalitarian appeal was problematic in an age of populist rule, since it contradicted Sukarno's rhetoric of equality and rights. Members dissatisfied with Perwari's lack of attention on poor women's issues left to join Gerwani, a PKI- (*Partai Komunis Indonesia*, or Indonesian Communist party) affiliated socialist organization for women that was also well known as the "most active defender of the rights of women labourers and peasants" (Wieringa 2002, p. 340). Gerwani was established in 1950 as Gerwis, and rapidly became one of the biggest women's organizations with an estimated three million members at the peak of its movement in 1965 (Wieringa 2002, p. 179), the majority of whom were unskilled working-class women, also seen as "victims of exploitation and discrimination" who had been subjected to continued oppression by "feudal and imperial remnants" (cited in Martyn 2005, p. 65). Besides fighting for better wages and women's rights at the workplace, Gerwani members also conducted literacy classes as part of their campaign to liberate the female working masses. More crucially, Gerwani gave working-class women both representation and voice that had been denied to them by elite women. In their socialist fight for working-class, non-elite women, Gerwani made clever use of two famous "warrior princesses" in Java: Srikandi,[17] the militant wife of the hero Arjuna in *wayang* tradition, and Kartini herself, whose passionate fight for women's rights to education and equality was invoked through their magazine, *Api Kartini* (Kartini's fire). While it may seem ironic and contrary, the use of the class-conscious Kartini as Gerwani's socialist symbol—a working-class hero—was also appropriate, given the populist discourses of the time. Here then is the narrative of Kartini for *all* women, regardless of class.

The tensed and, oftentimes, conflicting relationship between Perwari and Gerwani is an indication of how the ambivalent narration of Kartini in the postcolonial context of the 1950s had been shaped by divisive and contesting female voices and perspectives that attended the tropes of class and social inequalities. Although both women's organizations shared the same goal of achieving Kartini's feminist ideas, they also parted ways because of class-driven disparities that ranged from articulations of femininity (i.e. Gerwani's militant femininity versus Perwari's bourgeois femininity) to formations of membership and leadership as well as the ways Kartini was appropriated; for Gerwani, she symbolized the fight for women's equality, but for Perwari, Kartini's *priyayi* ideas and legacy were also important. Both narrative strands also highlight the Janus-faced ambivalence of language found in Kartini's writings all those years ago: on the one hand, there is her articulation of women's rights and equality, but on the other hand, there is her silence on the non-elite, Other woman. Ultimately however, the narrative strand that would go on to survive the violent transition into Suharto's New Order state is that of Kartini's *priyayi* elitism. As we will see, the violent "purge" carried out in 1965–66 by Suharto's masculinist military army and the resulting fall of Gerwani also contributed to the shaping of a new ambivalent narration of Kartini.

The infamous tale of the 1965 coup, in which six of the army's top generals had been tortured and castrated by wild, dancing, naked Gerwani women before being killed by PKI members on 30 September, has been woven into the textual tapestry of contemporary Indonesian history. What truly happened on that day may never be known, but when accounts of what happened to the generals hit the media circuit, angry Muslim mobs, supported by Suharto's military forces, went on a killing spree that left over a million dead and a nation traumatized in its wake. Thousands of Gerwani members went missing; they were raped, imprisoned, tortured, and killed. Gerwani itself was crushed and later banned. Wieringa's seminal study (2002) has since revealed the gendered and sexual underpinnings of the coup, including how the perception of sexually uncontrollable and powerful Gerwani women had struck fear into men's hearts and "set off the powder keg" (p. 8). However, the fact that they were poor, lower-class women seeking power was also deemed unacceptable.[18] Suharto was not just seeking to tame communist power and female transgression, but also to ensure that Indonesians of the lower class—approximately "21 million peasants and workers armed and independent of army control" (Wieringa 2002, p. 8)—stayed where they belonged. Deemed dangerous for rebelling against their ascribed *kodrat wanita* (woman's destiny), Gerwani members were further stereotyped by Muslims as atheists, non-believers or *kafir*. I argue here that while gender and sexual politics contributed much to the violent purge of 1965–66, the women of Gerwani bore the brunt of it as they belonged to not just one but *three* marginalized identity groups in Java: *kafir*, women, and lower class. Gerwani—representing the non-elite Other woman—was thus effectively silenced and erased from public sight. At the same time, its violent demise paved the way for the renewed subjugation of women under Suharto's rule, where women peasants and labourers were taught, at great cost, to know their place in the social, gender and religious order. The re-establishment of the status quo also meant the return to the proper order of things and with it, the affirmation of masculine, Islamic, and Javanese elite power. In the revised narratives of the New Order state, a new type of elite womanhood was constructed, one that supported Kartini's *priyayi* background with its emphasis on Javanese upper-class hegemonic power even as it undermined her feminist vision with its insistence on *kodrat wanita*. A new ambivalent narrative of Kartini was thus born.

The New Order Elite Woman: Gender, Class and Race

If the 1950s-mid 1960s saw the proliferation of women's organizations, alliances as well as their hopes and dreams under the bright auspices of nationhood, then the late 1960s onwards saw a marked decline in women's activities and organizations, all of which were brought under the firm control of the New Order government. Under Suharto's paternalistic-patriarchal rule, the state inscribed a much more restrictive narrative about the Indonesian woman and her identity, role and place in the nation space. Scholars have recognized the role played by the masculinist New Order regime in constructing the ideal woman whose femininity is not only based on domesticity and docility, but also emphasizes *kodrat wanita* (Blackburn 2004; Robinson 2009; Suryakusuma 1996; Tiwon 1996; Wieringa 2002). Against the backdrop of recovery from the traumatic violence of 1965–66, Indonesian women found themselves being pushed back to their "appropriate" places in the home, and their independence, rights, agency and voice severely curtailed. Meanwhile, lower-class women who had been subjected to the horrors of the "purge" had to undergo re-education under the watchful eyes of the New Order government; they were effectively silenced and subdued. In this new gendered narrative, the "maniac" women peasants and labourers running loose across the country were vanquished, erased and made unspeakable, and in their place a "model" femininity was constructed and made visible (Tiwon 1996): the "new" elite woman—educated, refined, and above all, contained and obedient to the tenets of *kodrat* in her circumscribed role as wife and mother. Indonesian women, it seems, have been returned to the feudal traditions that prescribed *priyayi* femininity. In line with this gendered ideology, Kartini—the original Javanese *priyayi* "princess" and now, an idealized *Ibu*[19] (mother)—was refashioned to create a "new kind of prison for women like the lower-class labourer" (Tiwon 1996, p. 54), and in the process revealed the hierarchical relationships among women as well as the ways in which they were informed and shaped by the gender politics of the time.

The ambivalent narration of Kartini took new shape through two major state-controlled women's organizations of the time: Dharma Wanita (Woman's Duty, henceforth DW), a compulsory association whose members comprised of civil servants' wives, and the PKK (*Pembinaan Kesejahteraan Keluarga*, or Family Welfare Guidance Programme), which aimed to re-educate lower-class, rural women about their role and place in the New Order. Intended as a gendered support system for husbands working in the civil service, DW also encouraged its members "to display and enjoy their high status" (Liddle 1996, p. 155) as they carried out their public service duties. By projecting images and representations of "new" elite women as gendered citizens in the national imaginary, DW played a vital role in promoting woman's ordained roles of wife and mother under the doctrine of State *Ibuism* (motherhood) which, according to Suryakusuma, is a concept that "derives the most oppressive aspects of both bourgeois 'housewifization' and *Priyayi* [white-collar Javanese] Ibuism" (1996, p. 101). Ideologically, State *Ibuism* endorses women's dependency on men and simultaneously reifies the Javanese preoccupation with social hierarchy, for a woman's position (and power) in DW hinges on her husband's rank and status in the civil service. Of significance here too is the manner in which the members of DW were exhorted to be the model leaders of their gender; these upper-class or elite women and wives of civil servants were expected to help their less fortunate sisters in lower-income, rural households, a concept closely aligned with Kartini's *priyayi* vision decades earlier. This is also why the PKK leaders were made up of DW members.

If DW resembled a "prestigious club" that showcased the wives of the elite tier of civil servants, the PKK then was for non-elite women who were further subjected to the structures of silence imposed by both elite men and women at the top of the social hierarchy. A nationwide organization that targeted women at the grass-roots level, the PKK was coordinated by the Department of Home Affairs and managed as part of the village government. Here too, as in DW, both class and "wifehood determined leadership" (Robinson 2009, p. 74). The flow of female power, defined by marriage status and class, not only observed the social hierarchy in place but also constituted a return to Kartini's conception of the *priyayi* woman's role as leader and educator for the rural masses:

> The wife of the Minister of Home Affairs automatically headed PKK at the national level. The same criterion operated at the lower levels of government down to the village, where the local PKK chapter was entrusted to the wife of the village head. ... The PKK provided ideological indoctrination for women, disseminating official gender ideology among rural women. (Robinson 2009, p. 74).

Under the leadership of DW members, the PKK held activities that included courses on cooking, sewing, etiquette and flower arrangement as well as family planning, nutrition and health (Robinson 2009), all of which were designed to raise an awareness about middle-class life and status; at the same time, the courses reinforced the notion of *kodrat wanita* as rural women—still haunted by the traumatic violence suffered during the "purge"—were re-educated about their secondary albeit natural role and position in the gender binary as mothers and wives in the domestic home.[20] Robinson (2009) also points out that the official gender ideology contradicts women's everyday lives and reality, especially in relation to non-elite women whose "economic activity is critical for their families' survival" (p. 74), a burden not shared by the members of DW.

Non-verbal structures of language such as representation, image and performance also contributed to the ambivalent narration of Kartini in Suharto's New Order regime. These structures were perpetuated and circulated through DW members who, as bearers of the "light" of State

Ibuism as a national ideology and discourse, had to project a certain image that was in keeping with their social position. As Taylor observes, the "Suharto-era *kain*, tightly wrapped, worn with high-heeled sandals, imposed a small gait and upright posture, signalling upper class status" (2008, p. 13). This image was fostered by Suharto's *priyayi* wife, Raden Ayu Siti Hartinah, who was distantly related to the Mangkunegara royalty of Solo.[21] The wife of the most powerful man in the nation and thus, the woman with the highest authority and status among Indonesian women, Siti Hartinah not only led the DW as First Lady, she also embodied Javanese *priyayi* femininity and fashioned herself accordingly. Although all the wives of Indonesian presidents wore the requisite national costume that is the *kebaya*, Siti Hartinah distinguished herself by using the *Kutubaru* style, a shorter hip-length type of *kebaya*, in addition to a scarf (*slendang*) worn across the chest and knotted at the waist; notably, the *kutubaru* style has been associated with aristocratic Javanese women in the palaces (Adriati, Zainsjah, and Damajanti 2018; Suciati and Sachari 2017). Even Siti Hartinah's hair bun (*konde*) followed the traditional Javanese style. At the same time, the state made special use of national celebrations like Kartini Day and *Hari Ibu* (Mother's Day) to showcase and endorse State *Ibuism*. On these occasions, the members of DW stood out as representatives of elite Javanese wifehood and motherhood in their "exaggerated version of the *kebaya*, with high heels, heavy make-up and fancier buns" (Mahy 2012).

The structures of performativity and mimicry that underscored the celebration of Kartini's birth were further reproduced and circulated by Indonesian women everywhere through Kartini lookalike and cooking contests (Mahy 2012; Wieringa 2002). Kartini might have been remoulded to fit the male fantasy of submissive, maternal femininity, but the material, performative bodies of Indonesian women—under the leadership of DW and the PKK—also lent "truth" to this fantasy and made it come alive on Kartini Day. Through bodily performance and appearance, the members of DW were a visual and visceral reminder of Javanese upper-class hegemonic power; they demonstrated to the Indonesian public who was really in charge of the country, a message reinforced on Kartini Day when women across Indonesia were urged to don the requisite *kebaya* and restyle their hair in the manner of a Javanese woman (see also Robinson in this volume, p. 139). Taylor (1997b) reminds us of the visual significance of the national costume, which was particularly charged with racial and gendered tones during the Suharto era, for the "female body as the wearer of 'national costume' denies the plurality of regional cultures"—a point to bear in mind in the following analysis of race—even as it shows how "women are the keepers of the national essence, whilst men forge new paths into the nation's future" (p. 113).

While class divisions among women informed much of my analysis here, I also consider briefly how race is equally key to the New Order government's strategies of domination during the 1970s, a turbulent period that witnessed the state's expanding power and territorialization across the archipelago through the violent subjugation of Aceh (from 1976 till 2005) and the 1975 invasion of East Timor. In contrast to the populist policies espoused by Sukarno's Old Order administration, Suharto's New Order regime overtly supported masculinist, elitist *and* Javanese power at the heart of its rule. Under the neo-imperialist projects of the nation-state, the structures of mimicry and gender performativity underlining the ambivalent narration of Kartini worked not only to exclude lower-class women but also non-Javanese women from other regions, cultures and ethnicities. Remarkable parallels can indeed be found between the New Order's enforcement of phallocentric authority on women and its neo-colonial conquest and consolidation of paternalistic-patriarchal power over "feminized", uncontrollable territories like Aceh and East Timor. Likened to wild Gerwani women of the 1950s and early 1960s, these troublesome, rebellious regions had to be reined in by Suharto's masculinist military forces whose violent tactics included targeted mass raping of women. At the same time, Suharto's domination of these territories also involved the affirmation of Javanese, elitist and masculinist power, upon which his New Order Empire was built.

In her study on Aceh women and their response to the symbolism of Kartini, Siapno (2002) writes thus:

> Kartini had come to symbolize the worst aspects of 'Javanisasi' [Javanese hegemony]—from enforcing the Javanese *sarung-kebaya* dress to the imposition of Javanese-style structure at all levels of administration, from heads of regencies (*bupati*), head of districts (*camat*), down to village heads (*lurah*). ... [As] the Javanese are 'immoral', thus Kartini is delegitimized as an improper heroine. (pp. 150–51)

In addition to capturing Aceh's opposition to Java as the elite, ruling centre and its official gender ideology (which contradicts Aceh's matrifocal traditions), Siapno's observation above is also significant for another reason, in that it reveals how the imposed structures and forces of "Javanisasi" have contributed to the subjugation and displacement of non-Javanese Indonesians as the periphery. Within this narrative, Kartini has ironically become the detested emblem of "Javanisasi" and must thus be resisted against. Similarly in the newly occupied East Timor, known then as the "27th Province", Suharto's government introduced Kartini Day and installed branches of DW and PKK in order to, purportedly, improve women's lives and support their rights even as it continued to deploy rape as a weapon of war (Hill 2012). Unsurprisingly, these measures failed to appeal to East Timorese women since they were perceived to be "totally without benefit ... due to its close relationship with ruling party Golkar and the Army" (Hill 2012, p. 218). Under such circumstances, Kartini's symbolism would have rung hollow for the East Timorese women who had been living in fear of violence and rape. Based on the complex Javanese system of hierarchy and order, Suharto's neo-imperialist projects had reinforced the marginalization of women along the lines of race, gender and class. As members of the disenfranchised and suppressed peripheries, non-Javanese women from the rural, lower-income groups were thus positioned at the lower end of the race and social hierarchies, in marked contrast to the Java-centric, upper-class and elite femininity represented by DW.

Conclusion

The historical appropriations of Kartini's memory and symbolism are rooted in an ambivalent narrative of female progress and female subjection that began with the Janus-faced language found in Kartini's letters: on the one hand, there is her impassioned cry for women's rights to education and work as well as the eradication of feudal customs like polygamy and arranged marriage, but on the other hand, there is her complicit silence on the plight of lower-class women that include the *selir*. Her vision of the educated *priyayi* woman bringing light to the masses as both mother and educator of Java's future leaders not only implicitly excluded lower-class women by conforming to the hierarchies of class, rank and privilege, but it also complicated the celebrated trope of her progressive feminism. This is seen during Sukarno's Old Order in the uneven developments in women's education, occupation and social mobility as well as in the contestations and divisions among women's groups like Perwari and Gerwani. The ambivalent narration of Kartini took on a different shape under Suharto's New Order regime, one based on gendered submission and motherhood as well as Javanese *priyayi* elitism; however, non-elite, lower-class women continued to be silenced and marginalized, and were subjected to the authority of *both* men and women of the elite class through state organizations like DW and the PKK. At the same time, the ambivalent narration of Kartini deepened when she became the imperialistic emblem of "Javanisasi" and was despised by non-Javanese women from the suppressed peripheries, notably Acehnese women.

Kartini's Janus-faced legacy has since travelled into the post-New Order period and been subjected to the forces of democratization of state and society as well as of globalization. The growing space for debate and contestation is reflected in the proliferation and fragmentation of voices and viewpoints on Indonesian women's identities and roles within the nation space and abroad as well as on Kartini herself. As noted by the editors in this volume's Introduction and by Robinson (Chapter 6 in this volume), opinions about Kartini are more polarized than ever, with many centred on the fractious issues of class and race. Furthermore, class barriers still persist and have been reinforced by global capitalism which, among other things, have contributed to the commodification and exportation of women's labour as migrant workers and domestic helpers. In 2014, the peasant women of Kendeng Mountains fought against a local cement company with global market ties that had opened a mining factory on their land; they called their resistance movement "Kartini Kendeng". It goes to show that lower-class women still invoke Kartini's name even as they remain one of the most vulnerable and exploited subaltern groups in the country. More than ever, these developments on the ground—together with current debates and discussions—attest to the ongoing construction of Kartini as the site of ambivalent narration, and the powerful manner in which it continues to "[hold] culture at its most productive position, as a force for 'subordination, fracturing, diffusing, reproducing as much as producing, creating, forcing, guiding'" (Bhabha 1990, pp. 3–4).

NOTES

1. Gouda (1995) and Hawkins (2007) are two such studies that call attention to Kartini's class consciousness. While Gouda's study is confined to female education in the colonial era, Hawkins examines Kartini's ambivalent identity and position within the context of colonial relations with the *priyayi*.

Taylor (1989) also briefly touches on Kartini's "ambitions to promote her own class" (p. 305).

2. Coté, for instance, notes how "Kartini withheld or delayed providing information to Rosa that she had discussed with Nellie van Kol ... while the correspondence with Rosa was clearly more important than that with her erstwhile companion, Marie Ovink-Soer" (2014, p. 25).

3. *Kabupaten* bears dual meanings: 1) as the district under the *bupati*'s administration, and 2) as his residence. Here, I use the term to refer to the *bupati*'s residence.

4. Geertz is famous for his views about the three cultural streams (*aliran*) that define Javanese life: the *priyayi*, the *santri* and the *abangan*. The *santri* uphold Islamic teachings and are considered pious Muslims while the *abangan* are also Muslims, but are more strongly influenced by Hindu elements in Java. During colonial rule, the *santri* led a commercial life and were distinct from the *priyayi* and village peasants (Geertz 1956, p. 99). Although this classification is not exactly clear-cut—there are *santri* villagers and *abangan* traders, these three streams nonetheless demarcate general religious, class and cultural differences. I have avoided using the cultural streams as my study is focused on social formations. Geertz's research, based on a central Javanese town-village complex that he calls Modjokuto, reveals interesting findings about early twentieth-century Javanese social formations and interactions that have provided me a useful model for my study here.

5. Sutherland (1975, 1979) argues that the *priyayi* were a heterogeneous group whose differences ran along the lines of region, language, family background, and other variables. They were also divided into high-ranking and low-ranking *priyayi*. The former, known as *pangreh praja*, were the aristocratic descendants of the traditional administrative class while the latter were made up of a "new rising class of non-traditional *priyayi*" (Koentjaraningrat 1985, p. 77) who gained upward mobility through education or ties to the ruling centre. Sukarno belonged to the latter group of low-ranking *priyayi*.

6. Historically, the practice of polygamy was confined mainly to those with affluence and status; it was actually quite "rare in most of rural Java" (Koentjaraningrat 1985, p. 139). As a result, *priyayi* households were usually large, with up to four wives (as prescribed by Islam) and ten or more children. For details about polygamy in Indonesia, see Nurmila (2009).

7. Interestingly, numerous inconsistencies can be found in Kartini's thinking about the Javanese people in her memorandum. For example, she condemns the nobility's "deep-rooted false notion" (2014, p. 812) of superiority because—in keeping with her view of social progress through education—it "inhibit[s] progress" (p. 812), but at the same time, she also draws the line between the nobility and the masses by criticizing how the "fine [priyayi] sentiments" and "idea" of abstinence are "lost to the masses" who think that

"'Not eating, drinking or sleeping is the aim of life! rather than— 'Through suffering, (effort, self-restraint and self-denial) one achieves a refined state" (p. 816). While we should bear in mind that Kartini, highly aware of the racial politics of the time, was pitching her ideas and arguments accordingly to her Dutch readers, I also argue that her writing reveals a keen awareness of the differences between the "nobility" and the "masses".

8. The Dutch term for the coastal area near Semarang.

9. Again, Kartini's conflicted attitude towards the Javanese nobility can be discerned here. In her earlier letter dated 18 August 1899, she tells Stella that she "had never given any thought to the fact that, as you say, I am of high birth", stating that "there is nothing so ridiculous, nothing sillier, than people who allow themselves to be honoured on the basis of their so-called 'high birth'" (2005, p. 30; 2014, p. 75).

10. Not much is historically known about the *nyai*, but she can nonetheless be found in the Chinese-Malay literature of early twentieth-century Dutch Indies. Popular examples include Thio Tjien Boen's *Tjerita Njai Soemirah* (1917) and Kwee Tek Hoay's *Rose of Cikembang* (1927). For an interesting discussion of the *nyai* in Dutch and Chinese-Malay fiction, see Hellwig (2012), pp. 99–125.

11. Coté observes how Kartini "had hidden the true nature of her family from her 'lieve moedertje' [dear mother] (Marie Ovink-Soer) in the course of a relationship that stretched over almost one decade and had included extensive discussions on Dutch feminist discourse" (Kartini 2014, p. 156n111).

12. See, as an example, Kartini's letter dated 14 July 1903 to Abendanon-Mandri (Kartini 2014, pp. 616–21), which reveals her bitter sense of humiliation and shame about her upcoming marriage to Djojo Adiningrat, whose *padmi* had passed away. Kartini was to fill the opening left by the deceased *padmi*.

13. Considering her antagonism towards polygamy in earlier letters, Kartini's resolute silence about her co-wives could be attributed to her continued and, perhaps, suppressed sense of shame and humiliation. See Kartini's letter dated 14 July 1903 (Kartini 2014, pp. 616–21). Taylor's Afterword in this volume also touches on how social and cultural factors might have contributed to Kartini's silence on the *selir*.

14. For details about women's education in the colonial period, see Blackburn (2004), pp. 33–51.

15. Although calls were made for educated *priyayi* women to help lower-class women and the Javanese people, they were also hampered by *adat*, which prohibited them from working outside their homes especially after marriage. Another obstacle was the *priyayi* women's ingrained prejudice towards the simple, rural women (Gouda 1995).

16. Diah (1955) also claims that women at the time had the freedom to choose their occupation and were given equal pay. However, this claim could be more accurately applied to elite, career women. It should also be noted that

Diah's idealized perception of the working Indonesian woman was influenced by her own well-to-do *priyayi* background, which enabled her to also obtain higher education at a New York university.

17. A skilled archer, Srikandi is one of the two wives of the *wayang* hero, Arjuna, whose other wife is Sumbadra, who symbolizes womanly submission. For more about these two female archetypes in Javanese tradition, see Carey and Houben (1992), pp. 12–37. Wieringa (2002) also draws on their mythology and meaning in her analysis of sexual politics in Indonesia.

18. See Wieringa (2002) for details on how Gerwani antagonized conservative women's groups and sectors of society with their "unwomanly" ambition to participate more fully in state politics.

19. Indonesians already knew Kartini as *"Ibu"* through the song, *Ibu kita Kartini*, during Sukarno's Old Order (see Robinson's Chapter 6 in this volume), but the New Order reinforced this connection by linking it to State *Ibuism* and *kodrat wanita*.

20. Based on State *Ibuism*, PKK introduced five principles to rural women in the following order: 1) producer of the nation's future generations, 2) faithful wife and companion, 3) mother and educator of children, 4) housekeepers, and finally, 5) citizen (Hull 1996, p. 95). However, these principles defined women across the board, including DW members, and reflected the systematic reduction of the feminine in the New Order.

21. Siti Hartinah also provided Suharto—a humble farmer's son—*priyayi* credentials as well as connections to the Javanese elite, upper-class circles. According to Vatikiotis, despite being linked to the *priyayi* world through his wife, Suharto remained "conscious of his farmer's roots" even as his wife "attempted to elevate his social origins to the ranks of the aristocracy" (1998, p. 10).

REFERENCES

Adriati, Ira, Almira Belinda Zainsjah, and Irma Damajanti. 2018. "Women's Perspective on the Surakarta Kebaya based on Biographies of Gusti Noeroel and Utami Suryadarma". *Journal of Visual Art and Design* 10, no. 2: 142–54.

Bhabha, Homi K. 1990. "Introduction: Narrating the Nation". In *Nation and Narration*, edited by Homi K. Bhabha. London: Routledge.

Blackburn, Susan. 2004. *Women and the State in Modern Indonesia*. Cambridge: Cambridge University Press.

———. 2008. "Introduction". In *The First Indonesian Women's Congress of 1928*, translated and with an introduction by Susan Blackburn. Clayton, Victoria: Monash University Press.

Carey, Peter and Vincent Houben. 1992. "Spirited Srikandhis and Sly Sumbadras: The Social, Political and Economic Role of Women at Central Javanese Courts in the 18th and Early 19th centuries". In *Indonesian Women in Focus: Past and*

Present Notions, edited by Elsbeth Locher-Scholten and Anke Niehof. 2nd ed. Leiden: KITLV Press.

Coté, Joost. 2014. "Reading Kartini: A Historical Introduction". In *Kartini: The Complete Writings, 1898–1904*, by Kartini. Edited and translated by Joost Coté. Clayton, Victoria: Monash University.

Diah, Herawati. 1955. "Indonesian Career Women". *Women's International Club Journal* 3, no. 6: 235–38.

Elliot, Janet. 1997. "Equality? The Influence of Legislation and Notions of Gender on the Position of Women Wage Workers in the Economy: Indonesia 1950–58". In *Women Creating Indonesia: The First Fifty Years*, edited by Jean Gelman Taylor. Clayton, Victoria: Monash Asia Institute, Monash University.

Geertz, Clifford. 1956. *The Social Context of Economic Change: An Indonesian Case Study*. Cambridge, MA: Center for International Studies, Massachusetts Institute of Technology.

Gouda, Frances. 1995. "Teaching Indonesian Girls in Java and Bali, 1900–1942: Dutch Progressives, the Infatuation with 'Oriental' Refinement, and 'Western' Ideas About Proper Womanhood". *Women's History Review* 4, no. 1: 25–62.

Hawkins, Michael. 2007. "Exploring Colonial Boundaries: An Examination of the Kartini-Zeehandelaar Correspondence". *Asia-Pacific Social Science Review* 7, no. 1: 1–14.

Hellwig, Tineke. 2012. *Women and Malay Voices: Undercurrent Murmurings in Indonesia's Colonial Past*. New York: Peter Lang.

Hill, Helen. 2012. "Gender Issues in Timor-Leste and the Pacific Islands: 'Practical Needs' and 'Strategic Interests' Revisited". In *New Research on Timor-Leste: Proceedings of the Communicating New Research on Timor-Leste Conference*, edited by Michael Leach et al. Melbourne: Swinburne University Press.

Hull, Valerie J. 1996. "Women in Java's Rural Middle Class: Progress or Regress?" In *Women of Southeast Asia*, edited by Penny Van Esterik. DeKalb, Illinois: Center for Southeast Asian Studies, Northern Illinois University.

Kartini. 2005. *On Feminism and Nationalism: Kartini's Letters to Stella Zeehandelaar, 1899–1903*. Edited and translated by Joost Coté. 2nd ed. Clayton, Victoria: Monash Asia Institute, Monash University.

———. 2014. *Kartini: The Complete Writings, 1898–1904*. Edited and translated by Joost Coté. Clayton, Victoria: Monash University.

Koentjaraningrat, Raden Mas. 1985. *Javanese Culture*. Oxford: Oxford University Press.

Kukathas, Chandran. 2009. "The Dilemma of a Dutiful Daughter: Love and Freedom in the Thought of Kartini". In *Toward a Humanist Justice: The Political Philosophy of Susan Moller Okin*, edited by Debra Satz and Rob Reich. New York: Oxford University Press.

Liddle, R. William. 1996. *Leadership and Culture in Indonesian Politics*. Southeast Asia Publications Series 29. Sydney: Allen & Unwin.

Mahy, Petra. 2012. "Being Kartini: Ceremony and Print Media in the Commemoration of Indonesia's First Feminist". *Intersections: Gender and Sexuality in Asia and the Pacific* 28. http://intersections.anu.edu.au/issue28/mahy.htm (accessed 10 September 2017).

Manderson, Lenore. 1983. "Introduction". In *Women's Work and Women's Roles: Economics and Everyday Life in Inonesia, Malaysia and Singapore*, edited by Lenore Manderson. Canberra: Australian National University.

Martyn, Elizabeth. 2005. *The Women's Movement in Postcolonial Indonesia: Gender and Nation in a New Democracy.* London: RoutledgeCurzon.

Mohammad, Goenawan. 2005. "Foreword". In *On Feminism and Nationalism: Kartini's Letters to Stella Zeehandelaar 1899–1903*, by Kartini. Edited and translated by Joost Coté. 2nd ed. Clayton, Victoria: Monash Asia Institute, Monash University.

Nurmila, Nina. 2009. *Women, Islam and Everyday Life: Renegotiating Polygamy in Indonesia.* London: Routledge.

Robinson, Kathryn. 2009. *Gender, Islam and Democracy in Indonesia.* London: Routledge.

Shiraishi, Takashi. 1990. *An Age in Motion: Popular Radicalism in Java, 1912–1926.* Ithaca, NY: Cornell University Press.

Siapno, Jacqueline Aquino. 2002. *Gender, Islam, Nationalism and the State in Aceh: The Paradox of Power, Co-Optation and Resistance.* London: RoutledgeCurzon.

Suciati, and Agus Sachari. 2017. "National Fashion Image of Indonesia's First Lady". *Journal of Arts and Design Studies* 56: 1–12. http://www.iiste.org/Journals/index.php/ADS/article/download/37740/38826 (accessed 19 January 2018).

Suryakusuma, Julia I. 1996. "The State and Sexuality in New Order Indonesia". In *Fantasizing the Feminine in Indonesia*, edited by Laurie J. Sears. Durham: Duke University Press.

Sutherland, Heather. 1975. "The Priyayi". *Indonesia* 19: 57–77.

———. 1979. *The Making of a Bureaucratic Elite: The Colonial Transformation of the Javanese Priyayi.* Southeast Asia Publication Series 2. Singapore: Heinemann.

Taylor, Jean Gelman. 1976. "Raden Adjeng Kartini". *Signs: Journal of Women in Culture and Society* 1, no. 3: 639–61.

———. 1989. "Kartini in Her Historical Context". *Bijdragen tot de taal-, land- en volkenkunde* 145, no. 2–3: 295–307.

———. 1993. "Once More Kartini". In *Autonomous Histories, Particular Truths: Essays in Honor of John R.W. Smail*, edited by Laurie J. Sears. Madison, WI: University of Wisconsin; Center for Southeast Asian Studies.

———. 1997a. "Introduction". In *Women Creating Indonesia: The First Fifty Years*, edited by Jean Gelman Taylor. Clayton, Victoria: Monash Asia Institute, Monash University.

————. 1997b. "Costume and Gender in Colonial Java". In *Outward Appearances: Dressing State and Society in Indonesia*, edited by Henk Schulte Nordholt. Leiden: KITLV Press.

————. 2008. "Identity, Nation and Islam". *IIAS Newsletter* 46 (Winter): 12–13.

Tiwon, Sylvia. 1996. "Models and Maniacs: Articulating the Female in Indonesia". In *Fantasizing the Feminine in Indonesia*, edited by Laurie J. Sears. Durham: Duke University Press.

Vatikiotis, Michael R.J. 1998. *Indonesian Politics Under Suharto: The Rise and Fall of the New Order*. 3rd ed. London: Routledge.

Vreede-de Stuers, Cora. 1960. *The Indonesian Woman: Struggles and Achievements*. The Hague: Mouton.

Wieringa, Saskia. 2002. *Sexual Politics in Indonesia*. Houndmills: Palgrave Macmillan; The Hague: Institute of Social Studies.

Wong, Aline K. 1979. "The Changing Roles and Status of Women in ASEAN". *Contemporary Southeast Asia* 1, no. 2 (September): 179–93.

Woodward, Amber. 2015. "Historical Perspectives on a National Heroine: R.A. Kartini and the Politics of Memory". Independent Study Project (ISP) Collection (Fall). Paper 2189. http://digitalcollections.sit.edu/isp_collection/2189 (accessed 10 August 2016).

5

Unpacking a National Heroine: Two Kartinis and Their People[1]

Danilyn Rutherford

> As Head of the Country, I deeply regret that among the people there
> are still those who doubt the heroism of Kartini.... Haven't we already
> unanimously decided that Kartini is a National Heroine? (President
> Suharto in *Tempo* 1987, p. 23)

On 11 August 1986, as Dr Frederick George Peter Jaquet cycled from
Den Haag to his office in Leiden, no one would have guessed that he
was transporting an Indonesian national treasure. The wooden box
strapped to his bicycle looked perfectly ordinary. When he arrived at
the Koninklijk Instituut voor Taal-, Land- en Volkenkunde, the scholar
opened the box to view the Institute's long-awaited prize: a cache of
postcards, photographs, and scraps of letters sent by Raden Adjeng Kartini
and her sisters to the family of Mr J.H. Abendanon, the colonial official
who was both her patron and publisher. From this box so grudgingly
surrendered by Abendanon's family spilled new light on the life of this
Javanese nobleman's daughter, new clues to the mystery of her struggle.

Dr Jaquet's discovery, glowingly reported in the Indonesian press,
was but the latest episode in a long series of attempts to liberate Kartini
from the boxes which have contained her. For decades, Indonesian and

foreign scholars alike have sought to penetrate the veils obscuring the real Kartini in order to reach the core of a personality repressed by colonial officials, Dutch artists and intellectuals, the strictures of tradition, and the tragedy of her untimely death. The promise and the mystery of Kartini have given rise to a fluorescence of questions on all aspects of her life. Why did she give up her plans to go to Holland? Did she really predict her own death? Was she a feminist or a nationalist? Is Indonesia living up to her dreams?[2] President Suharto's pronouncement notwithstanding, Kartini has sparked a conversation which seems unlikely to cease.

Whence the enthusiasm, the obsession with Kartini? From her birth on 21 April 1879 to her death in childbirth in 1904, Kartini scarcely ventured beyond the borders of the community in which she was raised. When she died, she left little behind except a handful of essays and a series of letters written to Dutch pen pals during the last four years of her life.[3] The obvious origin of Kartini's importance lies with those Dutch friends, who presented the young Javanese, with her flowing Dutch prose, as an emblem of the benefits of enlightened colonial rule. After Kartini's death, Abendanon compiled and edited some of her letters, which he published in Holland in 1911 under the title, *Door duisternis tot licht* or "From darkness into light." Aggressively promoted by Abendanon and other *ethici*, who used the proceeds to fund a charity in her name, the book quickly became a bestseller. It had already reached its third edition in 1912. Translations in English (1920), Arabic (1926), Japanese (1955), and French (1960) followed (Sutrisno 1989, pp. XIX, XVIII), along with the Volkslectuur version of 1922, *Habis gelap terbitlah terang*,[4] through which the colonial state introduced Kartini to the generation of Malay-educated schoolchildren who would live to identify her with the founding of their nation.[5]

Kartini the heroine was born in this process of translation as the truth beckoning from beyond the texts. While the lure of translation keeps Kartini alive, the institutions which produced and disseminated her stories have more to do with her heroism than the insights her letters may contain. But this is not to say that the debates about the "real" Kartini are without significance. We can learn a great deal by examining the Kartini that various periods in history have produced. In plumbing Kartini's heart, writers stake a political claim to a powerful symbol. To appropriate Kartini for a certain nation, party, class, or gender, writers must present a convincing answer to a simple question. Who are Kartini's people? Who did this heroine rightfully represent?

Pramoedya Ananta Toer's *Panggil aku Kartini sadja* and Sitisoemandari Soeroto's *Kartini: Sebuah biografi* (1977) provide two answers to this question. On a number of points their responses agree. Both writers claim Kartini for the Indonesian people as a pioneer of their yet-to-be-discovered nation. Both argue that Kartini's colonial patrons obscured the true power of her thought. Yet their views of Kartini's people and her thought are as different as the historical contexts in which they wrote. While their Kartinis may not embody all of the differences between the Old Order and the New Order, they reflect an important shift in legitimating ideologies. Pramoedya locates his Kartini and her people in a history of struggle. Soeroto locates hers in the naturalized categories and boundaries of the State.

The History of the Books

Before turning to the texts, it seems worth pausing for a moment on their construction. On the surface, the books have much in common. The tables of contents cover a similar range of topics: Kartini's background, the era in which she lived, her thoughts on colonial society, the later impact of her work. Both books are written in Indonesian with smatterings of Dutch, English, and Javanese. Both writers end each chapter with extensive footnotes, listing foreign scholars, interviews with Kartini's family, and her letters to substantiate their claims. Both Pramoedya and Soeroto begin their books by describing what inspired them to undertake research on Kartini. Both present their project as a long and arduous task.

It is in this account of origins that the differences between the books begin to come into view. Pramoedya, recognized by many as Indonesia's greatest living writer, published his introduction to Kartini's life and thought in 1962, three years before the violent demise of Sukarno's Old Order. Pramoedya saw his book as part of the struggle of the new Indonesian nation to free its history from colonial frames. Composed at the turn of the century, Kartini's letters gave Pramoedya a place to begin to rewrite his nation's past from the perspective of the ruled. Confined to Java by a dearth of resources and time, Pramoedya spent from 1956 to 1961 scouring the National Archives and National Museum in Jakarta, and gathering materials from private libraries, newspapers, and Kartini's son. As informants died and documents vanished, Pramoedya conducted his research as a race against time. Only with the financial and moral support of Indonesian friends and institutions could he endure the four long years it took to complete the work.

Soeroto, who published her biography in 1977, gives her mission a different twist. Fortune and patriotism launched this journalist and mother on her career as a biographer. Driving with her husband from Jakarta to Central Java in March of 1964, Soeroto got a sudden urge to stop in Salatiga to interview Kardinah, the late Kartini's younger sister, for a feature on Kartini's birthday. The inspiring picture Kardinah painted was confirmed that May when Sukarno made Kartini an official National Hero. It was an embarrassment to the nation that no one had written Kartini's biography, Soeroto concluded. Somehow, she worked up the courage to embark on a task that no Dutch nor Indonesian scholar had dared to undertake. Since there were "no Indonesian books on Kartini",[6] most of Soeroto's material came from Holland, including her copy of *Door duisternis tot licht*, called by Soeroto "DDTL." A chance encounter with Rob Nieuwenhuys in 1971 brought her a trunkload of his research notes to use in her efforts; other Dutch scholars sent materials as well. Soeroto interviewed Kartini's family, as well as General Nasution, who told her many "amusing stories" about the exploits of Kartini's son in the army. After four years of research, Soeroto had nearly ruined her eyesight, but her task was complete. Immediately popular, Soeroto's book was lauded as a "monumental" work by Bouman, a respected scholar of Kartini and one of the Dutch sources Soeroto cited.

We can learn something from the ways in which Pramoedya and Soeroto attempt to validate their findings. Pramoedya's task was to capture those glimpses of Kartini which had slipped through the net of Dutch scholarship. While he may not have had "hard" facts to replace them, he challenged the conclusions of foreign "experts". Soeroto's task was to combine the experts' conclusions and piece together Kartini with all of her glory intact. Dutch scholarship proves Kartini's virtues; if foreigners think so highly of Kartini, should not Indonesians feel the same? Soeroto collected, verified, and interpreted all of her data, but the emphasis was clearly on collection. With Soeroto's book being cited by the next round of Kartini revisionists,[7] her "facts" are recycled in yet another form.

Differences in method aside, both Pramoedya and Soeroto attempt to use their evidence to reveal the real Kartini behind the myth. In Soeroto's text, the myth is that Kartini was a "goddess", not a living woman who was great enough to inspire a nation. Her goal is to show those instances where, despite her greatness, Kartini suffered and faltered too.

In Pramoedya's text, the myth is twofold: Indonesians either reject Kartini as a colonial product or accept her as a nationalist without knowing why. His goal is to show that Kartini was the first "Indonesian thinker" able to represent her people in modern terms. Soeroto presents the facts that make Kartini a real person and even more glorious for this reason. Pramoedya presents the contradictions which created Kartini's consciousness and the Indonesian nationalism which followed. By demystifying Kartini, both contend that they will reveal a woman with a relationship to her people much stronger than the myths imply.

Kartini's Heritage

> This feeling developed in Kartini's heart, because she knew that in the field of progress, she was their valid heir. She felt called by history to work for eternity, to serve the people *(rakyat)* of her country. Without a doubt, it is clear that this call, indistinct or clear, had also been heard by her forebears. (Pramoedya 1962, vol. 1, p. 32)

> Didn't Kartini, as a descendent of Tjondronegoro, have a right to be a pioneer, to be an example knocking on the door of the old fashioned world that impeded the current of progress? Progress not just for women, but for men too so that both would move forward and the Javanese people *(bangsa)* would be perfected? (Soeroto 1977, p. 74)[8]

The first step in uniting Kartini with her rightful people is to anchor her firmly in the past. For both Pramoedya and Soeroto, the key to the "real" Kartini lies in her connection with a distant, glorious epoch. As a hero of the Indonesian nation, Kartini is heir to its tradition; from the legitimating soil of national myth grows Kartini's family tree. It takes some creative pruning, but both Pramoedya and Soeroto manage to graft the branches on which their Kartinis will bloom.

In Soeroto's case, the task is straightforward. Inventively interpreting the genealogies of Javanese kings, she fixes Kartini's roots in Majapahit, the Indies' most powerful precolonial state. Fourteen generations back, Soeroto discovered a paternal ancestor, Prabu Bromowijoyo, who could connect Kartini with the New Order's cartographical forebear. Much is at stake in this cartography, and Soeroto takes an angry detour to refute Berg's claim that Majapahit extended no further than East Java. Majapahit's boundaries have to have equaled the borders of modern Indonesia to prove the new state's historical legitimacy. Destiny placed

Kartini within these ancient boundaries, and destiny had a hand in her nationalism, which is also grounded in concrete, timeless truths. While Soeroto generally defers to the "proof" presented by Western scholars, this particular scholar has to be wrong.

Pramoedya also links Kartini to the ancient past, but he proceeds somewhat differently. Soeroto begins with blood lines and ends with a geography unsullied by the influence of the Dutch. Pramoedya begins with geography and ends with the blood spilled by rebels who fought to keep Jepara free. Pramoedya returns not to Majapahit, but to Mataram, the last Javanese kingdom to resist the Dutch East Indies Company, and depicts a long line of princes who made a stand. Her struggle links Kartini to those who preceded her; she is legitimated through conflict, not through the map. As the heirs to this spirit of resistance, Kartini and her people find their true bond.

Where Soeroto writes of Java's ancient era, we see an image of beauty and tranquility. "Molek, indah, kaya raya", Majapahit was a land of art and music, of peaceful and respectful relations between the rulers and the ruled. Colonial domination disrupted this pretty picture by stripping Java's leaders of their prestige. Under the rule of the Dutch, the Javanese degenerated. Apathetic and ignorant, they simply waited for commands and sat back while their new masters sucked their land and their spirit dry.

Against this depressing backdrop, Kartini's grandfather rose like a shining star in the colonial bureaucracy. Recognizing his talents, the Dutch rapidly promoted Tjondronegoro IV to positions of responsibility and authority, granting him his father's title at the tender age of twenty-five. From his vantage point as Bupati of Demak, Tjondronegoro IV saw the unhappiness around him and asked himself, "How did we fall so far behind?" The answer was obvious: a lack of education was to blame. So he taught himself Dutch and strove to enlighten his family and his inferiors. He hired a Dutch governor to teach his children science; he himself attended to their morals, promoting the age-old virtues of Javanese culture. His efforts paid off: not only were his sons respected servants of the Dutch and of their people, they were accomplished linguists and scholars to boot. Honoured with Dutch medals for their service, Kartini's grandfather and uncles bequeathed her a spirit of service and duty, along with the intellect her letters would later reveal.

When Pramoedya writes of Kartini's predecessors, he paints a more turbulent picture. Precolonial society was not governed by peace, but by a crude form of feudalism in which the people exchanged their freedom for protections in times of war. With the pacification of Diponegoro, the relations between the people and their leaders took a different form. Kartini's grandfather fought for his people through "reports and administration", no longer able to wage open combat (1962, vol. 1, p. 24). Whereas for Soeroto's Tjondronegoro, colonialism is the cause of ignorance, for Pramoedya's, ignorance is the cause of colonialism. Instead of "Why are we stupid?", he asks himself "How did we lose?" Pramoedya's Tjondronegoro answers "Western science", but he turns it towards different ends. Service and knowledge are not Kartini's birthright; it is the battle for the people which she is destined to carry forward into the era of the modern colonial state.

But Pramoedya does more than insert Kartini's noble forebears into the parade of Javanese heroes. He inserts her maternal ancestors into a parade of their own, aligning Kartini not only with the people's defenders, but with the people themselves. In Kartini's genealogy flow the competing streams of nineteenth-century colonial feudalism and twentieth-century capitalist exploitation. Kartini's mother was born in Jepara to the foreman of a private sugar factory. This grandfather belonged to the first generation of labourers produced when Holland liberalized the Indies economy. Where Soeroto brushes aside Kartini's mixed blood, Pramoedya makes it a key element in her consciousness. His Kartini inherited her father's love for learning, but she inherited more than her nose from his lower-class wife. Personal conflict and her society's contradictions gave Kartini a reason to leave her noble status behind, and to say "Just call me who I am."

Kartini's Childhood

> As his children grew up, Bupati Sosroningrat always cared for their spiritual development.... From their earliest years, he made a habit of bringing them on his visits to the villages, so they would understand the lives of the little people [*rakyat kecil*] and a feeling of love towards them would grow. (Soeroto 1977, p. 37)

> Kartini's nursemaid was domestic strife, a polygamous struggle. (Pramoedya 1962, vol. 1, p. 58)

Their genealogies complete, Old Order Kartini and New Order Kartini are ready to enter the scene. Our two Kartinis descended from very different forebears; they had very different childhoods as well. Where Soeroto paints a picture of domestic bliss, documenting Kartini's happy progress under her father's care, Pramoedya presents us with the stress of her mixed heritage, portraying the conflict between the common and the noble that drove Kartini into her father's care. Their early experiences prepared the two heroines for different relations with their people and different perspectives on the system in which they lived.

Drawing on Kardinah's memories, Soeroto recounts New Order Kartini's early years in richly detailed episodes. From the very beginning Kartini was ahead of her age. At eight months, she was inquisitive and adroit; at nine, she showed intellect and a talent for observation; at twelve, maternal instincts and a strong sense of justice. Soeroto intersperses these episodes with the series of rituals that Kartini's family—"who held rightly to Javanese tradition" (1977, p. 31)—performed for the young heroine. With these stories, Soeroto not only demonstrates Kartini's talents; she shows her acting and speaking Javanese, albeit with an adorable lisp.

Soeroto's tapestry of mundane facts reinforces the "reality" of New Order Kartini and locates her in the timeless world of Javanese culture. Her childhood is thoroughly imaginable for a good New Order Javanese. Of course, Kardinah could hardly have witnessed all of these events, but who could have invented such stories? What's more, with this happy picture, Soeroto negates any link between Kartini's common parentage and her later nationalism. Ngasirah's status was both legal and public; Kartini and the children of the noble wife were treated alike; the two wives got along well. The children may have spoken to Ngasirah in low Javanese, but their relations were perfectly cordial. It was Mr Abendanon, in an effort to appeal to a European audience, who deleted the Bupati's second wife from Kartini's letters. Kartini herself had nothing to hide. In all, the picture is a pretty one; just as in the days of Majapahit, what a pleasant life the family must have led!

Dispensing with her mother, Soeroto traces New Order Kartini's charitable sentiments directly to her father. It was Sosroningrat who took Kartini and her sisters to the villages and cultivated their love for the poor. Again relying on Kardinah's memory, Soeroto weaves a myriad of details around the trips: the expedition to see the fire victims, the travels through the flooded lands, the free banquets on Idul Fitri appear in sharp relief. We can almost see the gratitude on the faces of the happy peasants, the pleasure on the faces of the noble girls. The impact of this upbringing is clear. Soeroto writes:

> We can see how, thanks to the guidance of her father, a high *priyayi* with a feeling of responsibility and love for the people, the noble daughters from their earliest days were close to the lives of the people and how this implanted in them a love for their People [*Bangsa*], their brown skinned race, a feeling which throughout their lives could not be shaken by their friendship with the Dutch, no matter how close.... Cultivated in Kartini and in her younger sisters, this love directly influenced her as an adult, so in the end it became her goal to carry her People [*Bangsa*] in the direction of Progress and Welfare! (1977, p. 31)

Passed down from her father, Kartini's concern for her people is part and parcel of the selfless nobility of her ancestors. The Dutch may bring modern temptations, but New Order Kartini can resist their charms.

Old Order Kartini did not have the benefit of such an unproblematic upbringing. From the beginning, her life was rent by conflict. Her mother, Ngasirah, was valued for her body, not her birth or etiquette; the Bupati kept her outside the main house, far from the gaze of disapproving visitors. Between Ngasirah and the Bupati's noble wife, the Raden Ayu, there was little love lost. Kartini stayed out of the crossfire by turning to her father for companionship; Ngasirah finally left or was ordered away. Kartini's relationship with her stepmother never warmed; her relationship with her real mother was cut short. Through her father and her brother young Kartini gained the love and wisdom she craved.

These childhood tensions led to new contradictions when Kartini's father introduced her to the colonial world. One day, during a visit to the villages, the family met a young grass cutter. Kartini looked from the grass cutter to her young nephew, seeing their similarities and the gap between their lives. Her heart went out to the boy, yet she could not blame the person directly responsible for his suffering, for that person was her beloved father. In a flash, Kartini grasped the roots of her mother's suffering and the inhumanity which she now witnessed: the enemy was the system, not the people within it. What served in Soeroto's account as one more example of Bupati Sosroningrat's lessons becomes Old Order Kartini's moment of awakening.

Old Order Kartini's heroism lies in her ability to transcend the contradictions of her life and experience. Torn between love and justice, she produces a critique of the linguistic hierarchy which prevents people from communicating as human beings. Soeroto's Sosroningrat connects New Order Kartini to her people by teaching her the importance of *noblesse oblige*. Pramoedya's Sosroningrat separates Old Order Kartini from her people, but in the process creates the conditions which lead her to enlightenment. That her critique comes to focus on the status of women does not undermine Pramoedya's argument. Kartini's pledge to "work" for the "people" ("*rakyat*") marks the failure of feudal categories: noble women should never "work," especially not for the common folk. In confounding these categories, Kartini lays important foundations.

> From her sharp observation come not just knowledge and insight, but honest love for them which in the end will develop into patriotism: that is wide, positional Nationalism! (Pramoedya 1962, vol. 1, p. 115)

Kartini's Confinement

> Maybe Kartini, with her education, was destined to become the woman to have her eyes opened by seeing the DARK world here and the LIGHT world there. (Soeroto 1977, p. 74)

Where Old Order Kartini "awoke" through a forbidden identification with the *rakyat*, New Order Kartini had to leave the outside world to harken to her calling. New Order Kartini's happy days as a mischievous, carefree girl ended abruptly at puberty. Like other noble girls of the time, Kartini could not appear again in public until she was safely married. New Order Kartini suffered bitterly in her "gilded cage". Cut off from the classroom she loved, contemplating the horrors of marriage to a perfect stranger, she often thought of death. Yet it was suffering and confinement that led to this Kartini's enlightenment. While trapped in the house, she devoured books and newspapers, she listened to her father's conversations, she scrutinized the behaviour of his guests. She had long hours to absorb all that she read and observed. In short, "she became an adult before her time!" (Soeroto 1977, p. 71).

As New Order Kartini reflected on her position, she thought of the other girls who were suffering the same fate. Why had no one spoken out against the excesses of feudalism? Something had to be done. Inspired by the memory of her grandfather, Kartini experienced a renaissance of the spirit. The struggle in her soul between the forces of modernity and feudalism finally tilted in favour of the Light. She would be the one to take up the battle to improve the position of women, all to the glory of their people! She would work for her people to save other girls from her fate.

> She wanted to change the situation that she could no longer bear. She wanted with all her soul, because she was driven by a feeling of responsibility to devote her life to humanity—to decrease the suffering of Woman through the Progress of her People [*Bangsa*]! (Soeroto 1977, p. 75)

Old Order Kartini had already experienced enlightenment when she entered the gilded cage, but her suffering served to deepen her dedication. Given her relationship with her father, the field of women's education became an arena where Kartini could declare battle on feudalism without challenging his prestige. Suffering deepened her awareness, but it did not form it. Pramoedya insists that his nation's obsession with the tragic in Kartini's life only obscures the full meaning of her thought.

Kartini Leaves the Cage

Their awakening complete, our two Kartinis were prepared to confront the world and present their programme for change. After their release from confinement, the Kartinis pursued somewhat different goals, even if their activities were identical. New Order Kartini was revolutionary but respectful, holding fast to the good *priyayi* values her father taught her. Old Order Kartini used her grasp of Dutch language and Javanese art to fight the colonial system, pushing to their limits the boundaries which her environment presented her.

New Order Kartini began her campaign at home by freeing her sisters from the rules of respect. She put her studies into practice and built a personal regime on the basis of *"Kemerdekaan, Persamaan, Persaudaraan"*, that is, *Liberté, Egalité et Fraternité* (Soeroto 1977, p. 79). The territory of this new nation did not extend far. Revolutionary slogans aside, the regime deferred when it came to her parents, for Kartini recognized the respect her elders deserved. Her critique of Dutch officials who demanded Javanese deference focused on their greed and inauthenticity, not on the colonial hierarchy itself. These men were *"gila hormat"*, or *"crazy for respect"*; they succumbed to their desires, just like the greedy bupati who excessively extracted the *"cultuurprocent"*. How unnatural it was for the Dutch not to want people to speak to them in their own language. Javanese "happily use *kromo inggil*, the highest speech level, to those of their *bangsa* with a higher status"; having to speak it with a foreigner who responds in "market Malay" puts them to shame (Soeroto 1977, p. 117).

Given her upbringing, New Order Kartini had no trouble differentiating between good and bad uses of Javanese. Nor, it seems, did she find it difficult to recognize good and bad Malay. The good uses of Dutch were particularly obvious. Dutch gave Indonesian a way to order from the menu of foreign knowledge. Entrees as complex as the French Revolution could be served up in perfect Indonesian as long as one knew the code. For all the importance of this code, New Order Kartini knew that it could never fulfill the need for character and culture. Following her father's training and her ancestors' wisdom, she gave her people modern knowledge, but at the same time promoted Javanese values. This programme is clear in her Note on education: schools should teach Dutch, but they should give priority to the students' mother tongue (Soeroto 1977, p. 298). New Order Kartini may have "liked" Dutch, but she clearly knew its place.

Old Order Kartini confronted a more complex set of problems in her work for the *rakyat*. She had to choose her audience and the language in which she would address them. For New Order Kartini, Dutch was as transparent as a contact lens and no more likely to distort. For Old Order Kartini, Dutch was a politically charged weapon which had to be handled with care. Through Dutch, Old Order Kartini could enter the European world and criticize its occupants; she could represent the *rakyat*'s demands. Her writing could reach educated *pribumi*, allowing them to look at the Indies objectively and change what they saw. Kartini saw the potential of Malay, Pramoedya insists, but recognized that this language of gossip badly needed reform (1962, vol. 1, p. 137). Used by Dutch officials to shame their Javanese counterparts, Malay created colonial barricades, not doors, as Kartini saw when she compared it to Czech (Pramoedya 1962, vol. 1, p. 138). Soeroto marvels that New Order Kartini even knew about Russia (1977, p. 468). Pramoedya gives his Kartini an international awareness of the place of language in social struggle.

Both Kartinis put their visions into action through their work with Javanese artisans. Once again, the two women defined their project very differently. New Order Kartini inherited her love of Javanese art as a matter of course. Her father had taught her the beauty of her culture, its roots in the past, and the responsibility of "introspective patrons" to show their people its true meaning (Soeroto 1977, p. 115). High culture, like the boundaries of the state, harkened back to legitimating origins.

The duty of the elite was to preserve authenticity, keeping "Java" in its original shape.

Old Order Kartini also found the truth of her people in their art, but she saw this relationship very differently. Connotations, not denotations, gave art its value; historical experience gave culture its meaning. The gamelan was more than specifically Javanese music. It called to mind Kartini's ancestors and their brave and valiant deeds. The gamelan could also evoke a glorious future when the struggle would begin anew. Because of this connection between art and resistance, Kartini made the promotion of Javanese handicrafts a political activity. She not only saved the wood carvers from exploitation, she protected and cultivated their voice. In addition to preserving their identity, art could improve the people's character. By "returning art to the people in an improved form", education made the people strong (Pramoedya 1962, vol. 1, p. 118). As Pramoedya writes:

> For the first time in the history of Modern Indonesia, a person knew the function of art for education, and art as a way of knowing the character of the people, even their history in dark eras gone by. (1962, vol. 1, p. 118)

Unlike New Order Kartini, who valued culture as if it were a fixture of nature, Old Order Kartini saw art as the product of her people's struggle, an essential element of their character, won in history, not given by fate.

Kartini is Silenced

Neither Pramoedya nor Soeroto gave their story a happy ending. Both Kartinis rejected scholarships and married polygamists for the sake of their ailing fathers. Both eventually died in childbirth, their voices silenced, their ambitious plans permanently deferred. This series of tragedies followed a series of betrayals by people they loved and trusted. New Order and Old Order Kartini faced a similar set of villains, but these villains had differing motives for their deeds.

The "human tragedy" of New Order Kartini can be traced to the fateful day she gave up her plans to study in Holland. The colonial government, through her trusted Mr Abendanon, engineered her downfall. With her other Dutch friends, Abendanon could accept Kartini's criticism as long as she remained in the Indies because it came from such a "pure and honest heart" (Soeroto 1977, p. 121). But if Kartini had gone to Holland, who knows what would have happened? If Kartini was brave enough to confront the Dutch while under their control, who knows what she might have said if freed? Her alliance with Van Kol, the prominent Social Democrat, literally raised red flags. Abendanon later felt guilty, but that day on Klein Scheveningen he had no choice but to persuade Kartini not to go.

While the colonial government was to blame, New Order Kartini was not without responsibility for her fate. She could have rejected her patron's advice; she could have forged ahead. By wavering at the moment when her dream was in reach, Kartini paved the way to her marriage and her death; she would always regret this decision. Yet Soeroto embraces this "flaw" in Kartini which opens her to tragedy and pain. God's Will determined Kartini's destiny, but her sacrifice for her sick father is a natural response which makes Kartini even more sublime. With Cora Vreede de Stuers, Soeroto wonders if perhaps it was a good thing that Kartini died young. Abendanon might never have published DDTL if he had not felt remorse at her death. Would Kartini have meant as much to her nation if she had lived happily to a ripe old age?

While the incident on the beach sealed New Order Kartini's fate, Abendanon muffled her voice once again when he compiled DDTL. He edited freely to avoid offending the Kartini Fund's potential donors. We may never know the full scope of Kartini's criticism of the Dutch, nor of her awareness of the plots they mounted to thwart her. Many of her friends refused to cooperate with Abendanon; some even burned Kartini's letters. Luckily there are other sources of information to add to our picture of Kartini, even if we can never know her completely.

Old Order Kartini was censored too, but her repression began much earlier. Abendanon and her father never took her seriously. The Dutch government never bothered to read her "Note on Education", which Annie Glaser neglected to send to Holland. To the Dutch, "Kartini was like a coffee tree that produced well out of Dutch efforts to 'civilize' Indonesians—served up in all her sweetness ever since they began Dutch primary schools" (Pramoedya 1962, vol. 1, p. XI). If Abendanon prevented her trip for political reasons, this led to no moral crisis; his fascination with Kartini was political from the start. Of course Abendanon's compilation of her letters paints a distorted picture; the Malay version published by the Dutch blurs her image even more. Both books omit many of Kartini's letters to Stella, the socialist and feminist who was Kartini's most radical friend. These letters must have undermined the Dutch image of Kartini the tragic but grateful victim by introducing Kartini the fighter.

But the Dutch were not the only force which kept Old Order Kartini under wraps. In Pramoedya's version of his heroine's tragedy, an internal censor is a work as well. Kartini's decision to betray her convictions sprang in part from her relationship with her father. But this is not a victory of "natural" affinities; the tragedy was necessary, given Kartini's location in the history of her nation's consciousness. If Kartini had had a wider base of support, if she had been able to get closer to her real people, her life might have ended differently. But Kartini would never have understood the system had it not been for the contradictions in her soul. Love and conflict enabled Kartini to see her world through different eyes and to "humanize humanity", in the words of her hero Multatuli (Pramoedya 1962, vol. 1, p. 143). Love for her father, whom she would not yet deny, brought this struggle to an end.

Kartini Becomes a National Pioneer

What occurred after New Order Kartini's death can hardly come as a surprise, given Soeroto's foreshadowing. We are told by page XVII what will be proven in the end: Kartini embodied the spirit of nationalism "YEARS BEFORE THE FOUNDING OF BOEDI OETOMO IN 1908!" (Soeroto 1977, p. 438). Should we doubt this claim, we can flip to the speech that the leaders of De Indische Vereniging gave in Leiden in 1911 as soon as they had read DDTL.[9] Kartini's life so inspired these Indonesian students that they pledged to make her words their guiding light. This light did not fail their organization. The Vereniging survived the decade to become the Perhimpunan Indonesia under Mohammad Hatta and other "pioneers of our independence" (Soeroto 1977, p. 404). For the Father of the Revolution, Kartini's spirit steered a course through the *Sumpah Pemuda* to the War of National Liberation. Even today's family planning programme can claim Kartini as its ancestor; her critique of the Regent with fifty-three wives is simply "Two are enough!" in a slightly different guise (Soeroto 1977, p. 421).

If this trajectory is not enough to prove Kartini's nationalist credentials, Soeroto can turn to her heroine's sisters, who give a first-hand account of Kartini's spirit and its miraculous journey. Kartini's essence spread by contact and worked its way into everyone's soul. "We younger siblings carried on our older sister's work because her struggle was in our blood" (Soeroto 1977, p. 420).[10] Her ideas percolated through the Indies, finally reaching the educated youth whom Kartini inspired to unite. Kardinah recalls:

> A feeling of uplift was in the air. Everywhere sparks of the national movement had begun to appear. We always struggled to keep these sparks alive, until several years later appeared the movement that was later named the Nationalist Movement. (Soeroto 1977, p. 421)

Can there be any doubt that Kartini was its cause?

If we are still not convinced that Kartini was indeed the "pioneer of National Progress", the work of foreign scholars should persuade us. Soeroto lines up excerpts from George Kahin, W.F. Wertheim, J.S. Furnivall, and J.Th. Petrus Blumberger to testify to Kartini's role as the "MOTHER OF NATIONALISM", a fact which should not upset men because, after all, "mothers gave birth to us" (1977, p. 413).[11] "If well-known scholars say Kartini was a precursor of nationalism, based on proof, how can we not value her as much?" (1977, pp. 438–39).[12]

Pramoedya's historical method is somewhat more sophisticated: just because Kartini preceded later nationalists, Pramoedya does not claim that she inspired them. While Pramoedya credits Old Order Kartini as the first modern Indonesian thinker, her position at a particular juncture in history made her so. In the transition from forced-labour feudalism to modern bureaucracy, two phenomena were born: one was the ethical policy, a new instrument of colonial control, and the other was nationalism, the child of colonial education which would grow up to reject its parent. As the marker of this transition, Kartini deserves a place in history, whether or not there were concrete connections between Kartini and the revolutionaries who followed her.

Old Order Kartini may not have "caused" the national awakening, but her thought reflected the forces that would shape it. She followed Malay newspapers and knew of the expanding ranks of educated youth. She advocated reforming Malay, bringing the accuracy of her beloved Dutch to this language that would become Indonesian. She planned to write for the colonial press. "It has always been my intention to raise a loud voice", she wrote, "because only publication can bring the improvements that we wish in this situation which so badly needs uplifting" (Pramoedya 1962, vol. 2, p. 97). Had Old Order Kartini lived to participate in the movement, she might have cooperated with leaders who later challenged the feudalism she abhorred. Even if Kartini only reached Indonesians through *Door duisternis tot licht*, her thought heralded their nation's birth and its contradictions. Pramoedya writes:

> She knew that, at this time, she was the product of feudal upbringing with her father as the law and the source of law, representing not only the King but the Gods. Kartini was not going to disappoint her father or reduce his right over her as his daughter. But she was also aware of the future which had to be seized with effort and with struggle. (1962, vol. 2, p. 185)

Kartini had to accept her tragedy, but she anticipated what history was to bring.

Who are Kartini's People?

What insights can we gain from Soeroto and Pramoedya's answers to our original question? Explicitly or implicitly, who did and do these fine young women represent?

For New Order Kartini, the people were not a problem; she came by her constituency quite naturally. By inheriting her father's refined values, she came to love the rural people and care for their welfare; through suffering, she took up the fight to free other women so they could participate in this charitable mission. Kartini had no need to choose between *rakyat* or *ningrat*; all Indonesians, whether common or noble, could find their true identity in her family's virtues, the legacy of Majapahit, and the map. With these virtues to guide her, New Order Kartini proceeded with her social programme. She fought colonial temptations and criticized those who gave in. She revealed those whose desire and inauthenticity upset the natural order, whether the culprit was the "prestige crazy" Dutchman or his greedy native underling. Unlike modern Indonesian girls, New Order Kartini was never tempted to imitate the West. With an ancient, authentic map to guide her, her path and her people remained clearly in the light.

Old Order Kartini came by her people more painfully. Where New Order Kartini suppressed imagination—saving plenty for Soeroto and her "facts"—Old Order Kartini found her people in a battle between identification and compassion. This Kartini may have inherited her spirit of resistance from her ancestors, but her role as the mouthpiece of the *rakyat* sprang from the contradictions of her life. Her earliest experiences in a feudal household helped her to imagine the poor. The tension between her love for the people and her love for her father led Kartini to attack the foundations of the colonial hierarchy, not just its excesses. Where her grandfather was a reformer, Old Order Kartini was a radical, her identity grounded in struggle with the colonial power. In the dawn of a new era, Kartini did not just adopt a pre-existing position; she created her consciousness anew.

But this discussion of differences neglects a common feature of our two Kartinis. By presenting them in English, I have obscured the fact that both Kartinis inhabit an Indonesian language world. Old Order Kartini's *Rakyat* (people) differ from New Order Kartini's *Bangsa* (people, nation or race) and her *Masyarakat* (community or society); all three differ from the Dutch *Volk* or the American (We The) People. As markers of regimes with their own ideologies and agendas, these words each have a special salience. Soeroto's vocabulary cannot help but call to mind the destruction of the social forces which took Pramoedya's vocabulary as their emblem. For all their differences, these words serve a common purpose: they create a Kartini who writes in Dutch but thinks in Indonesian, a Kartini whose pen does not create, but reveals. In their search for origins, Pramoedya and Soeroto generate mythical figures. Grounding Kartini's people in place and in history, Pramoedya and Soeroto translate into Kartini's letters what they imagine must be there: a nation and a language waiting to be found.

Beyond the New Order: Historical Kartini and Her Texts

When we consider recent Indonesian history, our two Kartinis reveal much more than the fantasies of very different minds. Old Order Kartini and her New Order sister tell us much about Indonesia before and after the victory of the postcolonial state over civil society, a counter-revolution described by Ben Anderson in his essay, "Old State, New Society" (1983). Their characters call to mind the languages employed by Sukarno and Suharto, one signifying perpetual revolution, the other motionless order. To understand how these idioms have fared, we need only consider the fate of our two Kartinis' creators. Twenty-five years after his detention, Pramoedya is still under house arrest in Jakarta; his books remain banned (Watson 1973). Soeroto travels freely with her historian husband, giving speeches and granting interviews to the Indonesian press (Rambe 1979).

The ideological gap between the two Kartinis should come as little surprise. What seems more intriguing is the ease with which Pramoedya and Soeroto used identical excerpts to support very different arguments. Kartini, as a collection of letters, seems open to infinite readings. New Order Kartini may reign in today's Indonesia, but elsewhere other Kartinis have made their debut. Depicting the continuities, not the breaks, between the current and the colonial regime, these new Kartinis can tell us something of the features which have made Kartini such a durable symbol.

"In Her Historical Context" Kartini is a good example of the new generation. The latest in Jean Taylor's creations (which include "Far Reaching Policies" Kartini and "Child of Feminism" Kartini),[13] she spoke for the daughters of noblemen struggling to maintain their place in a changing society. This Kartini found her home at the dawn of an era when improved technology created new types of colonists who lived much more briefly in the Indies. With their wives and children, these officials and entrepreneurs created European enclaves, safe from the *"inlanders"* whom they regarded with curiosity and fear. To mix with their new masters, Javanese officials needed wives with European graces; ambitious fathers taught their daughters Dutch to prepare them for the task. Taylor's Kartini was a product of this process. Like Djajadinigrat, another "modern" *priyayi* of her day, Kartini presented an elite response to the demands of the modern colonial state. Her goals and her ability to formulate them arose from the sociological conditions of her time; her dream was to educate the members of her class so that they could fill the shoes of the Dutch.

Tsuchiya Kenji's "Keroncong" Kartini occupies a position in discourse as well as in history. This Kartini combined Dutch nostalgia and modern "science"; she was both a product and a producer of cultural idioms. While Taylor sheds some light on the letters' social context, Tsuchiya dissects the elements of Kartini's texts which make her a candidate for a nationalist reading. With Pramoedya, Tsuchiya argues that Kartini represents the "first modern element in Indonesian intellectual history" (Pramoedya 1962, vol. 1, p. XIII; see also Tsuchiya 1986), yet he explains aspects of Kartini's consciousness that Pramoedya takes as given. Looking at Kartini's prose, not her policies, Tsuchiya places Kartini at the end of the "empty years" following the demise of the last Javanese court poet. The conflicting strains in Kartini's character are not *ningrat* and *kromo*, but sentiment and realism. Writing at the beginning of the modern era,

Kartini created herself and her people by using Dutch to bring her world into view.

In Kartini's letters, she used her Dutch telescope to differing effects. Focused on the natural landscape, Keroncong Kartini painted sentimental pictures in space. Taking the transcendent viewpoint of a theosophical God, Kartini evoked a beauty anyone could claim. Like *keroncong* music and *hindia molek* art, these sentimental prose pictures mirrored the consciousness of the Dutch of the time: their nostalgia for an imagined past in a period of rapid change, their ambiguous attachment to this land they so briefly made their home. Focused on the social landscape, Kartini presented a biting critique of colonial society. No longer is hers a perspective that anyone can occupy; it is a vision that creates an "us" and a "them". Kartini's greatest contribution was to synthesize the social and the aesthetic, bringing words and images together to plant the seeds of a national consciousness. No longer the beautiful Indies, the place was Java, a cultural landscape unique to a people and a time. "Almost accidentally" the idiom for a new imagined community arose; it was Kartini, in her isolation, who first explored this position between Dutch and Javanese and brought this new idiom into being.

The most interesting elements of Keroncong Kartini are features that other Kartinis lack. Tsuchiya points to Kartini's loneliness as a Javanese viewing her society from outside the Javanese language world. Because of Kartini's isolation, the community she directly encountered was limited indeed; she had few companions who could share her point of view. Without this community, Kartini could never fix herself at the end of her lens; her writing is often garbled and repetitive as a result. For all their crises, New Order Kartini and Old Order Kartini enjoy a stable identity, a peculiarly Javanese soul. Tsuchiya's Kartini has to stake a claim on this soul, and its stability cannot be assured.

Perhaps more importantly, Tsuchiya points to an awkwardness between Kartini and the common people that neither Pramoedya nor Soeroto seems to note. Missing from the Indonesian versions are the strange stares that met Kartini during her jaunts to the villages in her father's motor car. Kartini imagined herself living in a hut, and relished the novelty of the notion; it was "as if" her sister were one of the workers precisely because it was not the case. It was colonial language, not personal experience, that allowed Kartini to imagine the people's soul; for Kartini, as for the "heroes" who followed her, a strangeness about the people remained. One of Holland's legacies to the new nation was Javanology, a science which made Dutch the revealer of the "truth" of Java; Kartini saw her people through a Javanological screen, but she felt the excess the Dutch categories left behind.[14] For all its beauty and political importance, Pramoedya's dream of Kartini is a dream, her identification with the peasants, a fantasy. Kartini could criticize Dutch officers all she liked, but she remained within the limits of their prose.

"Educating the Javanese": Kartini's Festival of the Indies

Kartini's letters are the product of imagination: Kartini pictures herself in the eyes of Dutch friends and she pictures the world beyond her walls. It is the ambiguity of Kartini's position in her pictures which allows Pramoedya and Soeroto to imagine Kartini as they do. Kartini's writing, like mestizo culture, lacks an unequivocal origin; thus, Kartini becomes a symbol for the founding of any number of collectivities.[15] Just as Kartini turned *hindia molek* into the Javanese landscape, Soeroto and Pramoedya project Kartini into their own social landscapes and make her image—and her people—their own.

Nowhere is this phenomenon more obvious than in Pramoedya and Soeroto's acclaim for Kartini's Note to the Dutch government entitled "Educate the Javanese!" (Kartini 1974). Soeroto believes it marks the "peak of Kartini's career as a theorist on the problems of Javanese society" (Soeroto 1977, p. 295). Pramoedya takes it as a courageous declaration of Kartini's views.

> With refined words, she faced the colonial government and laid out what she felt was the right of her people, the right not to say "amin." (1962, vol. 1, p. 166)

Both depict the Note as a coherent manifesto, reflecting their young heroine's plan of action. Soeroto sees Kartini promoting the Javanese language; Pramoedya sees her demanding her people's rights. Selectively cutting and pasting the document, both generate a message to prove what Kartini really meant.

In reassembling "Educate the Javanese!" to fit their fantasies, both Soeroto and Pramoedya leave a good deal of information out. A closer look at the uncut text reveals what a strange manifesto it is. Some curious images appear in the parts of the Note that Pramoedya and Soeroto discarded. As in her letters, Kartini writes of knowledge and prestige as if they were pretty things one might eat. The Javanese are children, dazzled by the baubles of pomp and prestige, but their appetites can be turned to Kartini's advantage. If the government acts enthused, the Javanese, just like preverbal children, will appropriate their idol's desires (Kartini 1974, p. 89). The Regents will take Kartini's "medicine" if the government coats her proposal with sugar and presents it in a shining wrapper (Kartini 1974, p. 89). Things get even stranger when Kartini switches perspectives and points her social telescope at Holland. There she finds dear Dutch children eager to learn of the beautiful lands and warm brown people they will rule. In addition to "global education", Kartini proposed a Javanology roadshow, a "Festival of the Indies" complete with handicrafts, grass huts, and "real Javanese" (1974, p. 92). Pramoedya and Soeroto set aside these images as well. Kartini and the community which shares her perspective occupy a very strange place indeed.

Elsewhere in the document, we find other indications of the limits of Kartini's imagined community. Kartini makes her case by citing empirical evidence. "Cases are known", Kartini tells us, of a Javanese girl who benefitted greatly from kind Dutch women (1974, p. 93) and a wise Javanese prince who sent his children to school (1974, p. 89). On closer inspection, all of these "cases" derive from a single life—Kartini's own. Referring to herself as if to a random member of her collective, Kartini is both the representing and the represented in her text. The argument is circular: her life is her own best evidence for promoting improvements in the conditions of her life.

Kartini's idiom may seem unusual, but "Educate the Javanese!" bears a resemblance to later writing of the Indonesian "awakening". Whether they read Kartini or not, in the 1910s, leaders of the *"pergerakan"* or movement also used Ethical language to mobilize their groups.[16] They created a hierarchy of the spirit but limited its scope to the *inlander* elite; they reversed the metaphor of *dukun* and doctors, this time degrading the Dutch. *As* a *priyayi* woman, Kartini lived a confined life. Her journeys were short, her fellow travellers were very few; the only people available to fill her hierarchy were her family and a few Dutch friends. Even more than the ideologues who followed her, Kartini cannot keep straight who is "us" and who is "them". Her mixed-up audience evokes mixed-up metaphors. The *dukun* are the educated (Javanese or Dutch?) who take their secrets to the grave, greedily hoarding their knowledge (Kartini 1974, p. 88). Kartini is the doctor, but she is also a patient. "Teach the people in the Netherlands to ask themselves, 'What would the Netherlands be without the Indies?'", she writes, "and the Indies should be taught to ask, 'What would the Indies be without Holland?'" (Kartini 1974, p. 94). Kartini can no more imagine one without the other than she can cut her father's "secret telegraph cable to her heart" (Kartini 1964, p. 48). Caught between linguistic worlds, Kartini is not sure where to go; Indonesia has not yet learned to speak.

Conclusions?

With Tsuchiya's help, we can take a different view of Kartini and her myths. The "real" Kartini and all the Kartinis who followed her are products of the penetration of certain politics into certain texts. Her ambiguity presents both a challenge and a resource; she is a question which can only be silenced through force. We can never know Kartini's true intentions; even if we could return to her Jepara, her secret core lies everywhere and nowhere in her texts. What we can trace are the powers which have staked a claim on Kartini to turn her symbolic force to their benefit. Grounded in history and territory, Pramoedya and Soeroto's versions of Kartini's truth reflect different moments in Indonesia's past. New Kartinis will continue to be born as long as power demands it; we may follow this process, but we are unlikely to bring it to a close.

An Afterthought

> Raden Ajeng Kartini freed herself from the narrow oppression of tradition, and the simple language of these letters chants a poem "From Darkness into Light." The mist of obscurity is cleared away from her land and her people. The Javanese soul is shown as simple, gentle, and less hostile than we Westerners had ever dared to hope. For the soul of this girl was one with the soul of her people, and it is through her that a new confidence has grown up between the West and the East. The mysterious "Quiet Strength"[17] is brought into light, it is tender, human and full of love, and Holland may well be grateful to the hand that revealed it. (Couperus 1920)

In a photograph featured in the Kartini Fund's Annual Report of 1926, a line of little girls, clad neatly in batik, takes turns washing their hands. The setting is a wellfurnished classroom, its shelves adorned by toy cars, pictures, and plants. The focal point is the gleaming modern faucet; to the left, a Dutch woman gazes at us placidly while another inspects the little girls' hands. It is a perfectly staged scene, but for one strange detail.

Staring blankly at the camera, her back turned to her teachers, a little girl has pulled up her *kain* to reveal a snowy white petticoat underneath.

An important set of characters is missing from this story. Along with a host of Western scholars and journalists, the colonial government spawned Kartinis of their own. Years before the publication of *Habis gelap terbitlah terang*, people in Holland flocked to Kartini lectures, chaired Kartini committees, and contributed to Kartini schools designed to bring *meer licht* to the Javanese soul. These Dutch men and women imagined a Kartini who represented all of the people of her colour. They rejoiced at the love at the core of that "quiet strength"; now there was nothing to fear. What could better reflect what they found in Kartini's soul than the underwear beneath the little girl's *kain*?

The story of these Dutch Kartinis is an important one, for that little girl's bloomers reflect modern contradictions as well as colonial ones. Along with the structures of the colonial state, modern Indonesia has inherited many of its anxieties. The strangeness Kartini depicted remains today. A history of that strangeness and the institutions which have created and confronted it could explain why so much is at stake in the identification of Kartini with her people. Such a history would open onto much wider terrain. In appropriating Kartini, the New Order controls just one of the moments when its own Dutch "foundations" might show.

NOTES

1. This chapter is a reprint of Danilyn Rutherford, "Unpacking a National Heroine: Two Kartinis and Their People", *Indonesia* 56 (1993): 23–40. Minor alterations have been made to conform to ISEAS' style.
2. See Vreede-de Stuers (1977) and Zainu'ddin et al. (1980) on Kartini's feminist credentials. To learn what Kartini would think of today's Indonesia, see Katoppo (1979).
3. In addition to "Educate the Javanese", discussed later in this article, Kartini's published works include "Een Gouverneur Generaalsdag", which appeared in *De Echo* in 1900, and "Van een vergeten uithoekje", published in *Eigen Haard* in 1903. Her earliest published work, "Het huwelijk bij de Kodja's", was an ethnographic depiction written by the sixteen-year-old Kartini for the 1895 edition of *Bijdragen tot de taal-, land- en volkenkunde van Nederlandsch-Indie*.
4. Pramoedya describes plans by the leadership of Perhimpunan "Jong Java" to translate Kartini's letters into Javanese, Sundanese, Madurese, and Balinese. According to Pramoedya, this project, discussed in the 1920s,

never materialized. The first "local language" translations Pramoedya mentions are R. Sutjidibrata's Sundanese edition, published in 1930, and Ki Sastrasugunda's Javanese edition, published in 1938. See Pramoedya (1962), p. 131. According to the foreword to the 1922 edition of *Habis gelap terbitlah terang*, Dr Abendanon himself asked the Volkslectuur committee to produce a Malay translation.

5. Simamora describes one woman's memory of reading Kartini when she was growing up during the 1920s. Ibu Aruji went on to found a women's battalion during the National Revolution. Ibu Aruji's memories have as much to do with Kartini's present status as with her impact in the past. See Katoppo (1979), pp. 145–50.

6. That is, according to Soeroto. When she began the project in 1964, a number of Indonesian works on Kartini had already been published. Subandrio's brief account of Kartini appeared in 1950; Pramoedya's three-volume "introduction" came out in 1962. Soeroto lists Pramoedya in her bibliography, but she does not mention his book in her text. It was after 1965 that Pramoedya's books became scarce; this paper can only illustrate indirectly the reasons why.

7. Zainu'ddin (1980) leans heavily on Soeroto.

8. Throughout this chapter, I will call attention to the different ways that Pramoedya and Soeroto translate what appears in Kartini's texts as the Dutch term "*volk*". John M. Echols and Hassan Shadily's *An Indonesian-English Dictionary* defines *rakyat* (then *rakjat*) as "people, the populace, public" (1961, p. 257). Variations include "*rakyat jelata*", "the masses, the common people, proletariat", and "*rakyat jembel*", "the poor". *Bangsa* is given eight definitions, including "nation, people", "race", "nationality", "family, category, sex", "social class, group", "type", "kind" and "breed" (Echols and Shadily 1961, p. 30). These words have significantly different political connotations. Pramoedya's vocabulary evokes the people as "public", a "populace" united in a struggle against common oppression. Soeroto's evokes the people as a "family", bound by the innate, taken-for-granted ties that link creatures of one "race", "breed", or "type". The relationship of these different terms to Pramoedya and Soeroto's very different Kartinis should become clear in the course of this article. For now, one should keep in mind who is speaking wherever these words appear. "*Rakyat*" and "*bangsa*" first gained political currency well after Kartini's death. "*Rakyat*" and "*bangsa*" are Pramoedya and Soeroto's words; they could not have been Kartini's.

9. See "Kartini's Ideals Taken as Compass for 'De Indische Vereniging'" (Soeroto 1977, pp. 426–30).

10. Letter from Ibu Kardinah to Soeroto, April 1984.

11. "That a woman in fact progressed first need not disappoint Indonesian men. For whoever truly feels like a nationalist should be proud ... precisely because the one who pioneered the rise of our nationalism was a woman

[*seorang wanita*]: the class of mothers [*kaum ibu*] who gave birth to us..."
(Soeroto 1977, p. 413). Replacing "a woman", "*seorang wanita*", with "the
class of mothers", "*kaum ibu*", Soeroto makes the "MOTHER" of Indonesia
out of a young woman generally portrayed as objecting to this equation.

12. Soeroto (1977, pp. 438–39) begins this chapter with a much more modest
claim. "Many well-known foreign scholars do not forget to mention Kartini
and her role in their books." In fact, Kartini appears in the excerpts which
"prove" Soeroto's point as a symptom of Western education, one factor among
others responsible for the development of nationalism. This does not concern
Soeroto. Her logic makes the historical symptom into the Mother of the
Nation; best of all, these scholars have hard facts and esteemed reputations
to back them up.

13. Taylor's work exemplifies our heroine's ongoing demystification by academics.
See Taylor (1974), where she calls Kartini's thoughts on education "wide-
ranging", "enlightened", and "highly visionary", in that her position "moved
beyond that of her society, which by leaders comprehended only men" (p. 83).
In Taylor (1976), Kartini's most important contribution becomes her ability
"to apply the doctrine of then contemporary feminism to her own society"
(p. 639). Taylor (1989) casts a different light on Kartini by comparing her
with a man of her class rather than other leaders of her gender.

14. See Tsuchiya (1990) for the history of Javanology and its role in the demise
of Java's written tradition. To understand the appeal of Javanology, it seems
important to consider the anxieties which led the Dutch to focus the "light"
of science on the "dark" world of the cultural unknown. Shiraishi (1989)
describes the technological, economic, and social roots of both the village
underworld and the Dutch ethici who, at the turn of the century, accelerated
colonial penetration and control. Kartini's awkwardness is not identical to that
of her Dutch lady friends, but her response clearly adopts the technologies
which emerged to combat their fears.

15. Derrida (1986) deconstructs another myth of national origins.

16. Shiraishi (1990) interprets the language of the *pergerakan*. Tjipto (veteran of
the Kartini Debating Club!) depicts an alternative hierarchy based on Javanese
virtues drawn from the Dutch linguistic world (p. 126). Tjokro, like Kartini,
is a "satriya under the government" (p. 62); just as Kartini stands defiantly
beside the Resident while other wedding guests crouch, Tjokro stands beside
the government representative while he bellows at the crowd. The *dukun/
doctor* reversal appears in Mas Marco's radical attack on the "Ethical" policies
of the colonial state (p. 83).

17. Couperus (1920) gives this English translation of his famous term "*Stille
Kracht*". It is already a "simple, gentle, less hostile" rendition of what is
elsewhere translated as "The Hidden Force".

REFERENCES

Anderson, Benedict. 1983. *Imagined Communities: Reflections on the Origin and Spread of Nationalism*. London: Verso.

Couperus, Louis. 1920. Foreword to *Letters of a Javanese Princess*, by Kartini. Translated by Agnes Louise Symmers. New York: Knopf.

Derrida, Jacques. 1986. "Declarations of Independence". *New Political Science* 15: 4–15.

Echols, John M. and Hassan Shadily. 1961. *An Indonesian-English Dictionary*. Ithaca, NY: Cornell University Press.

Kartini, R.A. 1964. *Letters of a Javanese Princess*. Translated by Agnes Louise Symmers. New York: W.W. Norton.

———. 1974. "Educate the Javanese!". Translated by Jean Taylor. *Indonesia* 17: 83–98.

Katoppo, Aristides, ed. 1979. *Satu abad Kartini: Bunga rampai karangan mengenai Kartini*. Jakarta: Grafitas.

Pramoedya Ananta Toer. 1962. *Panggil aku Kartini sadja: Sebuah pengantar pada Kartini*. 3 vols. Jakarta: Nusantara.

Rambe, Hanna. 1979. "Sejenek bersama Sitisoemandari". In *Satu abad Kartini*, edited by Aristides Katoppo. Jakarta: Grafitas.

Shiraishi, Takashi. 1989. "Before Dawn: A Note on 19th Century Java". Typescript.

———. 1990. *An Age in Motion: Popular Radicalism in Java, 1912–1926*. Ithaca, NY: Cornell University Press.

Soeroto, Sitisoemandari. 1977. *Kartini: Sebuah biografi*. Jakarta: Gunung Agung.

Sutrisno, Sulastri. 1989. Introduction to *Surat-surat kepada Ny. R.M. Abendanon-Mandri dan suaminya*, by Kartini. Edited by F.G.P. Jaquet. Translated by Sulastri Sutrisno. Jakarta: Djembatan.

Taylor, Jean Gelman. 1974. Introduction to "Educate the Javanese!", by Kartini. Translated by Jean Gelman Taylor. *Indonesia* 17: 83–85.

———. 1976. "Raden Adjeng Kartini". *Signs: Journal of Women in Culture and Society* 1, no. 3: 639–61.

———. 1989. "Kartini in Her Historical Context". *Bijdragen tot de taal-, land- en volkenkunde* 145, no. 2–3: 295–307.

Tempo. 1987. "Ayunda tidak pernah menyerah", 12 December 1987.

Tsuchiya, Kenji. 1986. "Kartini's Image of the Javanese Landscape". *East Asian Cultural Studies* 25, no. 1–4: 59–86.

———. 1990. "Javanology and the Age of Ranggawarsita: An Introduction to Nineteenth Century Javanese Culture". In *Reading Southeast Asia*, edited by Takashi Shiraishi. Ithaca, NY: Cornell Southeast Asia Program.

Vreede-de Stuers, Cora. 1977. "Kartini, petit 'cheval sauvage' devenu héroïne de l'Indépendence indonésienne". *Archipel: Études interdisciplinaires sur le monde insulindien* 13: 105–18.

Watson, William. 1973. Introduction to "Bukan pasar malam", by Pramoedya
   Ananta Toer. Translated by William Watson. *Indonesia* 15: 21–26.
Zainu'ddin, Ailsa Thomson. 1980. "Kartini—Her Life, Work and Influence".
   In *Kartini Centenary: Indonesian Women Then and Now*, by Ailsa Thomson
   Zainu'ddin et al. Clayton, Victoria: Centre of Southeast Asian Studies, Monash
   University.
Zainu'ddin, Ailsa Thomson, Kadar Lucas, Yulfita Raharjo, Christine Dobbin, and
   Lenore Manderson. 1980. *Kartini Centenary: Indonesian Women Then and Now*.
   Clayton, Victoria: Centre of Southeast Asian Studies, Monash University.

6

Call me Kartini? Kartini as a Floating Signifier in Indonesian History

Kathryn Robinson

Introduction

Every year on 21 April, Kartini's birthday, Indonesia celebrates *Hari Kartini* (Kartini Day). A day of civic celebration, it is marked by ceremonies, especially in schools and government institutions; and by reflections in the mass media on the state of women's social participation, challenges and achievements. This annual event has come to be focused, in often contradictory ways, on the "place of women" in modern Indonesia. Kartini's literary writings have been "mined" to give multiple and even contradictory characterizations of her voice, and hence of her historical significance.

This chapter tracks the evolution of the trope of "Kartini" as a national heroine. "Kartini" has become a concept that organizes the idea of "Indonesian women", a signifier that is deployed politically, and culturally, as part of a system of meaning-making. Her life and ideas have emerged as a "floating signifier"[1] in Indonesian political, social and cultural discourse. While the term may appear to have a fixed referent in a historical personage, "Kartini" is given different meanings in different times, and is neither static nor solid. It shifts and slides in the process of making meanings that express contesting political discourses. In particular, this chapter addresses the varying, shifting "Kartinis" associated with official and dissident gender politics in post-independence Indonesia in the following contexts: Sukarno's Old Order, Suharto's New Order, the contested space of *Reformasi*, and the contemporary post-*Reformasi* multimedia environment of *jaman now* (the "now" generation). In this chapter, I use "Kartini" to refer to instances of the floating signifier, while references to the historical Kartini are unmarked (i.e. Kartini).

Knowing Different "Kartinis"

Kartini has become a historical figure because of the publication of her letters, written over four years of her short life (see Introduction to this volume). Hence we know her mainly as a literary figure.

Her *bupati* father allowed her to attend the local Dutch-language primary school, and this enabled her to interact in a colonial social milieu where she developed friendships with Dutch people, including many who visited her home. She corresponded with several of them, and we know her through her letters, in particular those she wrote to Rosa Abendanon-Mandri, the wife of a colonial official, and her earlier correspondence with Stella Zeehandelaar, a Dutch feminist whom she'd never met.

As Goenawan Mohamad (2004) points out in his introduction to the Indonesian edition of her letters to Stella Zeehandelaar, letters are a very particular literary and communicative genre. The writer presents a persona that is fashioned in the epistolary relationship. In Kartini's letters we can experience the different tone of the letters sent to her "pen pal" Stella, closer to her in age and with an avowed leftist political position, and her letters to Abendanon-Mandri which, in some places, read like love letters, full of adoration, expressions of longing and love (see Watson 2000, pp. 25–26). This correspondence grew out of a meeting and a delight in shared conversation and intimacy, but also involved sharing the feminist ideas that Kartini had honed in her earlier correspondence with Stella.

Kartini was a young woman of her age and social class. Born at the end of the nineteenth century, a time of extraordinary social change in the Netherlands East Indies (NEI) and globally. Indeed, she lived her short life poised between two eras, two cultures. As Hildred Geertz writes:

> She was forced to the conclusion that some basic changes had to be made
> in Javanese society in order to bring it into accord with the ideals of social

equality and progress, but at the same time, the more she understood Western culture, the more she became convinced that her own ancient Javanese civilization was in itself of the highest value and should not be abandoned for a shallow modernity. (1964, p. 9)

As with many iconoclasts, her progressive stance has roots in prior generations. Historian Jean Taylor (1989) locates Kartini's *priyayi* (native administrative class) family in an era when developments in the NEI made it rational and advantageous for *priyayi* children to be schooled in Dutch: for the sons to seek advancement in the civil service, and for the daughters to be fashioned into suitable wives for these modern Javanese officials. Her grandfather was one of the first *priyayi* officials to learn Dutch, a practice passed down through his son (Kartini's father) and grandchildren.

Her command of Dutch meant she was able to freely converse with colonial officials, many of whom were caught up in the waves of late nineteenth-century thought: ideas of nationalism, freedom, social equality, women's rights and critiques of the class-driven values of European society. There was critical debate in the Netherlands at the time concerning the moral responsibility of the colonial government for the welfare of the natives, and the necessity of returning some of the wealth to them. This led to a shift in policy, articulated by Queen Wilhemina in 1901 (the "ethical policy") (see Cribb 1993). The ideas of the so-called *ethici*, the proponents of the policy, were published in the Dutch-language Indies newspapers, among which was *De Locomotief* (The locomotive), which Kartini read.

Her education ended abruptly when her father required her, according to the custom of her class, to be secluded at home (*pingitan*) prior to contracting an arranged marriage. Kartini wrote of this practice: "I entered my prison" (Letter dated 25 May 1899; Kartini 2014, p. 69). Paradoxically, during this period, her Dutch education enabled her to read widely, including Dutch novels such as *Max Havelaar* and *Minnebrieven* (Love letters) by Multatuli. She also read *De stille kracht* (The hidden force) by Louis Couperus and an anti-war novel by Berta von Suttner, *Die Waffen nieder!* (Lay down your arms!). She read political, cultural and scientific magazines and the Dutch women's magazine *De Hollandsche Lelie*, to which she also contributed.

Watson (2000, pp. 21–22) notes that the style of her letters was influenced by that of the Dutch novels she read: her literary style expresses an imaginative engagement with the world, in the manner of the novelist. Kartini was able to envisage a life other than the one she led, an intellectual space that perhaps her socialization as a Javanese would not otherwise have enabled.

It is Kartini's epistolary self—the product of her self-fashioning—that is available to us. Her letters reveal her to be a girl of the modern era, aware of a changing world, a world of ideas, and show a reflexive stance to her place within it. In the letters, she is very self-conscious about how she might be perceived/received: for example, she confesses to her friend that she will accept a proposal arranged by her father, as she is concerned that her refusal might have an impact on her father's and sisters' health. She begs her interlocutor not to judge her—but it turns out that the proposal is for her sister. In this vein, it has been noted that she does not reveal to the feminist Stella the information that she is the child of a minor wife (see Introduction and Chin's Chapter 4 in this volume).

Her modern sensibility encouraged her to critically and appreciatively appraise the European/colonial social world in which she was embedded, and also to adopt a critical and reflexive—but also appreciative—view of her Javanese culture. Her writings indicate that she was truly a product of the modernism of late nineteenth century: witness the tension between aristocratic privilege and attention to the rights of the "ordinary folk" in her social ideals and actions, as well as the modern sensibility of self-reflection and self-fashioning that emerged in her writing.[2]

Her explorations of self-expression and self-discovery, and the autobiographical tone of many of her letters, provide the fertile material for the many divergent interpretations of her life, her thoughts, and her significance as a political figure.

As noted in the Introduction to this volume, her literary corpus has been published in numerous editions, and the selections and translations reflect the hands of the editors and translators. They have established distinctive representations of her work that condition how she has been understood as a historical figure. Also, we only have her side of the correspondence. Rutherford (see Chapter 5 in this volume) notes that some of her correspondents burned their letters from her rather than have them published in a way that would have fulfilled the compilers' agendas.

Most contemporary public knowledge of Kartini comes, however, not from any edition of her letters or other writings, but from third party interpretations through historical biographies (such as Pramoedya 1962; Soebadio and Sadli 1990; Soeroto 1977), newspaper stories published each year around *Hari Kartini*, biographies, films as well as commemorative objects and practices, all of which have added layers of interpretation to her self-fashioning.

The 100-year anniversary of her birth sparked a number of conferences and compilation volumes evaluating her legacy (Katoppo 1983; Zainu'ddin 1986) and she is always invoked in accounts of women's activism in Indonesia (see for example Locher-Scholten and Niehof 1987; Suryochondro 1984). As a historical figure in the history of global feminism, she has captured the interest of many scholars working outside of Indonesia studies (see, for example, Connell 2010; Lawrence 2016). But for the people of Indonesia, she is most usually known through official versions of her biography and official speeches on *Hari Kartini*, especially in schools (see, for example, Katjasungkana 1997).

It is only in the last few years that the complete collection of her letters to Rosa Abendanon-Mandri, as well as her letters to Stella Zeehandelaar and other correspondents, have become available in compilation and in English translation, thanks to the scholar Joost Coté (Kartini 1992, 2005, 2014) whose translations indicate a very articulate and gifted writer.[3] His faithful translations expose us to the range of Kartini's voices.

As a floating signifier, "Kartini" emerges through these practices of re-presentation. As Danilyn Rutherford writes: "We can learn a great deal by examining the Kartini that various periods in history have produced. In plumbing Kartini's heart, writers stake a political claim to a powerful symbol" (Rutherford in this volume, p. 104). She has been appropriated for "nation, party, class ... [and] ... gender" (Rutherford in this volume, p. 104).

Her writing has been represented as the expression of a range of political positions, from emancipatory movements to the official representations of the "citizen mother" (Robinson 1994, 2009) of the New Order regime. Most recently, "Kartini" has been assimilated into arguments for woman-friendly interpretations of Islam. As a floating signifier, "Kartini" absorbs these fluctuating, and often competing meanings. *Hari Kartini*, the national holiday proclaimed in 1964, provides a focal point for the expression of these diverse interpretations, and is utilized for political debate about gender politics in Indonesia (Mahy 2012). However, the official performances and speeches on *Hari Kartini* usually do not critically delve into her original writings but attach contemporary political, cultural and social agendas to a recurring national symbol. The following sections discuss the emergence of the different "Kartinis" in the colonial and nationalist periods, and the manner in which these form a foundation for the re-presentation of "Kartini", especially on the eponymous national day, *Hari Kartini*.

Celebrating *Hari Kartini*

Hari Kartini has over the years become the focus for activities and discussions about the social participation and situation of Indonesian women, the kernel of which is a modernist narrative of "progress" towards a goal (e.g. women's emancipation, women's education, gender equity). Relations between men and women have been a site of political discourse and political contestation since the colonial period (Robinson 2009) and on *Hari Kartini*, Kartini is commemorated in ways that reflect prevailing government ideas about appropriate gender relations and gender equality. The annual commemoration of Kartini as a national heroine exposes shifts in political discourse and power relations. But while "Kartini" has been used to normalize the prevailing social positioning of women by governments, equally she has been used as a figure (*sosok*) to index challenges to existing gender orders and gender regimes (Robinson 2009) and as a vehicle for expressing feminist aspirations.

The following analysis considers the key themes that are invoked on *Hari Kartini* and the different kinds of articulations and shifts that attend these themes according to state ideology and agenda in the post-independence contexts of Sukarno's Old Order, Suharto's New Order, the Reformasi, and the post-Reformasi generation of *jaman now*.

Kartini as Educator: A Key Theme

The roots of contemporary significations can be found in the discursive strategies used in the initial edition of her letters, selected by Abendanon (Kartini 1911) from letters written to his wife and others. Abendanon was NEI Director of Education and represented what we may call (borrowing from the rhetorical strategy used by Rutherford (in this volume, p. 103) the "colonial Kartini". Abendanon edited the letters in a way that served his own interests of furthering the ethical policy agenda of educating the "natives" in a reformed turn-of-the century colonialism. Abendanon's compilation and editing focused on her expressed desire to become a teacher and her belief in the power of education, especially vocational education, to change lives, in particular, women's lives. The selected letters articulated views that corresponded with his own.

The title selected by Abendanon, *Door duisternis tot licht* (Through darkness into light)—translated in Indonesian as *Habis gelap terbitlah terang* (Kartini [1938] 1990)—deploys a metaphor that Kartini repeatedly uses in her writing to describe society, and individuals, moving from "dark" to "light" as they embrace modernity which, for her, is a movement from unfreedom to freedom. These were very much the sentiments that abounded in her lifetime, a time of the "dissolution of the nineteenth century" (Hobsbawm 1994). The term *emansipasi* (emancipation) (of women) is commonly associated with Kartini in contemporary political discourse.

For Kartini, reflecting on her own experience, education was the key to freedom, both for individuals and collectively for her countrymen, the "brown people" of the NEI. After her marriage, she opened a school for young children which became the inspiration for the Kartini school movement that was initiated by her sisters after her death (Coté 2008). Already in the colonial era, "Kartini's name became the banner for the struggle for women's emancipation through school education" (Vreede-de Stuers 1987, p. 53). Girls' education as well as its role in women's "freedom" is an enduring idea linked to "Kartini" and is one of the key themes commemorated on *Hari Kartini*, which is especially celebrated in all Indonesian primary schools.

"Old Order Kartini": A Nationalist Heroine

Kartini was selected by Sukarno as one of three women to be nominated as *pahlawan nasional* (national heroes; an honorific that is most usually given to men) in May 1964. *Pahlawan*, or hero, is a person who exhibits "courage and sacrifice in defending the truth for the nation and for religion; or warriors who exhibit extraordinary courage" (my translation of the definition in *Kamus Besar Bahasa Indonesia* (*Kamus* 1991, the official Indonesian dictionary). The category of *pahlawan nasional* generally designates individuals who took up arms in the cause of national freedom. Kartini is an apparently unusual choice, not only in being a woman but also in that she used, as is commonly noted, "the pen, not the sword". The two Acehnese heroines—Cut Nyak Dhien and Cut Meutia—who were named at the same time as Kartini, were warriors in the long anti-colonial struggle in Aceh. Kartini was selected because of her stance opposing discrimination against women, and especially because of her desire to elevate "native" women to the same status as Dutch women. As noted above, her writings are particularly passionate about women's education as the way to achieve these goals. Locher-Scholten and Niehof attribute her elevation to Sukarno's view that she embodied the "purity of the young Indonesian nation" (1987, p. 5).

Kartini was critical of aspects of the colonial order, but she did not have a nationalist consciousness: these ideas only began to take hold in Java several decades after her death (Kahin 1952). However, she did reflect on the critical social thought of her times in regard to the conditions of colonial rule, and expressed compassion for the poverty and backwardness of some of her country men and women. She was also critical of some of the excessive posturing of the colonial elite (e.g. making fun of Dutch colonial administrators who assumed the symbols of office of Java's traditional rulers). Because of her Javanese identity and her education and exposure to European thought, Kartini positioned herself as an enlightened *priyayi*, a native leader who could better encompass, understand, and respond to the needs of her people than Dutch officials. She supported the idea of a greater role for the *priyayi* in the administration of the colony, like the Dutch *ethici* with whom she mixed.

In contemporary Indonesia there is some controversy around the fact that of these three women national heroes, only the literary figure, Kartini, was selected for a national day (see Introduction to this volume). Historian Jean Taylor states that some have argued that "she was an apologist for colonialism, and that her revolt against Javanese feudalism was meaningless elsewhere in the archipelago" (2003, p. 297).

The song *Ibu kita Kartini* (Our mother Kartini) that is sung, especially by schoolchildren, on *Hari Kartini* was composed in 1931 by Wage Rudolf Supratman, who also composed the Indonesian national anthem, "Indonesia Raya". He originally entitled the song *Raden Ayu Kartini, bangunlah hai kawan* (Friends, let's rise up). This original version used her title, Raden Ayu,[4] which indicated her status as the daughter of a *bupati*, but this was apparently changed by Sukarno to *Ibu kita Kartini*, perhaps reflecting the egalitarian aura of the anti-colonial movement and the emotional identification of the Indonesian nation as female (Ibu Pertiwi).[5] The publication of her letters by Abendanon in 1911 made her available to the emerging group of young nationalists, as is reflected in the composing of this song. The nationalist credentials that flowed from the publication of her letters and her association with education and emancipation were the foundation of her adoption as a nationalist figure, the basis of the celebration of *Hari Kartini*. It has since become another key theme associated with Kartini.

"New Order Kartini": State Motherhood

The celebration of *Hari Kartini* was a signature of Suharto's authoritarian "repressive developmentalist" regime (Feith 1980). In seeming contradiction with Kartini's expressed views on emancipation, it became a day to reinforce the state gender regime (Robinson 2009). The patriarchal ideology of the New Order represented the president at the head of the national "family". This was reinforced through a familist state ideology: women were incorporated into the state as "citizen mothers" (Robinson 1994, 2009). Their primary roles and responsibilities as citizens were as wives and mothers; the legislated role of men as the head of the household "naturalized" the role of *Bapak Presiden* (Father President) at the pinnacle of the nation. *Hari Kartini* firmed up as a day to celebrate the state ideology of womanhood and this signification of "Kartini" emphasized her sacrifice, death in childbirth.

On *Hari Kartini* during Suharto's New Order, women would participate in activities organized by the corporatist women's organizations, Dharma Wanita (mandated for civil servants' wives) and PKK (*Pembinaan Kesejahteraan Keluarga*, Guidance for Family Welfare—organizing all women in chapters headed by the wives of village headmen). The activities celebrated motherhood (such as healthy baby competitions) and domestic arts (such as cooking competitions).

Commemorating "New Order Kartini" (Rutherford, Chapter 5 in this volume), women would wear Kartini costumes representing a romanticized Javanese elite culture: a long sleeved fitted blouse (*kebaya*) and a batik tightly-wrapped skirt (*kain panjang*); a large artificial flattened bun (*konde*) attached above the nape of the neck, emulating the hairstyle in iconic images of Kartini; and high-heeled slippers. This was a style of dress, feminist critics commented, that was far removed from the values of simplicity and practicality that came through in Kartini's writings and also in her quite extensive photo record.

My own first experience of *Hari Kartini* occurred in the mining town of Sorowako (South Sulawesi) where I was a researcher in the late 1970s.

The Indonesian managers' wives had established an organization for company employees' wives that mirrored the corporatist Dharma Wanita and PKK in its structure and function. They would organize activities on *Hari Kartini* such as healthy baby competitions and cooking demonstrations as well as the wearing of *kain kebaya* and *konde*, activities that reflected the New Order state agenda for women.[6]

The late Aristides Katoppo recounted an incident in this period when he was teaching a university class around the date of *Hari Kartini*, and one of the female students asked to be allowed to leave early so she could make the time-consuming preparations of make-up and costume for a Kartini lookalike competition. The irony was not lost on him of such a request coming from a young woman enjoying the privilege of higher education that was denied to Kartini—and he refused the request (Robinson 2009, p. 38). As "New Order Kartini" became part of civic education, *Hari Kartini* celebrations in schools mainly comprised (and still comprise—see below) dressing up and singing the song *Ibu kita Kartini*. However, *kain kebaya* is associated with Java, and in the spirit of *Binneka Tunggal Ika* (Unity in Diversity, the national motto), *Hari Kartini* has, since *Reformasi* and decentralization (in 2001), also become a day to wear the local version of "traditional" dress. This is perhaps a response to a critique of Kartini's "Javanese-ness" that has become even more pronounced in social media discussions post-2001, and which emerged in interviews I conducted with young people in late 2017—see below.

An article published in the South Sulawesi provincial metropolitan daily of the time, *Pedoman Rakyat* (1985), reported on the official celebration of *Hari Kartini* in Sidrap district (*kabupaten*) in 1985, at the height of the New Order. The report featured the speech of the ex-officio head of Dharma Wanita (the district head's wife) as she was conducting the ceremony at their local celebration of the "106th year" of *Hari Kartini*. Her speech expresses the essential character of the "New Order Kartini", in both the vision of the idealized role of women as wives and mothers, and the corporatist objectives of the official women's movement (Dharma Wanita) in mobilizing women to support state objectives. She declared:

> The struggle of women today must be continuously based on the spirit of RA Kartini. With this spirit women will be capable of playing their accompanying role (*peran serta*[7]) in bringing about the success of development (*pembangunan*). The spirit of Kartini is not revealed (*diwujudkan*) in fiery speeches and strong slogans, but it is hoped we will

try to apply, for the good of society (*mengamalkan*) Kartini's resolute and exemplary attitude (*sikap keteladanan dan tekad*). She was able to express a pure/holy heart (*hati suci*) in struggling for her nation (*bangsa*), in particular the collectivity of women (*kaum wanita*), even though she was the daughter of a *bupati* (a district official under Dutch colonial rule). She was able to break down (*mendobrak*) feudal custom in her struggle to reduce the people's ignorance (*kebodohan*) by establishing a school for young women and addressing the problem of the regulation (*pengaturan*) of children, which will influence family welfare (*kesejahteraan keluarga*[8]).

Her speech represents the quintessential New Order "Kartini", who is moved by a nationalist spirit and whose vision is held to support the gender ideology and, curiously, "family planning" policies of Suharto's New Order. Indeed, some passages from Kartini's manifesto "Educate the Javanese!" (Kartini 1974) could have been part of the platform of the New Order's corporatist women's organization, Dharma Wanita: educate women in order to uplift the masses (see also Chin in this volume). In New Order ideology, women had a primary role as nurturers of children, of future generations (*generasi penerus*).

In another re-signification of the New Order, rather than representing aspirations for women *yet* to be achieved, "Kartini" stood for women's social equality/social participation that independent Indonesia had *already* achieved under Suharto's New Order. This signification was manifest in an "educational" comic targeted at primary school-age children, *Album Ganesha* (1996).[9] This recounts Kartini's story, emphasizing her desire for and success in education, and the schools she and her sisters founded. It does not mention her disappointment in not being able to pursue her educational dreams, or her views on marriage (criticism of arranged marriage and polygamy), and only briefly notes her desire to improve the status (*derajat*) of women. The last frame of the story represents a group of working women (recognizable by their uniforms) with the caption:

> Now [it is] 90 years since Kartini's death. Thanks to her struggle, there are Indonesian women today who have become ministers, doctors, engineers, flight attendants and so forth. Every 21 April we celebrate *Hari Kartini* to remember the service of *Ibu kita Kartini* (Our mother Kartini). (*Album* 1996, p. 55)

In this view, "Kartini" is remembered as the heroine who laid out the vision for women of the Indonesian nation—which the New Order has achieved.[10]

Dissident "Kartini": *Hari Kartini*, a Flash Point for Protest in the Late New Order

State appropriation of "Kartini" has not gone unchallenged, and she emerged as an icon of protest and resistance to the Suharto regime in the late New Order. As the political climate "warmed up" in the mid to late 1990s, "Kartini" was frequently deployed as a trope in writings about women's social position, political rights, and also about social equality generally (see for example Witoelar 1996). Pramoedya's 1962 biography was reissued and launched by prominent feminist activist lawyer, Nursyahbani Katjasungkana (1997). In her speech, she noted that before reading the book, she knew only the song *Ibu kita Kartini* and the "small details" of her life that were related in speeches at official ceremonies on 21 April. Katjasungkana invoked the walls of *pingitan* (seclusion in adolescence) to symbolize the situation of contemporary Indonesian women.

On *Hari Kartini* in 1995, there was a well-publicized protest when women from Jogjakarta and other towns in Central Java made a pilgrimage (*berziarah*) to Kartini's grave in Desa Bulu 20 kilometres from Rembang. There they laid flowers, prayed, and gave speeches in an event lasting over three hours. They then proceeded to the Kartini museum in Rembang (her former house) where they intended to stage a further rally. The museum was in use by government officers holding the official celebration of *Hari Kartini*, so their protest was held in the museum yard (Raharti et al. 1995).

As was the common practice in this era, the protesters staged a street performance (*"happening art"*): five men, naked from the waist up, herded a handcuffed woman wearing a *kebaya* into a cage. They chanted: "this woman is under our groin (*selangkan*); this woman is under our power (*kekuasaan*)". One of the protestors, Luis Margiyani, stated to journalists: "The suppression (*penindisan*) of women was occurring 116 years ago in the era of Kartini but today the rape (*pemerkosaan*) of women is becoming more brutal" (Raharti et al. 1995).

The demands of the protestors were: 1) to stop child prostitution and sexual harassment (*pelecahan seksual*), and 2) to close down the corporatist women's organizations—Dharma Wanita, Dharma Pertiwi (the corporatist organization for military wives) and PKK—as well as the women's ministry (*Kementerian Negara Urusan Wanita*). They argued that the ministry was not doing anything to improve the social standing (*derajat*) of women because they ignored critical events such as the murder of labour activist Marsinah (Robinson 2009, p. 108) and the rape of overseas domestic workers (known also as TKW, acronym for *Tenaga Kerja Wanita*, which refers to female (overseas) workers). These incidents indexed critical issues faced by women—who entered the workforce in increasing numbers under the New Order policies (see Robinson 2009), in contradiction with the state gender regime that emphasized domesticity—but were largely ignored in government policy (Robinson 2000). The protestors were detained by the police at the local station in order to make them feel "responsible for disturbing the peace of the district administration" (Raharti et al. 1995).

Some of the first mass street rallies in 1997 that challenged the legitimacy of the Suharto regime were led and attended by women, using the strategy of housewives' protesting against the rising prices of commodities which made it impossible for them to fulfill their duties as managers of the household and provisioners for their families. They invoked and inverted the state ideology of the "citizen mother" by terming their movement *Suara Ibu Peduli* (the voice of concerned mothers). Women's designated subordinate role as housewives and carers in the state ideology and organization provided the ideological legitimacy of their challenge to the state (Robinson 2009).

In the tumultuous year of political change, 1998, *Hari Kartini*—just one month before Suharto resigned—became a focus for the hopes and demands of women for political reform. Newspapers reported demonstrations, especially at campuses, all over the country, including Jakarta, Bandung, Jogjakarta and Makassar (*Kompas* 1998). The newspaper *Republika* (1998) published its report under the headline "*Habis upacara, terbitlah demo*" (After the ceremony emerges/arises the demo)—a word play on the Indonesian title of the translation of Kartini's letters, *Habis gelap terbitlah terang*. The demonstrators were taking up a range of women's issues including the high price of milk and other basic commodities that had generated the first street protests against the Suharto regime in 1997. Like the demonstration in 1995 at Kartini's grave, they also highlighted the issues working women faced such as violence and exploitation, especially of overseas labour migrants. Kartini was equated with modern heroic figures like the labour activist Marsinah, who was murdered by security forces. The women protestors lent their voices to the issues featured in the student demonstrations that brought down Suharto, such as corruption and the economic crisis. A significant new element reported for the demonstrations in Bandung and Jogjakarta was that the women of Dharma Wanita joined the protests (*Kompas* 1998; *Republika* 1998).

Hari Kartini in Post-Reformasi Indonesia

In 1998, *Hari Kartini* became a focus for women's protests against the regime. As a floating signifier, "Kartini" was reclaimed and re-presented as a champion of women's rights and also of social equality. The effervescent period that followed the popular uprising that brought down Suharto in May 1998 involved a reworking, often ironic, of the political language of the New Order.

After 1998, "Kartini" continued to provide a focus for the unfolding debate about women's empowerment (*pemberdayaan*)[11] in the context of democratization. In an article in *Kompas*, activist Maria Hartiningsih (2000) questions the way Kartini had been understood and represented in the mass media, challenging the signification that had evolved under the New Order. According to Hartiningsih, the commemorative activities that focused on cooking, dressing in costume and make-up are a *"versi foedal[12] baru"* (a new version of "feudal" relations). The pinnacle of *Hari Kartini*, she writes, is usually a seminar addressed by a woman in a high position claiming to represent the spirit of Kartini in arguing for harmonious gender partnership (*kemitraan sejajar*[13]) and the view that the struggle of Kartini had already borne results (*telah berhasil*) with women taking on roles in the economy and in public life (e.g. as civil servants). In her view, the public representation of the *mitos* (myth) of *Hari Kartini* has destroyed history (*menhancurkan sejarah*) for the political legitimation of current leaders. She speculates that perhaps Kartini would cry to see how her ideas and dreams about the status and rights of women had been manipulated by a regime that placed women in the two "bunkers" (*kubu*) of wife and mother, reflecting the "feudal" *priyayi* view (challenged in Kartini's letters) that women's main role was to care for their husbands (*urus suami*). Maria Hartiningsih strongly represents the feminist ambitions of the *Reformasi*, damning the New Order regime for its destruction of women's identity, and economic and political rights.

Furthermore, Hartiningsih picked up a theme that was increasingly playing out on the social media at the time: she questioned Kartini's iconic status, asking why she was chosen as the symbol (*lambang*) for achieving Indonesian women's emancipation. Why not include other women, such as other nationalist women, and celebrate their achievements? This question would come to occupy a more central place in the debates surrounding Kartini, especially among the *jaman now* generation, and will be discussed in the section below.

In 2001, a broad range of women activists attended a forum on *Hari Kartini* at the iconic Hotel Indonesia (HI) (Robinson 2009, p. 150). Attendees ranged from the first Indonesian Minister for Labour, the leftist S.K. Trimurti (serving 1947–48)—who even as an octogenarian could deliver a rallying speech—to academics, journalists, middle-class activists and urban working-class women of the NGO Urban Poor Consortium. Megawati Sukarnoputri was president at the time, and the participants in the forum expressed great hope that the first woman president would prove responsive to the demands of women for change.

Hari Kartini has since lost much of the euphoria of the heady days of *Reformasi* while the fervent talk of *pemberdayaan* (empowerment) has been subsumed into the everyday of electoral politics and decentralization, but it nonetheless continues to be marked as a national day and provides a focus for the consideration of the state of gender relations in Indonesia. Post-*Reformasi* women have made important gains: improvements in electoral representation, and laws against domestic violence, for example, and *Hari Kartini* seems to have provided a "nudge" to the nation, or at least its media and officials, to take stock and look forward to new challenges.

"Kartini" *Jaman Now*[14]

What does "Kartini" mean to the post-*Reformasi* millenial generation, referred to in Indonesia as *jaman now*? "Kartini" as a free-floating signifier is now used for commercial as well as political and cultural ends, and "Kartini" in these differing guises has a strong presence on social media around *Hari Kartini*. Clothes, restaurants and all manner of goods are sold under the banner of "Kartini" at this time. Leading up to *Hari Kartini* in 2016, for example, I received a promotional email from Garuda Indonesia airlines which linked the idea of "Kartini" to the modern career woman flying professionally (GarudaMiles 2016). The image was a young woman travelling alone, in a modern sleeveless dress and with stylish short hair: no sign of Islamic dress such as the *jilbab* (tight veil) popular with many modern middle-class women, and no batik wrapped skirt, *kebaya* or *konde* that symbolized "New Order Kartini". In 2018, a smart Jakarta hotel offered 25 per cent off cocktails on 21 April and suggested that customers post "#KartiniNowadays" on social media. There are new "Kartini"-themed cultural products, including new books and a film in 2017, while TV talk shows interview celebrities on "Kartini" themes.

During a short visit to Indonesia in December 2017, I conducted group interviews in four cities. I asked about contemporary knowledge of, and ideas about, Kartini and about how *Hari Kartini* is celebrated in the early twenty-first century. The groups were: in Jakarta (feminist activists from three generations; all female), Kupang (university students, NGO activists and civil servants; male and female), Surabaya (university students; male and female), and Makassar (university students; female). It was clear that Kartini as a national or cultural figure is not at the top of their minds, especially outside of the period in which, as one of the students put it, "Kartini" is *"booming"*—around the time when the annual celebrations of *Hari Kartini* are held on 21 April.

None of the young people could recall attending events to mark *Hari Kartini* since they were in primary school, where they remembered the main form of celebration was to dress up, either in the iconic garb of Kartini—Javanese-style batik wrapped skirt and *kebaya*, or in local "traditional" costume (*pakaian adat daerah*); the latter accommodated the sensibilities of regional pride and the critiques of Kartini as "too Javanese". In this vein, one of the NGO workers in Kupang said that on *Hari Kartini* 2017, her child's kindergarten held a "fashion show" for mother and child dress-alike pairs. There were no celebrations reported on any of the campuses I visited. During the discussion held in Kupang, a male official from the government office for the empowerment of women (*Dinas Pemberdayaan Perempuan*) commented that there were many important days for women, including the UN day for the elimination of violence against women (*hari anti-kekerasaan*), a discourse he noted that was not available in Kartini's time. There was a distinct sense in his comments that *Hari Kartini* was a bit of a "old hat", and that other days highlighted issues that had more contemporary relevance for women.

Most of the scholarly literature that I consulted, some of which I have referred to in the first section of this chapter, contains discussion revolving around the different editions and interpretations of her writing, but this was a sterile starting point for discussions with the younger generation. None had read any of her writings, and only one (a student in Makassar) had read Pramoedya's 1962 novel *Panggil aku Kartini sadja* (Just call me Kartini), a text that has been regarded by one of my feminist activist friends in Jakarta as a critical source for understanding Kartini as a historical figure. It became clear that it is quite rare for young Indonesians to directly engage with either Kartini's own works, or the scholarly literature about her.

None of the young people in the group interviews had seen the recent (2017) film *Kartini*. One of the lecturers had viewed it, and her main (bemused and critical) comment was that it had been turned into a romance with Kartini having a secret boyfriend, which she felt was not revealed in any of the letters. But when I asked the students the question that I should have begun with—"Who among you regularly go to the cinema?", I found there were none. This was a clue to their consumption of media. Some said they had seen the trailer, which is on Youtube, and another had begun watching the 1982 Sjumandjaya film *RA Kartini* on Youtube, but only for about an hour.

But of course for the *jaman now* generation, everything happens on social media; it became clear that any celebration/commemoration of Kartini would happen in this way. In the period around 21 April when "Kartini" is *booming*, the *jaman now* generation post commemorative pictures of themselves using hashtags such as "#Kartini" or "#HariKartini". A search on Instagram using these hashtags revealed thousands of postings, mostly images of Kartini or of women, individually or with others, dressed in *sarong kebaya*.

There is a not insignificant photographic record of Kartini. Her image is of a decidedly modern-looking girl.[15] There is an iconic portrait that is frequently reproduced (e.g. on the cover of the book *Satu abad Kartini*, or One Hundred Years of Kartini; Katoppo 1983) and this is the content of many of the messages on Instagram. The other practice reported was that the young women took photos of themselves wearing *kebaya*, often with their mothers, and posted these on Instagram. Perhaps reflecting the sentiment of these Instagram postings, and of Kartini representing mother-child bonds, one young man in Surabaya claimed his mother as his "Kartini". However, there is a general agreement in all the groups of what "Kartini" stood for: the key significations for them are *"emansipasi"* (emancipation) or *"kesetaraan jender"* (gender equality).

In the formal mass media, *Hari Kartini* is still marked by reflections on "the state of women" in Indonesia. For example, the news magazine *Tempo* and the major newspapers as well as TV stations publish material relating to "Kartini" around the third week of April each year, such as reflections by public figures on the state of Indonesia's women. In 2017, the *Tempo* spotlight on *Hari Kartini* focused on bringing to the public the life of a woman *pahlawan* from the anti-colonial struggle, Emmy Saelan (1925–49) from Sulawesi Selatan who was captured and executed by the Dutch (*Tempo* 2017). This would seem to be a response to the question raised by Hartiningsih in the late 1990s, and which has been increasingly articulated among the generation of *jaman now*: *Why Kartini?* (Hartiningsih 1999; see also the Introduction to this volume).

When I asked the groups of students about the modern women whom they saw as iconic or representative figures, perhaps in the spirit of the era of decentralization, they mentioned names of women originating from their local areas. So, in Kupang, one put forward the name of local celebrity politician, Ibu Susi Pudjiastuti, Minister for Maritime Affairs and Fisheries in the cabinet of President Jokowi (2015–19), and this received general acclaim from the group. One of them commented on the fact that she had achieved high office and business success despite having only high school education. In Surabaya, the hero was Sri Mulyani Indrawati, a high-profile Indonesian economist who had been Minister of Finance in Susilo Bambang Yudhoyono's government (2005–10) and a director of the World Bank; she returned to Indonesia to join Jokowi's cabinet in 2016.

A young woman in Makassar who was active in *pencinta alam* (environmentalist) groups reported one of the most creative celebrations of *Hari Kartini*. She described an occasion where a group of young women climbed a mountain around the time of *Hari Kartini* and put on the *kebaya* when they reached the summit—symbolizing that women can do anything and also celebrating something that had not been done before: for these young women of *jaman now*, "Kartini" signifies women achieving something for the first time—a very sophisticated reading of her story.

Old Meanings Don't Die: The Archaeology of "Kartini"

One of the important points observed in the interviews discussed above is that the New Order-style significations of "Kartini" have continued to endure, especially in government institutions. As indicated by the mother-daughter dress up competition described above, there is still pressure for women in some situations to dress up in the celebratory *kebaya* and batik skirt. A woman pathologist sent her story along to be shared in one of the groups I convened. She and her workmates in a hospital laboratory were instructed last year by their (male) boss to wear *kain kebaya* on *Hari Kartini*, instead of their usual lab coats. She protested on the grounds that this costume was unsuitable for their work, and she alone of the team did not comply. She noted the irony of educated professional women being instructed to dress in a way inappropriate to their work to celebrate "Kartini".

In the 2017 *Tempo Hari Kartini* special edition, in addition to the story on a woman *pahlawan* discussed above, there was a sponsored page (Infotorial) from the Minister of Youth and Sports in Jokowi's cabinet, which made clear that the New Order "Kartini" has not gone away. The Minister, Imam Nahrawi, describes Kartini as an "exemplary female figure (*sosok perempuan*), a mother figure (*sosok ibu*) who made a great contribution to the nation, and the birth of talented future generations" (*Tempo* 2017). Kartini, the Minister holds, is a good inspiration for the youth generation, in that she has shown that the way to achieve women's equality (*kesetaraan perempuan*) is through education. He further comments that he hopes the celebration of *Hari Kartini* is not only ceremonial, but also serves to "remind the people (*masyarakat*), especially men, that behind every successful man is a fantastic women (*perempuan hebat*)" (Kementerian Pemuda dan Olahraga 2017). The signification of woman's role as standing behind the man lives on! This single issue of *Tempo* not only indicates the longevity of significations that serve masculine power, but also showcases the contestation about the singularity of Javanese Kartini, Kartini the author, as standing for women *pahlawan*.

Kartini, Marriage and Feminism

A critical theme that has occupied women on *Hari Kartini*, regardless of the ruling government in place, is the issue of marriage. As noted earlier, Kartini was well known for her passionate critique of polygamy and arranged marriage. However, as Indonesian women increasingly articulate their views in public politics, the aspirations signified by "Kartini" are coming under critical scrutiny. A common critique is that while Kartini was able to articulate ideal conditions for the freedom of women, she was unable or unwilling to follow through in her own life (a view articulated, for example, by some of the young women I interviewed in 2017—see below). Kartini is frequently criticized or held to have fallen short of her own expressed goals in accepting her father's choice of spouse for her in an arranged marriage. Prior to this—when the sisters had heard that a marriage proposal was in the offing and Kartini thought it was for her, she expressed her regretful conclusion that she needed to follow her father's will as a loving and dutiful daughter. However, her support for women's equality and improving the status of women is perhaps the most common Kartini trope. Indeed, it was the "feminist Kartini" that caught my attention as an Australian feminist when I encountered her persona in the late 1970s, at *Hari Kartini* celebrations in Sorowako where I was conducting research. I invoked the association of Kartini and the idea of freedom in an article I published in 1987 which considered the changes I was observing in the Indonesian mining town, as women lost their independent role in the economy following the involuntary loss of village land to the mining venture. I explored the contradictions between the New Order government policy agenda for women, ironically celebrated on *Hari Kartini*, and "Kartini's vision" (Robinson 1987).

Agreeing to an arranged marriage on the face of it does indeed seem to be a capitulation to male authority. But my assumptions in this regard were challenged by conversations in Sorowako with women in the community who had experienced arranged marriages. In this community, which was experiencing very rapid change, the customary practices of families arranging marriages for their children was rapidly giving way to free choice marriage. But the women who had experienced arranged marriages did not see themselves as the losers compared to their younger sisters and cousins who were able to choose their spouses. Ironically, the potential negative consequences of free choice marriage under certain economic circumstances became starkly evident in the mining town where women had lost independent livelihoods, precisely under the conditions of modernity. At the time, this understanding challenged my own understanding as an Australian feminist, in that arranged marriages in all circumstances were inevitably bad for women. Of course, the situation of the village women in the mining town was very different from that of Kartini, who found herself moving into an established household to replace a similarly high-status deceased first wife of an older man. But Kartini herself articulated the tension between differing goals (to be free and to be a dutiful daughter) and the risk of choosing to go against her father's will. She clearly understood the economic basis of women's freedom in her arguments for vocational education which manifested in her strong support for her sisters to train as nurses and her own desire to be a teacher. That is, critical comments on her story and her account of her choices reveal an underlying assumption of marriage as a personal relationship, which is primarily the case in modern capitalist society; but it also reveals the lack of understanding of marriage as a social relationship that involves relations far beyond the conjugal pair, as has been the case in the communities of the Indonesian archipelago until recently (Jones 2002, p. 228; Idrus 2016). Nonetheless, as noted above, a prevailing value associated with Kartini is that she stands for emancipation of women, for the possibility of women making choices in their lives, and the associated idea that she aspires to equality or equity (*kesetaraan*) between men and women—including within marriage.[16]

Islamic "Kartini"

The shifting representation of "Kartini" as a touchstone for women's rights issues has not escaped the current trend of public expressions of piety and civic values in Islamic terms. The piety movement in Indonesia has generated a strong strand of Islamic feminism which argues that social equity, including gender equity, is a fundamental Islamic value (Robinson 2009). Organizations that adopt Islamic feminist positions came together at the *Kongres Ulama Perempuan Indonesia-KUPI* (Congress of Indonesian Women Islamic Scholars) held in Cirebon in April 2017, also the "Kartini" season (*KUPI* 2017; Upi 2017). The congress draws its relevance from the signification of *Hari Kartini* as the time to take stock of the situation of Indonesian women and address the agendas for change. The congress argued for the legitimate place in Islam for women's religious authority (*ulama perempuan*). But *ulama perempuan* (female *ulama*) is also understood to mean scholars (male and female) who take the position that Islam, and the interpretation of Islamic doctrine, is inherently favourable to gender equity. The congress discussed sources and practices of women as religious authorities, while participants addressed the Islamic positions on issues such as child marriage and polygamy and also the environment (Robinson 2017). Congress materials referred to Kartini and her Islamic education and values in their recovered history of women's religious authority (Marcoes 2017). The organizers invoked "Kartini" as symbolizing a historic moment in the struggle of women for emancipation (*emansipasi*), and also put forward the idea that she was influenced by Islamic ideas as well as the more generally asserted influence of her Dutch friends.

In the current climate of Islamization, there have been many articles and social media postings in recent years seeking the roots of Kartini's ideas in Islam as well as (or even instead of) Western thought (see, for example, Marcoes 2017; *Tribun Jateng* 2017). Of particular interest is her religious study under Kyai Haji Mohammad Sholeh bin Umar. That is to say, in this view, "Kartini" is represented as an antecedent of current

Islamic feminism, thereby strengthening the argument that the historical roots of Indonesian women's movement (as represented by Kartini) have always been inflected by an interpretation of Islam that is sensitive to Islamic protection of women's rights, for example, in marriage.

Conclusion

Although Kartini's written corpus is increasingly available to us, the meanings associated with the signifier "Kartini" shift and develop in the context of broader social debates about gender relations and women's social roles. The establishment of *Hari Kartini* as a national day celebrated with routinized ritual performances and texts (including the song *Ibu kita Kartini*) make this the cornerstone of debates about, and interpretations of, "Kartini". Her iconic image, with increasing presence on social media, stands as a reminder that Indonesia has a history of debates about women's social roles; but as a "floating signifier", her image and the popular *mitos* of her story do not accompany a linear trajectory of women moving from bondage to emancipation as the title chosen by her first compiler, Abendanon, might imply. As an officially sanctioned annual event, *Hari Kartini* occupies a unique position in Indonesian political and cultural life, a moment when the nation celebrates womanhood (albeit in shifting guises) and provides women activists and supporters of social and gender equity an opportune moment to reflect on gender relations in Indonesia through the floating signifier "Kartini", at a time when government and media attention are assured.

NOTES

1. I am using this term in a manner akin to the way it was used by Stuart Hall in his discussion of race (Hall 2014).
2. See discussions of the emergence of modernism in, for example, Williams (1989).
3. There had been some questioning of her skill as a writer, based on earlier translations.
4. This title has been loosely translated as "princess" in the English edition of her letters (see Geertz 1964).
5. "Ibu Pertiwi" references a god (*dewa*) who controls the earth but is also a synonym for the nation (see *Kamus* 1991).

6. The discussion of *Hari Kartini* in the Suharto era and beyond relies on my own field observations as well as news clippings and other materials that I have collected contemporaneously over the years during visits to Indonesia and on internet searches. Hence it is a somewhat "serendipitous" collection, rather than the result of a massive systematic online search which would have yielded an enormous amount of material.

7. This is one of the quintessential terms of the New Order gender ideology, which can be seen as the opposite of *emansipasi*. She also uses the term *pembangunan* (development), the key term of the New Order developmentalist ideology.

8. *Kesejahteraan keluarga* (family welfare) is another key term that is used in the name of the corporatist group PKK.

9. Subtitled "*komik pengetahuan yang menyenangkan*" (knowledge/educational comic that is fun).

10. The rates of girls' education, in particular at primary and junior secondary school levels, did markedly improve under the New Order.

11. *Pemberdayaan* (empowerment) was a signature term of the political revolution of *Reformasi*. The Minister for Women in the first Reform cabinet, Khofifah Indar Parawansa, insisted on changing the name of the Ministry to *Kementerian Pemberdayan Perempuan*.

12. *Feodal* in Indonesia refers to historical hereditary unequal relations and related power differences; it is not strictly speaking about feudalism in the European sense.

13. This was the New Order formulation for its gender policy.

14. *Jaman now* is the term used for millennials in contemporary Indonesia.

15. It is hard to imagine that the few photos of Cut Nyak Dhien, some of which showed her as an abject captive of the Dutch, would prove to be so popular on Instagram.

16. Watson (2000) makes an interesting argument that Kartini's horror of polygamy and lack of enthusiasm for marriage was in fact a revulsion against sexuality, rather than axiomatically expressing a feminist understanding of gendered power. He also argues that she seemed to be content with her father's choice of spouse.

REFERENCES

Album Ganesha: Komik pengetahuan yang menyenagkan: Edisi khusus sejarah, January 1996.

Connell, Raewyn. 2010. "Kartini's Children: On the Need for Thinking Gender and Education Together on a World Scale". *Gender and Education* 22, no. 6: 603–15.

Coté, Joost, ed. and trans. 2008. *Realizing the Dream of R.A. Kartini: Her Sisters' Letters from Colonial Java*. Ohio: Ohio University Press; Leiden: KITLV Press.

Cribb, Robert. 1993. "Development Policy in the Early 20th Century". In *Development and Social Welfare: Indonesia's Experiences Under the New Order*, edited by Jan-Paul Dirkse, Frans Hüsken and Mario Rutten. Leiden: KITLV Press.

Feith, Herbert. 1980. "Repressive-Developmentalist Regimes in Asia: Old Strengths, New Vulnerabilities". *Prisma: Indonesian Journal of Social and Economic Affairs* 19: 39–55.

GarudaMiles. 2016. "GarudaMiles Tribute to Modern-Day Kartini", 11 April 2016. Promotional email. In the author's possession.

Geertz, Hildred. 1964. "Kartini: An Introduction". In *Letters of a Javanese Princess*, by Kartini. Translated by Agnes Louise Symmers. New York: W.W. Norton.

Hall, Stuart. 2014. *Race: The Floating Signifier*. Produced by Media Education Foundation. Produced, directed and edited by Sut Jhally. San Francisco, CA: Kanopy Streaming. Streaming Video.

Hartiningsih, Maria. 1999. "Mengais nilai simbolis dari tokoh simbolis, Kartini". *Kompas*, 18 April 1999. Online article. In the author's possession.

———. 2000. "Tak lekang dimakan zaman: Surat-surat Kartini". *Kompas*, 2000. http://www.kompas.co.id/kompas%2Dcetak/millenium/data 2000/sura50. htm (accessed 21 March 2000). In the author's possession.

Hobsbawm, Eric. 1994. *Age of Extremes: The Short Twentieth Century 1914–1991*. London: Michael Joseph.

Idrus, Nurul Ilmi. 2016. *Gender Relations in an Indonesian Society: Bugis Practices of Sexuality and Marriage*. Leiden: Brill.

Jones, Gavin. 2002. "The Changing Indonesian Household". In *Women in Indonesia: Gender Equity and Development*, edited by Kathryn Robinson and Sharon Bessell. Indonesia Assessment Series. Singapore: Institute of Southeast Asian Studies.

Kahin, George McTurnan. 1952. *Nationalism and Revolution in Indonesia*. Ithaca, NY: Cornell University Press.

Kamus Besar Bahasa Indonesia. 1991. Departmen Pendidikan dan Kebudayaan. 2nd ed. Jakarta: Balai Pustaka.

Kartini, R.A. 1911. *Door duisternis tot licht: Gedachten over en voor het Javaansche volk*. Edited by J.H. Abendanon. Semarang: Van Dorp.

———. 1974. "Educate the Javanese". Translated by Jean Taylor. *Indonesia* 17: 83–98.

———. [1938] 1990. *Habis gelap terbitlah terang*. Translated by Armijn Pane. Jakarta: Balai Pustaka.

———. 1992. *Letters from Kartini: An Indonesian Feminist, 1900–1904*. Edited and translated by Joost Coté. Clayton, Victoria: Monash Asia Institute, Monash University.

———. 2005. *On Feminism and Nationalism: Kartini's Letters to Stella Zeehandelaar, 1899–1903*. Edited and translated by Joost Coté. 2nd ed. Clayton, Victoria: Monash Asia Institute, Monash University.

————. 2014. *Kartini: The Complete Writings, 1898–1904*. Edited and translated by Joost Coté. Clayton, Victoria: Monash University.

Katjasungkana, Nursyahbani. 1997. "Panggil aku Kartini saja". *ISTIQLAL*, 22 April 1997. http://www.radix.net/~bardsley/wied.html (accessed 24 November 2003).

Katoppo, Aristides, ed. [1979] 1983. *Satu abad Kartini 1879–1979*. Jakarta: Sinar Harapan.

Kementerian Pemuda dan Olahraga. 2017. "Kartini, perempuan dan generasi millenial yang hebat". *Tempo*, 24–30 April 2017.

Kompas. 1998. "Peringatan RA Kartini: Dirayakan lewat aksi keprihatinan di kampus-kampus", 22 April 1998. Online article. In the author's possession.

KUPI: Kongres Ulama Perempuan Indonesia. 2017. "Hari Kartini dalam nurani peserta KUPI", 24 October 2017. https://infokupi.com/hati-kartini-dalam-nurani-peserta-kupi/ (accessed 9 February 2018).

Lawrence, Annee. 2016. "'A Meaningful Freedom': Women, Work and the Promise of Modernity in a Reading of the Letters of Raden Adjeng [sic] Kartini (Java) Alongside Miles Franklin's *My Brilliant Career* (Australia)". *Hecate* 41, no. 1–2: 18–36.

Locher-Scholten, Elsbeth and Anke Niehof, eds. 1987. *Indonesian Women in Focus: Past and Present Notions*. Dordrecht: Foris.

Mahy, Petra. 2012. "Being Kartini: Ceremony and Print Media in the Commemoration of Indonesia's First Feminist". *Intersections: Gender and Sexuality in Asia and the Pacific* 28. http://intersections.anu.edu.au/issue28/mahy.htm (accessed 10 September 2017).

Marcoes, Lies. 2017. "Kartini, kiyai Sholeh Darat, dan KUPI". *Rumah kitab*, 28 April 2017. https://rumahkitab.com/kartini-kiyai-sholeh-darat-dan-kupi (accessed 3 September 2018).

Mohamad, Goenawan. 2004. "Kartini sebuah pesona". In *Aku mau... Feminisme dan nasionalisme: Surat-surat Kartini kepada Stella Zeehandelaaar 1899–1903*, by Kartini, pp. vii–xix. Translated by Vissia Ita Yulianto. Jakarta: Buku Kompas; Yogyakarta: Program Pasca Sarjana Ilmu Religi dan Budaya, Universitas Sanata Dharma.

Pedoman Rakyat. 1985. "Hari Kartini ke-106 di sidrap dipusatkan di desa Mojong", 1 May 1985. In the author's possession.

Pramoedya Ananta Toer. 1962. *Panggil aku Kartini sadja: Sebuah pengantar pada Kartini*. 3 vols. Jakarta: Nusantara.

Raharti, Sri, Bandelan Aminuddin, and Marcelino. 1995. "Demo Kartini ala Rembang". *Forum keadilan*, no. 2, 11 May 1995.

Republika. 1998. "Hari Kartini: Habis upacara, terbitlah demo", 22 April 1998. In the author's possession.

Robinson, Kathryn. 1987. "Kartini's Vision and the Position of Indonesian Women". *Mankind* 17, no. 2: 104–13.

————. 1994. "Indonesian National Identity and the Citizen Mother". *Communal/Plural* 3: 65–82.

————. 2000. "Gender, Islam and Nationality: Indonesian Domestic Servants in the Middle East". In *Home and Hegemony: Domestic Service and Identity in South and Southeast Asia*, edited by Kathleen Adams and Sara Dickey. Ann Arbor: Michigan University Press.

————. 2009. *Gender, Islam and Democracy in Indonesia*. London: Routledge.

————. 2017. "Female Ulama Voice a Vision for Indonesia's Future". *New Mandala*, 30 May 2017. http://www.newmandala.org/female-ulama-voice-vision-indonesias-future/ (accessed 16 April 2018).

Soebadio, Haryati, and Saparinah Sadli. 1990. *Kartini: Pribadi mandiri*. Jakarta: Gramedia.

Soeroto, Sitisoemandari. 1977. *Kartini: Sebuah biografi*. Jakarta: Gunung Agung.

Suryochondro, Sukanti. 1984. *Potret pergerakan wanita di Indonesia*. Jakarta: Rajawali.

Taylor, Jean Gelman. 1989. "Kartini in Her Historical Context". *Bijdragen tot de taal-, land- en volkenkunde* 145, no. 2–3: 295–307.

————. 2003. *Indonesia: Peoples and Histories*. New Haven: Yale University Press.

Tempo. 2017. "Martir pertama perempuan Republik", 24–30 April 2017.

Tribun Jateng. 2017. "Ikhtiar Kartini dan kiai Sholeh Darat", 20 April 2017. http://jateng.tribunnews.com/2017/04/20/ikhtiar-kartini-dan-kiai-sholeh-darat (accessed 16 April 2018).

Upi. 2017. "Indonesian Muslim Women Engage with Feminism". *KUPI: Kongres Ulama Perempuan Indonesia*, 6 December 2017. https://infokupi.com/indonesian-muslim-women-engage-with-feminism/ (accessed 9 February 2018).

Vreede-de Stuers, Cora. 1987. "The Life of Rankayo Rahmah El Yunusia". In *Indonesian Women in Focus*, edited by Elsbeth Locher-Scholten and Anke Niehof. Dordrecht: Foris.

Watson, C.W. 2000. *Of Self and Nation: Autobiography and the Representation of Modern Indonesia*. Honolulu: University of Hawaii Press.

Williams, Raymond. 1989. *The Politics of Modernism*. London: Verso.

Witoelar, Wimar. 1996. "Kartini dan Kartono". *Kompas*, 21 April 1996. http://www.kompas.co.id/9604/21/naper/asal.htm (accessed 7 March 2000).

Zainu'ddin, Ailsa G. Thomson. 1986. "'What Should a Girl Become?' Further Reflections on the Letters of R.A. Kartini". In *Nineteenth and Twentieth Century Indonesia: Essays in Honour of Professor J.D. Legge*, edited by David P. Chandler and M.C. Ricklefs. Clayton, Victoria: Centre of Southeast Asian Studies, Monash University.

7

Kartini and the Politics of European Multiculturalism[1]

Paul Bijl

Introduction

Luisa Passerini writes about the paradox of memory (and, we can add, forgetting) that we cannot look for something we lost unless we remember it at least in part (Passerini 2003, p. 239). When investigating cultural memory of colonialism in Europe, a first impression many people have is one of silence in the sense of oblivion (Ricoeur 2004): colonialism, in this conception, has vanished without a trace. In the Netherlands, people have claimed that Dutch colonialism in Indonesia is not taught in high schools, not talked about in the media, that photographs of colonial atrocities committed by the Dutch colonial army have been swept under the carpet and that the voices of those once colonized by the Dutch are never heard in the Netherlands. Yet if we investigate specific places and communities, a different picture emerges: histories of Dutch colonialism have been part of the school exams since the 1970s, colonial "scandals" (e.g. abusive labour conditions of coolies in colonial Indonesia) have been reported upon in newspapers since the nineteenth century, photographs of colonial atrocities were widely published and distributed in the early twentieth century, and the Netherlands has a rich tradition of publishing

Indonesian authors, both originally writing in Dutch and in translation (Bijl 2012, 2015). How can we account for this impression of silence and this abundance of sounds?

In this chapter, analysing current cultural memories of Kartini in Dutch contexts, I will argue that in investigating silences we need to pay attention to location as both sounds and silences are always unevenly distributed: while in certain locations there can be almost a cacophony of sounds, in others utter silence can be encountered. Second, I want to show how silences, once they have occurred or been produced, change position and meaning over time, sometimes being perpetuated and repeated, sometimes changing character as they move across contexts. By investigating these two aspects, I want to draw attention to silence's spatial (synchronic) and temporal (diachronic) dimensions. In this chapter, I will mainly focus on a prize named after Kartini which has been awarded in the city of The Hague since 2001 to stimulate emancipation of, at first, Dutch women of colour but eventually, at least in theory, everybody contributing to the emancipation of anybody. Silence as a phenomenon can be connected in two ways to this prize, one spatial, the other temporal. If we look at this prize synchronically in the Netherlands today, we discover it is floating in a sea of silence with respect to Kartini, whose name and work are currently almost completely forgotten in Dutch contexts. Second, there are silences within the makeup of the prize—particularly with respect to racism in the Netherlands, the problems of which remain almost wholly undiscussed—that merit a temporal analysis of silence in, respectively, Kartini's work itself, its reception in the Netherlands during colonialism and the archives of the Kartini prize, and to ask where these silences come from and how they developed over time.

The Location of Silence

Cultural memory of Kartini in the Netherlands is strongly divided between those who are completely unfamiliar with Kartini and those who seem to know her inside out. Most Dutch people I talked to, including several professors of modern Dutch literature, had never heard of Kartini and were sometimes slightly embarrassed about this. How could they never have heard about one of the most widely-known Dutch authors of the twentieth and twenty-first centuries? Was it really the case that parts of her letters were last published in Dutch in 1987 in an edited volume now out of stock while they could easily be ordered in Indonesian, English and French? Was there really such a thing as a Dutch-language author who had figured on Indonesian banknotes for many decades, who is part of the Indonesian high school curriculum, translated into eight languages and published by the United Nations, yet is hardly ever heard of in the Netherlands anymore?

On the other side, there were those who wondered if it was really necessary to embark on yet another project on Kartini. Not that we knew everything about her, but what about the rest of the Indonesian colonial past? The other Indonesian women writing at the time, for instance? What distinguished people in this second category from the others was that they were all working on Dutch and Indonesian colonial history, most of them professionally. Indeed, if we look at institutes that concentrate on the colonial past, Kartini is a household name. The Museum of the Tropics in Amsterdam, formerly the Colonial Museum, has a glass case largely devoted to her in its section on Dutch colonialism in Indonesia. In 2004, the museum opened a separate "Kartini wing" which connects the children's museum to the central hall. For several years a huge portrait of Kartini has been put up in one of the central squares of the city of Amsterdam (the Mr Visserplein) as part of a project in which all cultural institutes in the neighbourhood were invited to advertise their icons (Kartini functions as an icon of the Museum of the Tropics).

A second postcolonial context where Kartini can be found in the Netherlands is within the ageing circles of what is called "Indian letters" (*Indische letteren*). Focusing on Dutch-language literature from colonial Indonesia and the postcolonial Netherlands from the travel logs of the earliest days of the Dutch East India Company in the seventeenth century to the novels of the third generation of immigrants from the Dutch East Indies in the twenty-first century, this group of literary scholars and amateurs has regularly included Kartini in the literary histories it has produced (e.g. Nieuwenhuys 1982) and in several articles specifically about her in their own journal *Indische letteren*. In mainstream (European, white) Dutch literary history, however, she is nowhere to be found (e.g. Anbeek 1990; Schenkeveld-Van der Dussen 1993; Vaessens 2013).

Kartini is not only a familiar name in postcolonial circles, but also in some "multicultural" ones. There are two multicultural prizes named after Kartini. One is awarded by the Royal Holland Society of Sciences and Humanities (KHMW) for the best female first-year migrant student in a scientific or technical discipline in a Dutch university. Second, there is a Kartini prize awarded by an organization named PEP (Participation

Emancipation Professionals) and yearly given to an individual or organization which in the eyes of the jury should be prized for its emancipatory work in the city of The Hague. This Kartini prize (formerly the Raden Aju Kartini prize for foreign women) has been awarded since 2001 and has since seen many both subtle and fundamental shifts in terms of its target groups, its criteria and the many considerations behind its choices. This chapter will take this prize as its focal point as it embodies crucial tensions with respect to current Dutch cultural memory of Kartini, especially with respect to silence.

Before turning to this latter prize, I want to briefly give an explanation for Kartini's simultaneous remembrance and forgetting in Dutch contexts. Crucial here is, as Ann Laura Stoler has pointed out for French colonial memory, a compartmentalization of both history and literary history, within as well as outside the academy (Goss 2000; Stoler 2011). The study of Dutch literature, for instance, is importantly rooted in nineteenth-century nationalism when the Netherlands was imagined as a community of white people speaking Dutch and essentially living in a particular area of Europe. As was mentioned above, Kartini (a Javanese woman) was never part of any "Dutch" literary history, but also institutionally Dutch "colonial" and Dutch "metropolitan" literary history have been kept apart. The University of Amsterdam, for instance, has for years had three separate professorships in the Dutch department for the literatures of, respectively, colonial Indonesia, Suriname and the Dutch Antilles and South Africa. This shows that this literature was not disregarded, just treated in different compartments and forgotten in the privileged compartment of white, Dutch literature from Europe.

The Times of Silence

My starting point with respect to the Kartini prize is its silence on the society into which "foreign" women are supposed to emancipate, or, as it is often said in the Netherlands, "integrate" themselves. This silence will be connected to the silences in Kartini's own work and in the way she has been remembered in the Netherlands since it was first published in 1911. As will be made clear below, problems in the broader Dutch society, particularly concerning racism, are discussed in other initiatives taken by the city council of The Hague, for instance by the Bureau of Discriminatory Affairs (*Bureau Discriminatiezaken*), but the lines of communication that reach us when we engage with the Kartini prize's website make clear that the problems faced by the women who form the prize's main target group are first and foremost their own, personal deficits and those of the communities they are supposed to belong to. In 2014, the website of the prize states that "Everything [sic] that contributes to an equal position and participation of men and women in The Hague can win the prize" (Kartiniprijs). Examples given are: a company which consciously aims for more women at the top of its organization, a woman starting a garage, a neighbourhood signing an agreement against domestic violence, a group of foreign fathers entering the fray against honour killings, and girls who break down role patterns.

Essentially two phenomena are pointed out through these examples: on the one hand successful citizenship, apparent from economic initiatives, and, on the other hand, challenges that are supposed to thwart these initiatives. Crucial is that in Dutch contexts in 2014, these obstacles are strongly gendered and ethnicized: "domestic violence" is mostly connected to immigrant families (Ghorashi 2010; when white Dutch fathers kill their family, for instance, the press usually talks of a "tragedy") and the concept of "honour killings" has been seen as solely applicable to immigrant communities, particularly from Muslim countries, since the 1970s (Schrover 2011). The website also offers background information about the name of the prize, and states that the prize is named after Kartini, who

> from a young age onwards resisted the traditional norms and values vis-à-vis girls which she experienced as repressive. Kartini became famous far across the borders of her own country. These days she is still seen as an important source of inspiration. (Kartiniprijs)

Two things are striking in this description. First of all, there is no mention of Dutch colonialism; on the contrary, the text talks about Kartini's "own country". Although this is, in a literal sense, in line with Kartini's writing (in which Java is often referred to as "our land" and "my land"), this can be a misleading statement in a Dutch postcolonial context, suggesting that Kartini could enjoy some form of citizenship while in fact those deemed legally "native" in the Dutch East Indies were living in what historian Cees Fasseur has called a "state without citizens" (Fasseur 1994, p. 54). Second, Kartini's uphill battle is described here solely in terms of a fight against tradition, harking back to a classical colonial opposition between modernity and tradition in which Europe, imagined as further on a developmental timeline, had a historical task to bring its colonies from, for instance, the Middle Ages or Antiquity into modern times (Bijl 2009). However, if we look at Kartini's writings themselves, a rather different image emerges in which, next to problems she had with Javanese sexual and gender culture, also European policies and culture were critically scrutinized by her, sometimes in an angry and sometimes in an ironic voice. In what follows I will first discuss Kartini's own analysis of the position of "native" women in colonial Java and then the appropriation of her writings in the Netherlands which forms the bridge between Kartini herself and the contemporary Kartini prize. In both cases I will focus on the topic of silence.

Silence in Kartini's Letters and Their Remembrance in the Netherlands

In the 1911 edition of her letters, which included reprints from 1912 and 1923 and is still the most widely available edition in the Netherlands (though only second-hand), Kartini addresses the topic of silence regularly. It has three distinct meanings. First, silence is presented negatively as what is expected of Javanese women, both in their everyday lives and in the face of setbacks and other unpleasant circumstances. "The ideal Javanese girl", she writes critically, "is quiet, as immobile as a wooden doll—speaking only when absolutely necessary in a whisper, inaudible even to ants—walking slowly, step by step, like a snail—laughing, soundlessly without parting her lips—it is not nice when one's teeth can be seen, one then looks like a fox" (Kartini 1992, p. 31). Kartini often describes her surroundings (the Javanese landscape, members of her family) as silent, but always with a critical undertone as this same silence is what she wants to shake off to become, as she calls it herself, a "modern girl". In a second set of contexts, however, silence becomes a positive notion, namely when it is a sign of a deeper or higher truth which cannot be expressed with words. Silence in these cases either gains religious connotations or is an expression of feelings which are transferred between people and somehow totally devoid of lies. "Silence is the interpreter of deep feeling", Kartini writes in a passage in which she claims that silence is not an absence, but can be just as meaningful as, if not more meaningful than, any sound (Kartini 1992, p. 277). In another letter, she writes that there is no spoken or written language through which the soul can express itself, but only a "silent, mysterious language, which is expressed in neither words nor letters, but which can nevertheless be understood and comprehended by anyone with feeling, and which is completely reliable because in its entire vocabulary that little word, 'lie' is unknown!" (Kartini 1992, p. 24). A third, also positively connoted form of silence addressed by Kartini, finally, is silence as a form of protest. About social events Kartini and her sisters object to, she writes that "[d]uring such occasions we are dead silent; we can neither talk nor laugh; indignation and compassion silence us" (Kartini 1992, p. 240). In another letter she writes: "We never speak of this anymore, but being silent does not always mean agreeing; giving up everything now that we have come this far we will not do and we have never had any plans towards this" (Kartini 1992, p. 62).

Silence in Kartini's letters, in short, is either a sign of oppression or a language of truth or protest. That silence played such an important part in Kartini's life can be made understood if we see her as standing in a contested space where multiple discourses were active, some of which (such as European feminism and colonial reformism) opened up new freedoms for her and others (e.g. parts of Javanese sexual politics and colonial racism) severely limiting her options. On the one hand, Kartini was discovering new languages that gave her more elbow room, yet on the other hand, other discourses thwarted her upward mobility. If we carefully read these letters, therefore, it becomes clear that the culture standing in her way cannot only be identified as Javanese with its "traditional norms and values" (such as forcing women into polygamous marriages), but also as Dutch with its "modern", European norms and values, including racism, orientalism and colonialist paternalism. "The Dutch laugh and ridicule us for our ignorance, but when we try to educate ourselves, then they adopt a defiant attitude towards us", she writes (Kartini 2005, p. 46), analysing situations like these as indications that many Dutch had "two measures" when it came to Dutch and Javanese students: "Two laws, one for us and one for them: no! *God save us from this*" (Kartini 2005, p. 46). This was, however, precisely the legal situation in colonial Indonesia up to the very end when after the Second World War the Dutch only started the prosecution of Japanese war crimes committed against Europeans, not against Indonesians.

Silence, however, plays a role in Kartini's letters in another crucial yet far less tangible manner than in the examples given above. Writing solely to Dutch people, there were limits to what Kartini could say, especially about the Netherlands and its presence in Java. One solution Kartini seems to have found to nevertheless address certain unsayable subjects is the use of irony. In ironic statements, people can say one thing that in that context means the opposite. So when Kartini writes to her pen friend Stella Zeehandelaar, "Before you lie the thoughts of someone who belongs to that despised brown race!" (Kartini 2005, p. 46), or when she comments on the attitude of some Dutch women whose help she and her sisters had asked for with the words, "[a]pparently they thought it was nice that we little Javanese [*Javaantjes*] asked for their help" (Kartini 2005, p. 28), she is of course repeating standard Dutch racist and paternalistic attitudes, but also silently subverting them, for the rest of her texts discredit any belief that she would refer to herself seriously as a little Javanese belonging to the despised brown race. It is at moments like these that Kartini does not explicitly thematize silence as a language of protest but actually uses this language: through her irony she asks the reader to read between the lines and notice precisely what is not audible yet still present.

In the Netherlands, the passages of Kartini's work in which she criticized Dutch colonialism never gained much attention. On the contrary, from the beginning this part of her letters has been effectively silenced. Already her first editor Abendanon criticized her, in his eyes, unrealistic ideals when he warns that "[i]t is easy to idolize those who cherish lofty thoughts. Yet when the realization of these thoughts involves nigh insurmountable societal difficulties, it is one's duty to curb one's enthusiasm. The consequences of going against the grain are not always foreseeable" (Kartini 1911, pp. I–II). Abendanon seemed to have liked the idea of helping a young Javanese woman, but not of her actually forming her own ideas. This was in line with the broader ambiguity in Dutch, "ethical policy" (comparable to the French *mission civilisatrice* and the British white man's burden) in which "native" people were seen as children who were developing themselves but who nevertheless remained "not white, not quite" (Bhabha 2004, p. 131). They were still considered a different race with a different culture and ideas of a shared humanity only partly and unevenly led to dispel the conception that "natives" and Europeans were fundamentally different.

An oft-repeated mantra about Kartini in Dutch publications during the colonial era was that she was a "pioneer" for Javanese women. In Dutch, the word is "baanbreekster", which literally means so much as "she who creates new roads or ways". Yet when it came to the old roads or the mountains that needed to be moved, reference was made only to Javanese culture. Dutch people clearly loved talking about how

Kartini experienced the "galling bonds" of *adat*, the word the Dutch used for "native" laws and customs. The *Bataviaasch Nieuwsblad* of 20 April 1912, for instance, writes about Kartini's family being "bound" to adat (Veerbaldt 1912) and still in 1984, the *Nederlands Dagblad* used the headline "Javanese woman sees the Western light" (Schutte 1984). Both articles were following the lead here of the title Abendanon gave to his anthology of Kartini's letters, namely *Through Darkness into Light*. Whereas the darkness was consistently interpreted in the Netherlands as Javanese tradition and the light as European modernity, a careful reading of Kartini's letters yields, as we have seen, a more complicated picture than the Dutch fantasy of "white men saving brown women from brown men" (Spivak 2010, p. 48). All in all, what is important in light of her later remembrance in Dutch contexts, including the Kartini prize, is Kartini's criticism, in words and silences, of Dutch (colonial) culture, particularly its racism.

Silences in the Kartini Prize

When the Kartini prize was installed in 2000, it was explicitly called by the mayor of The Hague "the foreign women prize" aimed at the "structural improvement of the position of foreign women and girls in The Hague" (Archive Importante). I will continue to use the problematic word "foreign", in Dutch *"allochtoon"*, as this was the category used by the prize, but not without some explanation. The word *"allochtoon"* was introduced in the Netherlands in the 1970s to distinguish between, on the one hand, immigrants and their children and, on the other hand, so-called "autochtonen", meaning people of whom both parents had been born in the Netherlands. Literally, *"autochtoon"* means "from the same soil" and *"alltochtoon"* "from a different soil", hence my choice to translate *"allochtoon"* as "foreign". In everyday practice in the Netherlands, however, *"allochtonen"* these days are most often all people of colour (black, Arabic, Asian, etc.), while "autochtonen" are people supposedly without colour (whites). The conception behind this usage of words is that only white people can be considered truly "Dutch" while people of colour cannot. All in all, this means that even if you are a sixth-generation Suriname-Dutch, black citizen, you are still often considered an *"allochtoon"* and therefore a foreigner. People of colour are also often named after their (or their great-great-great-grandparents') country of origin, so as "Turkish" or "Moroccan" or "Surinamese", for instance.

Hyphenated identity positions (Turkish-Dutch, etc.) are not available in the Netherlands.

In the first years of the Kartini prize, nominations were limited to individual women of colour, groups of foreign women of colour and organizations specifically working with and for these women. In the 2001 report by the first jury, the reasons for installing the prize are further illuminated by the chair and member of the city council for the liberal political party VVD, Mrs Lilian Callender (Archive Importante). The Hague, she writes, is a multicultural city, yet participation of foreign women is neither "proportionally distributed" nor always visible. "Foreign women" here is said to mean women from outside Western Europe, particularly from Suriname, the Dutch Antilles (located in the Caribbean), Turkey and Morocco. Regularly, the report states, we are confronted, correctly or not, by less positive stories about these groups of women: forced migration, head scarves, single and/or abused women, women in women's refuge centres and teen mothers. The prize, however, was meant to show the strength of these women: despite the odds, many of them had successful careers or were active in neighbourhoods or involved in organizations for refugees, for instance. The Kartini prize was meant, Mrs Callender concluded, to put these women in the spotlight, to nuance the image of "pathetic" (the text itself uses commas) foreign women and to offer shining examples to young people to take responsibility for themselves and the communities they are part of.

In the programme booklet distributed on the occasion of the first prize ceremony, held on 21 April 2001, a section on Kartini illuminates why she was chosen to name the prize after (Archive Importante). Kartini, the booklet states, was unconventional and modern and irritated people who wanted to leave the status quo unchanged. Speaking and writing perfect Dutch, she was however forced into a marriage, which made her aware of the unjust laws and customs in her small community. During her lonely imprisonment she was inspired by European feminists and social thinkers. Kartini was planning to continue her education in Europe, but both the government in Batavia (present-day Jakarta) and her father thwarted her ambitions and forced her to remain in the domestic sphere.

What connects Kartini to the prizewinners, in other words, are tough circumstances and a woman trying to better her situation by not accepting the conditions of her situation. However, in line with the cultural memory of Kartini in the Netherlands, problems addressed are almost exclusively not those of white, Dutch culture, but of the immigrants' culture to which a prizewinner was supposed to belong. What was the broader conversation in the Netherlands about women of colour around 2000? Several historians have traced the histories of discourses on immigrants in the Netherlands in the twentieth century. According to Marlou Schrover, multicultural policies, introduced in the Netherlands during the 1960s and 1970s, "promoted the otherness of immigrants", just like in several other European countries (Schrover 2010, p. 329). This created opposition between a Dutch "self" and a foreign "other" that led to a freezing of both "Dutch" (white) culture and the cultures of immigrants. Multiculturalism, Schrover holds, homogenizes differences between members of a perceived culture, ignores cultural dynamics, presupposes a collection of cultures which are equally valued and leads to immigrant organizations which present a monolithic and static image of their communities. It also leads to ideas of a unified, always-already character of Dutch culture. After the 1970s, Schrover sees a steady breakdown of multicultural policies and subsidies. Whereas at first migrant organizations were seen as essential for smoothing relations with the rest of Dutch society, in 1981 the government decided that migrants should turn to general organizations rather than have subsidized organizations of their own: subsidies were reduced; in the 1990s further reductions were introduced and in 2000 subsidies were (temporarily) stopped altogether. By that time, the attack on multiculturalism was much more visible due to a rather intense public debate. According to Schrover "the policy focus shifted from social-economic participation towards reducing social and cultural distance between migrants and Dutch society" (Schrover 2010, p. 348).

Halleh Ghorashi has written similarly about Dutch discourses on immigrants, but focuses specifically on women (Ghorashi 2010). According to her, a shift has occurred around the year 2000 from "absolute invisibility to extreme visibility" of migrant women, particularly from Islamic countries. Ghorashi detects a "culturalist" approach to migrant women in the Netherlands, meaning that they are seen as oppressed by their own culture, trapped in their own home. While, just like Schrover, she detects a shift from 1970s multiculturalism to the present emphasis on "integration", she holds that several other factors have remained the same; next to culturalism is also a prevalent idea of the immigrant as deficient with respect to Dutch society (in terms of language, education, etc.) and as an absolute other who therefore never can become Dutch. Especially migrant women are often imagined as helpless creatures that need to be isolated from "their" cultures to turn them into decent citizens. Possible competencies are not recognized while only certain causes of non-participation in the broader society are recognized and others, like societal exclusion through racism, are not.

How does the Kartini prize fit this image sketched by Schrover and Ghorashi? In line with the post-1970s departure from multiculturalism which had reached an end point around 2000, the prize in 2001 sought to stimulate "integration", which in Dutch contexts implies that *"allochtonen"* have to adjust to a reified Dutch culture and society which are deemed unproblematic. However, it did not only present the women it decorated as absolute others or as helpless creatures, but as capable citizens, though often obstructed by outside forces. When the prize was installed in 2001, it was not the first or only prize for women's emancipation in the city. The Victorine Hefting prize, awarded since 1988, was meant for women in the city who have in some way bettered the position of female artists in the city; the Hilda van Suylenburg prize, awarded between 1989 and 2005, was specifically for initiatives concerning elderly women; and the emancipation prize for companies, which existed between 1998 and 2005, was aimed at stimulating emancipatory employment policies. Around 2000, when these prizes already existed, the city thought it was necessary to found a specific prize for foreign women, thus contributing to their growing visibility as noted by Ghorashi.

However, throughout the history of the prize, people who were involved from various sides expressed concerns whether it should be there in the first place and if so, what its character should be. Already in 1999, when the possibility of a prize specifically aimed at "foreign" women was discussed by the Committee for Wellbeing, Public Health and Emancipation of the city, doubts were voiced (Archive Importante). Was a separate prize for foreign women necessary? Why could they not be awarded any of the other emancipation prizes? On the other hand, one of the commission members argued, the emancipation process was less advanced in the case of foreign than in the case of native women. Another committee member was of the opinion, however, that there should be no separate prize for specific "target groups" and that rather the city should stipulate that foreign women were more likely to receive one of the other prizes. The city's municipal executive (*wethouder*) for emancipation, Jetta Klijnsma, who later became the Dutch State Secretary (*staatssecretaris*) of Social Affairs and Employment (including Equality), said she could see the point of this last committee member, but also that with that argument you could question all emancipation prizes as they all targeted a specific group, namely women. In a letter one year later, she phrased her considerations as such:

> I expect that an emancipation prize specifically aimed at foreign women and girls will provide role models. Also, by inaugurating a specific prize justice will be done to the peculiar character of the emancipation process within foreign communities which often develops differently in terms of kind, content and dynamics than emancipation processes within native-Dutch communities. (Archive Importante)

A separate emancipation prize for foreign women was thus installed because this group needed it more than any other. However, in 2006, the doubts as expressed above, among other elements, led to a fundamental change in the policy of the city. Already in a 2004 report, the foundation which awarded the various emancipation prizes in The Hague between 2001 and 2013 (Importante: women's information point/centre for information) stated that "[t]he process of emancipation is a dynamic process which ... asks for a regular recalibration of visions, targets and strategies" (Archive Importante). Evaluating the four prizes mentioned above, it was most positive about the R.A. Kartini prize, as it was only this prize which could be clearly connected to policy priorities of the national government, namely, on the one hand, that members of groups that were discriminated against should participate in all sections of society and be accepted and appreciated for who they were, and, on the other hand, that the integration and societal participation of specifically migrant women and girls was in want of government support. On the basis of this report, the mayor of The Hague in 2006 decided to uphold the Victorine Hefting prize while abolishing the Hilda van Suylenburg prize, the emancipation prize for companies as well as the R.A. Kartini prize for foreign women and to replace these prizes with "one new, general emancipation prize which is not connected to a particular target group or age group" (Archive Importante). The new prize was named *R.A. Kartiniprijs*, indicative of the fact that indeed policy concerning emancipation had importantly shifted to women of colour.

As indicated above, everybody can these days win the prize, and if we look at winners of the last eight years we can definitely notice big differences from the "old" Kartini prize. Three winners fit the narrower categories of the old prize in the sense that they were awarded to people or organizations primarily working for women of colour. In 2007, Moroccan-

Dutch woman Rahma El Hamdaoudi was awarded for her work for Moroccan-Dutch women; in 2010, the prize was given to an initiative called "Unit MCI" which aimed at the prevention of honour-related violence and forced marriages; and in 2012 Ethiopian-Dutch woman Haimanot Belay received the prize for her work within the Ethiopian-Dutch community, especially with respect to topics the jury deemed important to women such as breast cancer, female genital mutilation and domestic violence. In 2008, however, the prize was awarded to a theatre performance "In the Name of the Fathers" in which a group of fathers, both white and of colour, reflected on current notions of masculinity and of fatherhood; in 2009, the white Dutch woman Hanneke Oortgiesen won for her work for the Parent and Child Centre (before 2003 the Mothers' Centre); in 2011 Surinamese-Dutch woman Roline Julen was awarded the prize for her work with teen mothers and other disadvantaged young people; and in 2013 to the Matroesjka foundation which also works with (single) young mothers. These winners show the broadening of the Kartini prize since 2007, although the 2014 winner again emphasized a division between the emancipated white population of the city and communities of colour who were deemed to still have a long way to go: Radjesh Madarie, a Surinamese-Dutch LGBT activist, was awarded that year because the jury saw in him a role model for the migrant LGBT communities in The Hague who does important work particularly among Hindu Surinamese-Dutch (Kartiniprijs).

The current website of the Kartini prize (www.kartini.nl) has quite extensively documented all years of the prize's existence and includes all jury reports, information about the nominees and winners as well as the regulations and background information on Kartini. What is striking is that in none of these documents is the word "race" or "racism" mentioned (Kartiniprijs). This is in line with the other findings as presented above, and with the way in which Kartini has been remembered in the Netherlands: the problems of Kartini, just as the problems of women of colour, were and are sought in relation to their own behaviour and in relation to the communities to which they supposedly belong, while the white majority of the Netherlands is left out of the picture and not addressed. This does not mean that attention for racial discrimination is completely absent in The Hague. If we look at the document which outlines the city's "Emancipation and Anti-Discrimination Policy" for the years 2004–6, we see that according to The Hague "emancipation and discrimination are two sides of the same sheet of paper" (Archive Importante). Anti-discrimination is called "tracking down and taking away obstacles which people encounter on the road to emancipation". One important instrument to attain this goal is to fight prejudices, and the way to do this, the document states, is to highlight positive examples, so no emphasis on victimization and no "moralistic, finger-waving approach". Again, it is not the white part of the population which is sought to be addressed, only various minority communities of colour. Moreover, the document names two separate organizations that will work on emancipation and anti-discrimination, respectively, Importante and the Office of Discriminatory Affairs. Since 2013, Importante no longer exists, its tasks having been taken over by a new organization named PEP: Participation Emancipation Professionals, which now awards the Kartini prize. Whereas on PEP's website, the words "race" and "racism" are almost completely absent (PEP), the Office of Discriminatory Affairs uses these words more than sixty times on its website and clearly states in the FAQ section that: "Most complaints of discrimination are about discrimination on racial grounds (about two-thirds of the total)" (Bureau Discriminatiezaken). All in all, we can see that in The Hague there is not so much silence on issues of race and racism, but that the sounds and silences on these topics are unevenly distributed. Although the city itself claims that emancipation and anti-discrimination are intimately connected, in practice they are relegated to different organizations that each speak a different language.

A productive frame of interpretation to give meaning to this division of labour is provided by Fatima El-Tayeb in her book *European Others: Queering Ethnicity in Postnational Europe* (2011). According to El-Tayeb, there is an ideology of "racelessness" in Europe, meaning that there is a strategy of denial that conceptions of race play any part whatsoever in European contexts (other than in American contexts, for instance). In Dutch contexts it is often the case that race is thought to be only brought up by racists. The wish is sometimes the father of the thought here: some people who make this particular claim would like to see the Netherlands as a post-racial society but in fact rush ahead and forget that in the postcolonial Netherlands race keeps on playing a part. Research has shown again and again that race plays a part in getting access to the labour market, for instance. This state of affairs also provides an explanation why Importante, PEP and the Kartini prize hardly use the words "race" and "racism": on the one hand, these concepts disturb the liberal idea of equal opportunities for those who know how to grasp them, but on the other hand, they disrupt the prize's founding thought to focus on positive, not negative, aspects of people's lives.

Conclusion

These findings on the remembrance of Kartini in the Netherlands make clear that it would make no sense to speak of her memory or forgetting in binary terms, for she is both present and absent in Dutch contexts at the same time, depending on where you look for her. Silence's location, its synchronic dimension, I argue, is crucial, and depending on where you keep your ear to the ground, you will either hear nothing or an abundance of sounds. Moreover, moments where silences are encountered should indeed be considered not as absences, but as active processes, for as Foucault writes:

> [silence] is an element that functions alongside the things said, with them and in relation to them within over-all strategies. There is no binary division to be made between what one says and what one does not say; we must try to determine the different ways of not saying such things, how those who can and those who cannot speak of them are distributed, which type of discourse is authorized or which form of discretion is required in either case. (Foucault 1998, p. 27)

These words are strongly applicable to some of Kartini's (thoughts on) silences. Signs of oppression and protest, her silences were produced and conditioned by the discourses dominant in the society of colonial Java in which she lived. This is especially true for her critique of Dutch racism that she mostly attacks through irony, thereby simultaneously (re) producing racist sounds and critical silences. These silences about Dutch racism, however, were not heard in the Netherlands yet nevertheless perpetuated. Diachronically, they form a consistent element in Kartini's remembrance throughout the twentieth and twenty-first centuries and these days inhibit addressing the role of racism for women of colour who are awarded the Kartini prize. What is needed is a rereading of Kartini's texts, in which her critique of Dutch racism lies hidden as an *"oubli de réserve"* (Ricoeur 2004, p. 414), a meaningful silence that may help the Dutch talk less about "integration" and more about living together.

NOTE

1.   This chapter is a reprint of Paul Bijl, "Colonial and Postcolonial Silence: Listening to Kartini in the Netherlands", in *Beyond Memory: Silence and the Aesthetics of Remembrance*, edited by Alexandre Dessingué and Jay M. Winter

(London: Routledge, 2015). Minor alterations have been made to serve the purposes of the present volume and to conform to ISEAS' style.

REFERENCES

Anbeek, Ton. 1990. *Geschiedenis van de Nederlandse literatuur tussen 1885 en 1985*. Amsterdam: Arbeiderspers.

Archive Importante. Municipal Archive, The Hague.

Bhabha, Homi. 2004. *The Location of Culture*. London: Routledge.

Bijl, Paul. 2009. "Old, Eternal and Future Light in the Dutch East Indies: Colonial Photographs and the History of the Globe". In *Mediation, Remediation, and the Dynamics of Cultural Memory*, edited by Astrid Erll and Ann Rigney. Berlin: De Gruyter.

———. 2012. "Colonial Memory and Forgetting in the Netherlands and Indonesia". *Journal of Genocide Research* 14: 441–61.

———. 2015. *Emerging Memory: Photographs of Colonial Atrocity in Dutch Cultural Remembrance*. Amsterdam: Amsterdam University Press.

Bureau Discriminatiezaken. https://www.discriminatiezaken.nl/ (accessed 15 September 2014).

El-Tayeb, Fatima. 2011. *European Others: Queering Ethnicity in Postnational Europe*. Minneapolis: University of Minneapolis Press.

Fasseur, Cees. 1994. "Cornerstone and Stumbling Block: Racial Classification and the Late Colonial State in Indonesia". In *The Late Colonial State in Indonesia: Political and Economic Foundations of the Netherlands Indies, 1880–1942*, edited by Robert Cribb. Leiden: KITLV Press.

Foucault, Michel. 1998. *The History of Sexuality I: The Will to Knowledge*. Translated by Robert Hurley. London: Penguin.

Ghorashi, Halleh. 2010. "From Absolute Invisibility to Extreme Visibility: Emancipation Trajectory of Migrant Women in the Netherlands". *Feminist Review* 94: 75–92.

Goss, Andrew. 2000. "From Tong-Tong to Tempo Doeloe: Eurasian Memory Work and the Bracketing of Dutch Colonial History, 1957–1961". *Indonesia* 70: 8–36.

Kartini, R.A. 1911. *Door duisternis tot licht: Gedachten over en voor het Javaansche volk*. Edited by J.H. Abendanon. Semarang: Van Dorp.

———. 1992. *Letters from Kartini: An Indonesian Feminist, 1900–1904*. Edited and translated by Joost Coté. Clayton, Victoria: Monash Asia Institute, Monash University.

———. 2005. *On Feminism and Nationalism: Kartini's Letters to Stella Zeehandelaar, 1899–1903*. Edited and translated by Joost Coté. 2nd ed. Clayton, Victoria: Monash Asia Institute, Monash University.

Kartiniprijs. https://www.kartini.nl/ (accessed 15 September 2014).

Nieuwenhuys, Rob. 1982. *Mirror of the Indies: A History of Dutch Colonial Literature*. Translated by Frans van Rosevelt. Edited by E. Beekman. Amherst, MA: University of Massachusetts Press.

Passerini, Luisa. 2003. "Memories Between Silence and Oblivion". In *Contested Pasts: The Politics of Memory*, edited by K. Hodgkin and S. Radstone. London: Routledge.

PEP: Participatie Emancipatie Professionals. https://www.pepden haag.nl (accessed 15 September 2014).

Ricoeur, Paul. 2004. *Memory, History, Forgetting*. Translated by K. Blarney and D. Pellauer. Chicago: University of Chicago Press.

Schenkeveld-Van der Dussen, M., ed. 1993. *Nederlandse literatuur: een geschiedenis*. Groningen: Nijhoff.

Schrover, Marlou. 2010. "Pillarization, Multiculturalism and Cultural Freezing: Dutch Migration History and the Enforcement of Essentialist Ideas". In *Low Countries Historical Review* 125: 329–54.

———. 2011. "Om de meisjes, voor de meisjes: Een historisch perspectief op problematisering en bagatellisering van onderwerpen die te maken hebben met migratie en integratie". Leiden: Leiden University.

Schutte, G. 1984. "Twee rebellerende freules". *Nederlands Dagblad: gereformeerd gezinsblad*, 11 July 1984.

Spivak, Gayatri Chakravorty. 2010. "Can the Subaltern Speak?" In *Can the Subaltern Speak? Reflections on the History of an Idea*, edited by Rosalind Morris. New York: Columbia University Press.

Stoler, Ann Laura. 2011. "Colonial Aphasia: Race and Disabled Histories in France". *Public Culture* 23: 121–57.

Vaessens, Thomas. 2013. *Geschiedenis van de moderne Nederlandse literatuur*. Nijmegen: Vantilt.

Veerbaldt, J. 1912. "Vrouwenbeweging: Nog eens: De emancipatie der Javaanse vrouw". *Bataviaasch Nieuwsblad*, 20 April 1912.

8

Afterword

Jean Gelman Taylor

The contributors to this volume deliver us a striking paradox. Internationally, Kartini ranks just after Anne Frank as the best known of authors who wrote in the Dutch language. But in the Netherlands today she is barely known or read. In Indonesia, Kartini is barely read but widely known. Kartini has a rich afterlife in hundreds of articles, speeches and exhibitions. UNESCO sponsored translations into English and French of some of her letters for its Collection of Representative Works of world literature. She is the heroine of at least two feature-length films. A national day is dedicated to her in Indonesia when her name is invoked in recognition of women's achievements. All this while, the letters she wrote and by which she was launched into transnational consciousness remain largely unread.

What we have here, as this book makes very clear, is that the historical personage has transmogrified into a reference point in discussions, debates and controversies on big topics. Kartini's name is invoked in studies of colonialism, racism, political ideologies, religion, gender, equality, human rights and women's emancipation. In specifically Indonesian contexts, her name is invoked in conversations on girls' education and careers.

Now, this is a very heavy burden to lay on the shoulders of one who lived a mere twenty-five years and six months. The years of Kartini's life that are part of the written record are 1898–1904. Within this short time span, if we read her letters we discover passage from a young girl's excitement at venturing upon the modern age, the noble ideals and dreams of the precocious, the transport of affections for new-found friends, energetic efforts to raise pride in Javanese culture, and the hope of forming ties with like-minded young people in Java. There is also maturation, ambitions adapted to meet changed circumstances, and then a life cut short just days after giving birth to her only child. Had Kartini been given a longer life we would perhaps have traced evolution in ideas and principles and achievement of goals. Over the decades since her death, commentators have analysed Kartini according to the sensibilities of their own historical time and priorities. And they have necessarily found the heroine wanting.

The contributors to this volume probe Kartini's afterlife. The book's focus is on appropriation. Name recognition lends itself to appropriations that do not rest on a deep knowledge of the author's words and so lead in many directions. Kartini becomes attached to the specific interests of commentators, politicians and scholars. Appropriation points to the future. Kartini ceases to be a person fixed in a specific historical time, a person revelatory of that time. Instead, she becomes a tool for examining Indonesian and Dutch societies in periods way beyond her own lifetime. The editors, Paul Bijl and Grace V.S. Chin, phrase this phenomenon in their joint Introduction as "many Kartinis". Kathryn Robinson, in her chapter, employs the intriguing term "floating signifier".

We are led to consider the power of editing from the beginning. This may be a form of silencing, which is a theme taken up by Bijl and Chin in their separate chapters. Coté's chapter "rescues" an important aspect of Kartini's plans and initiatives from the "cutting floor". She became the intermediary through whom Dutch acquaintaince in Java and the Netherlands acquired salon furniture, hand-crafted cabinets, screens and boxes from the woodworkers for which Jepara was—and still is—well known. When the gaps in the published letters were restored (and Coté has been a major force in this respect), we see the historical Kartini discussing designs, suggesting to the woodcarvers innovations that would appeal to a new, European clientele, setting prices, organizing packaging and sending the finished works by rail to Batavia and by ship to the Netherlands.

Coté's discipline is history, and it is his chapter that brings to the fore activities of Kartini that have been and are ignored by most critics, social media commentators, translators and academics. Indeed, in Cote's judgement, Kartini's greatest practical achievement was not the founding of little schools for a handful of girls in the homes of her father and then of her husband, but her exertions in fostering appreciation of Javanese arts and crafts. As a shrewd observer of her class (an attribute Chin contests) Kartini thought Java's new rich could be persuaded, once they perceived Dutch interest in their own culture, to place traditional Javanese crafts in their parlours as well as pianos imported from Holland.

Through his study of Kartini's customers, Coté addresses the book's theme of appropriation. Those Dutch people who placed orders through Kartini wanted furniture and household items decorated with Javanese motifs such as *wayang* figures. Coté argues that these tastes could only have developed because of a change in the nature of Dutch imperialism and new perspectives on the colonial relationship. Dutch patrons of Kartini's woodworkers were becoming aware and proud of the Netherlands' colonial possessions. They were attuned to the new European ideas of civilizational duty, in short, of ethical colonialism. Implementation required perpetuation of colonial guidance.

Bijl's chapter "Hierarchies of Humanity: Kartini in America and at UNESCO" probes deeper into the nature of imperial agendas and tutelage. He makes Western perspectives the central part of his research. Here Bijl finds a dualism. There is the liberating impulse from the Enlightenment in the recognition of the equality of all humanity, and there is *at the same time* the concept of stages in human development, a ranking of peoples, a positioning of "races" on a scale of humanity.

Bijl asks what did it really mean to acclaim Kartini as a "pioneer"? Implicitly and explicitly Kartini was deemed as being ahead of her people and her time. She had surpassed the majority of Javanese of the early twentieth century because of her contact with Dutch civilization. Reaching that higher rung on the ladder through her European schooling, her command of the Dutch language and her intimacy with leading proponents of ethical colonialism, she had qualified herself to lead others, to raise them up and nudge them closer to Europeans. And indeed Kartini imbibed these notions herself. The phrase "From Darkness into Light", which was the title given to the first published collection of Kartini's letters to her inner circle of Dutch acquaintance, was not authored by J.H. Abendanon, her editor, but taken from Kartini's own pen. The phrase is her descriptor of her personal journey. Bijl traces the pervasiveness of the ideal of uplifting humanity's masses beyond her admirers in the

Netherlands. He cites, in example, this sentiment in Eleanor Roosevelt's Preface to the UNESCO English-language edition of Kartini's letters: "they [the letters] will help us to understand what we of the Western world must understand if we are to be helpful to nations emerging from old customs into new". Ultimately, Bijl writes, it is almost impossible to be free of this perspective that is rooted, even unconsciously, in racism.

Bijl returns to this argument in his later chapter, "Kartini and the Politics of European Multiculturalism". Here he considers the Kartini prize established by the municipality of The Hague in 2001 to be awarded annually to an immigrant woman judged to have become part of Dutch society and to have made a meaningful contribution to it. Success, Bijl argues, is predicated on the winner having overcome her own culture and traditions. She remakes herself. She triumphs over everything that is wrong with *her*, with her own cultural inheritance and her fellow immigrants in the Netherlands. She has become Dutch. Bijl asks could it be that the racism migrants encounter in the Netherlands engenders their social exclusion, rather the migrants' attachment to their own customs being the cause?

Kartini, in the council's manifesto, is a shadow of her historical self. In his former chapter, Bijl reminds us that Kartini had to be raised to the status of princess to be of interest to Westerners. *Letters of a Javanese Princess* is the title given to Agnes Symmers' translation of seventy-eight of Kartini's letters. Both the translator and publisher overlooked her letter to Stella Zeehandelaar in which she wrote "Call me simply Kartini" (Kartini 1964, p. 36). Similarly, Bijl points to Knopf publishing house's preference for including in an anthology an essay on Kartini written by the Dutch novelist Louis Couperus rather than any original piece of writing by Kartini herself.

Danilyn Rutherford's compelling article "Unpacking a National Heroine: Two Kartinis and their People", first printed in Cornell University's journal *Indonesia*, asks how Indonesians have understood Kartini. Turning away from the Europeans and Americans who were thinking and writing in a world where colonialism reigned, Rutherford compares two biographies of Kartini published after the establishment of the Republic of Indonesia. Again, these texts differ in that they were not written in the colonizer's native language, but in the national language of the sovereign state of Indonesia. The first biography is Pramoedya Ananta Toer's *Panggil aku Kartini sadja* (Just call me Kartini). Unlike Western commentators, Pramoedya read Kartini's letters. His title is

Kartini's own words (albeit translated from the Dutch) in response to her penfriend's query on how to address her.

Pramoedya's analysis was published in 1962 in the tumultuous times leading up to the cataclysm that saw the extirpation of communism and people deemed associated with it by the Indonesian state, its armed forces and civilian para-militaries. Pramoedya was the short story writer whose fiction was peopled with figures from the village world of Kartini's maternal ancestors. He collected and published stories in Malay from the late nineteenth century. During his own incarceration in a labour camp on Buru Island (1969–79), he conceived and later wrote Indonesia's "birth of the nation" in the form of four historical novels. Later he was to publish, in letter and essay form, reflections on his own life and on the life of his nation, becoming, in a sense, a latter-day Kartini. From his studies, Pramoedya formed the view that Kartini was Indonesia's first modern intellectual. He also perceived hers as a voice of resistance. Kartini was, he wrote, a forerunner, not in the way the Dutch conceived of her as a pioneer of uplift on the path to Dutchness, but a forerunner of nationalism and commitment to self-determination within an independent nation-state.

Abendanon added to Kartini's "From Darkness into Light" the sub-heading "Reflections on and for the Javanese People" (Kartini 1911).[1] Rutherford draws our attention to Pramoedya's translation of the Dutch *volk* (people) into the Indonesian *rakyat*. Translation is never neutral. Each word imposes a decision on the translator. Pramoedya's choice of translation breathes class connotations, rather than imputations of shared ancestors and traditions. *Rakyat* are the common people, everyman and everywoman. With Pramoedya, the term implies entitlement, the entitlement of those long denied a share in the national good by the privileged. Pramoedya reflected on the passions of Sukarno, Indonesia's first president, who appropriated the Javanese Kartini as a symbol of Indonesia's nationalist struggle.

Chin notes that Sukarno instituted 21 April (Kartini's birth date) as Kartini Day in April 1946. It is worth drawing attention to this date. Sukarno had proclaimed Indonesia's independence barely nine months earlier in Jakarta. He made his declaration of Kartini Day from Yogyakarta, then the republican capital, at a time when Dutch military power was again spreading over the archipelago and hemming the republicans in behind "police lines". Very early in the public relations armoury of the independence struggle, Sukarno had selected the Javanese Kartini as a symbol for all Indonesians. In naming her Ibu Kartini (mother Kartini) instead of by her aristocratic titles (Raden Ajeng, later Raden Ayu), Sukarno dispensed with connotations of elite privilege, but also with any association that might suggest women's entitlement to men's rights. As mother of the people, she was a personage anchored in family and household, capable of being beloved and respected by all Indonesian ethnic communities.

Sitisoemandari Soeroto is the author of the second biography of Kartini that Rutherford discusses. Like Pramoedya, Soeroto was a writer and journalist, but unlike him she was female and enjoyed family circumstances that allowed her to expand the sources on which she drew in forming her understanding of Indonesia's national heroine. Where Pramoedya drew on sources accessible to him in Indonesia, Soeroto travelled to the Netherlands to explore Dutch archives and to conduct interviews to probe Dutch perspectives on Kartini. Again, Rutherford reminds us of the relevance of historical time. Soeroto's biography had its birth in 1977 in President Suharto's New Order. She translated *volk* as *bangsa*, nation, a word encompassing all Indonesians, obliterating social and economic inequalities. No longer was Kartini the advocate of struggle and resistance in Suharto's Indonesia. She had become the admirable promoter of girls' schooling, of the welfare of the family, and of society at large.

Schooling expanded very rapidly in independent Indonesia. Female students proceeded to higher study in universities and academies; women of all socio-economic groups became highly visible in the workforce. Kartini Day prospered under the Suharto government. Robinson examines it from several angles. The main ingredients—girls and women dressing up in "Kartini costumes", and speeches on women's roles in society—supported the New Order's directive that all should harmoniously work together for economic development. Robinson's research shows that these ingredients have persisted long after the downfall of Suharto. Suharto's Kartini continues in troubled times to present untroubling messages about girls' education and homemakers. The themes have flourished through *Reformasi* and post-*Reformasi* times, seemingly stronger than the grumbles and counterpoint: that Kartini is out of date, too Java-centric, that dressing up like Kartini slights other women worthies.

Robinson broadens consideration of Indonesian perspectives by interviewing young urban women. Today's sophisticated young women, cosmopolitans, millenials, those who see themselves as *"jaman now"* (today's generation), find Kartini Day passé. They acknowledge Kartini as promoter of education for girls, but they have not read what she wrote, nor want to, and they argue that there are other pressing issues today for them to confront: domestic violence, the use of rape for political intimidation, and the infraction of rights of LGBTI communities. Appropriations by Dutch and Indonesian alike have rendered Kartini irrelevant to contemporary Indonesia.

Here is a link to Chin's chapter in this book. Addressing twenty-first century concerns in "Ambivalent Narration: Kartini's Silence and the Other Woman", Chin finds Kartini a deficient or troublesome figure for a feminist perspective on Indonesian history. Chin's starting point is silence. She charges Kartini with classism, meaning a pride in her paternal *pryayi* (aristocratic) background. She points to Kartini's reticence on the very existence of her birth mother. Those reading Kartini's letters to the Abendanons before F.G.P. Jaquet published the full text of them in 1987 (Kartini 1987) did not know that Kartini was the daughter of her father's secondary-ranked wife. They understood her repeated assertions of the bitterness of polygamy for women as empathy rather than Kartini's own lived experience.

There is always awkwardness for the writer of English to find a term that conveys the status of wives in polygamous households. "Secondary wife" tells us that by rank she is the inferior, but it may imply a chronological status. We might assume that Kartini's birth mother was brought into a household in which the first wife already presided. Some writers employ the Indonesian term *selir* (concubine), but its generally negative connotations render it both inadequate and misleading. Kartini's birth mother, Ngasirah, was the lawfully married first wife in chronological terms, but secondary in status because of her class origins. The first wife in ranking, Raden Ayu Moerjam, was the first in social status because of her ancestry. She represented the family to the world, headed the household, and was publicly the mother of all the children born to the common father. Ngasirah bore eight of the eleven children in the family. Kartini was her fourth child. The two mothers lived in different quarters of the same house compound and shared in different ways a common daily life.

Kartini finally confided to Rosa Abendanon-Mandri that she herself was a member of the kind of family she condemned and was about to marry into another (Kartini 1987, pp. 307–11).[2] Historians of sensibility and emotion would point to 1903 as a time when substantiating degrees of courtesy and respect had prevailed. In a colonial society such as Java, the horror Europeans professed of polygamy as uncivilized, barbarous and oriental was well known, so there was a strong motive of induced shame to conceal. Javanese norms of propriety also account for her silence. There was the dignity and respect due to Raden Ayu Moerjam, to her father, and to conventions regarding what was fitting to be public or private.

Restraint always comes at a cost. So Kartini confides the facts of her life and the awful prospects of her approaching marriage in a great flood of mortification, personal aversion and apologies. She writes of lost ambitions, of failure to be a model independent woman. But perhaps we can rescue her from the classism and conformity with the mores of her time. Kartini describes the etiquette practised in families such as hers, which was descended from aristocrats and had connections to Java's royalty. We see a photograph of her with Roekmini and Kardinah, the two sisters closest in age and sympathies.[3] At first glance, Kartini, standing between her sisters, seems to occupy the focal point of the photograph. But it is Roekmini, seated, her feet on a footstool, who commands attention. The photographer or choreographer of this photograph has ensured that, despite the three girls being dressed identically, with the same jewellery and hairstyles, the viewer instinctively understands Roekmini to be the daughter of the Raden Ayu. She is the senior in status to her sisters, who must rank a little lower than she as daughters of the secondary wife. There was no way to overturn behaviour even within the family to accord with modern, Dutch ideas, but, in private space, Kartini tells us she released her younger brothers and sisters from the requirement to crawl into her presence and speak only with permission.

Silence has other costs. Chin tells us that politeness and social conformity cover up violence in all its emotional and physical forms. She considers polite manners in contemporary Indonesia and their apogee in the New Order organization, *Dharma Wanita* (Women's Duty). Through it, the wives of men senior in government service engaged in work for the public good, understood as "raising up" village women, encouraging them to have good morals, and to care for family and the welfare of the nation. Women's Duty sponsored classes for village women in cookery and sewing (which Kartini had also urged for promoting healthy living and livelihoods). They did not, writes Chin, campaign for higher wages for working women, nor speak out against attacks on women union leaders and ill-treatment of the vulnerable.

The legacy of the Suharto-era Kartini, Chin argues, continues until today. "Memory" and symbolism are rooted in silence regarding society's real evils, its denial of violence and trauma. Even today, appropriation of the historical woman and her transformation into a saccharine mother of all characterizes contemporary narratives of the feminist struggle in Indonesia. The socially inferior are marginalized. Among them Chin includes non-Javanese women. The Dutch saw Kartini as a symbol of Dutch success; Sukarno presented her as a non-elite nationalist; Suharto fashioned her as the domestic pioneer of development. Chin's chapter makes us ponder if this history of appropriations is the failure of a scholarship that lets government ideologies prevail.

Elite women in Indonesia have university educations and high level jobs; they travel overseas, and regard public roles and work as women's right. Chin reminds us that for the majority of Indonesian women work is a necessity. The entrenched social order and attitudes deny ordinary women empowerment. Elite women lead successful public lives and careers precisely because they are able to draw on the cheap labour of other women.

* * *

The disciplines of comparative literature and anthropology dominate Indonesian Studies in the West today. History, in decline as an academic discipline, is now merged into "studies" at both school and university levels. The propensity of historians to look backwards, to focus and prize primary sources, is no longer generally attractive. (And one can note here that Kartini, as a privileged young woman with servants, had time to write letters that stretched to forty pages and more.) The contributors to this volume have deftly shown what the idea or notion of Kartini can become when those promoting her as a national icon do not take the time to ground themselves in a knowledge of her writings. The very place of letters in intellectual history cannot be replicated in our own era of email, Facebook and Twitter.

Appropriation is what others have made of a historical personage. We remember that one meaning of appropriation is theft. And this volume shows us quite surprising outcomes, that feminist narratives and "progressive" narratives of history may be blind to society at large and around them. The contributors urge us to reconsider our own ethics as scholars. How do we approach issues of modernity/tradition, or, to use an Indonesian pairing, *ningrat/rakyat* (aristocracy/commoners)? Here are no malicious versions of history, but unwitting reinforcing of notions of cultural superiority and *noblesse oblige* or of received ideas that imbue the political sensibilities and ideological demands of specific times. There is the determination to attach an idea or a symbol to a specific political cause, such as "benign" colonialism or "progressive" feminism. Chin points up ironies. Kartini, she writes, was made to represent the worst aspects of Javanism and thereby made a most improper heroine for Acehnese or East Timorese women. Appropriation is about us, whether we are Europeans or Indonesians. It is a fascination with ourselves.

In all the case studies presented here, we learn that appropriation detaches individuals from their family, society and times. An icon must stand alone for ready identification with a cause. But detaching Kartini from her immediate family does a great disservice to understanding its place in Indonesia's history. Kartini's own sisters contributed to the image-making. Kardinah took exception to Pramoedya's representation of their sister as plebeian and wrote a rejoinder (in Dutch, in 1966) in that most venerable of publications, the *Bijdragen tot de taal-, land- en volkenkunde* (Journal of linguistics, geography and anthroplogy) (Reksonegoro 1966). Her younger sisters maintained a correspondence with Kartini's closest Dutch friends until 1936. We have, thanks to Coté's translation into English of the unpublished Dutch originals, an unbroken record of intimate correspondence between Indonesian and Dutch over thirty-seven years (Coté 2008).

This is unequalled in Indonesian history and indeed in many societies. In this continuing correspondence we trace an evolution in Indonesia's social history over time. The youngest sister, Soematri, started her epistolary journey as a ten-year old in 1901, addressing Rosa Abendanon-Mandri as "Dear Mevrouw", thanking her for presents and letters. Over the years of her own coming of age and increasing familiarity, Soematri moved to address Rosa Abendanon-Mandri as "Esteemed Friend" and, later, as "Dearest Mother" (*Liefste Moedertje*). As a marker of social history, we may consider how two sisters referred to their husbands in correspondence with their Dutch friends. Where Kartini in 1903 referred respectfully to her husband as the "Regent of Rembang", Soematri in 1918 casually called her husband "Achmad" (or by the contraction "Mad") in her letters to Rosa and to her girlfriend, Lien (Lien van den Berge-Kelder). She wrote comfortably, too, of "both our mothers" (Coté 2008, p. 286).[4]

We discover an older brother, Sosrokartono, in the ongoing correspondence. This third son was the one who realized the sisters' dream of going to Holland. Study in Holland, Kartini had anticipated, would rid the sisters of habits of deference and silence, and equip them to return as teachers and promoters of the common good. From Soematri's letters, we discern that Sosrokartono led a life in Holland troubled by alcohol and drugs, with attendant money difficulties. Time and again, Soematri thanked the Abendanons for rescuing her brother and settling his debts. The extended correspondence narrates an Indonesian history of emotions and sensibility.

Appropriation presents Kartini in isolation, alone. But a pioneer comes from somewhere; she does not spring unattached and individually. Kartini's male relatives and her sisters' husbands corresponded with the Dutch on colonial policy. To what degree did Kartini quote her male relatives, and in what way was she new or original? Robinson finds that many Indonesians who reflect on Kartini conclude she was a puppet of the Dutch, created by the colonial elite to represent "the best" in Netherlandic imperialism. Is this a critique that is exclusively designed against a woman? Where are the studies of Kartini's male contemporaries and those of later generations who, like her relatives and in-laws, worked within the colonial civil service, wrote reports to the Dutch hierarchy on the ills of colonial society, and proposed policy changes? They have not been disparaged in nationalist histories as puppets of the Dutch. Sukarno gave them more agency when he classified this group as "cooperators" (to distinguish them from the "non-cooperators", men who eschewed drawing a salary from the Dutch and who, like Sukarno, relied instead on a working wife).

Should we consider the arguments Henk Schulte Nordholt has made on being "modern" in the colony (2009)? He argues that modernity in its many forms was deeply attractive. It could be embraced by the new urban indigenous lower and middle classes who earned their living in jobs linked to the colonial authority. They pursued personal goals of ambition for themselves and their families. What Schulte Nordholt discusses is not just about emulation, looking up to the Dutch, but looking ahead. For, in order to acquire this modern lifestyle, Indonesians had to change how they spent their time, how they earned their living, and how they selected schools for their children. Schulte Nordholt estimates this group to number around 500,000 men and women by 1940.

Robinson introduces social media as a source on how contemporary Indonesians perceive Kartini. But social media can be found to display ignorance, prejudice, and an all-too-common aversion to the hard work of reading through all of Kartini's writings and reflecting on the sensibilities of late nineteenth and early twentieth centuries. Studies of Kartini overlook the historical fact that her maternal grandmother was a *Hajjah*. The title indicates she had travelled as a pilgrim to Mecca at a time when very few Indonesians, male or female, hazarded the long, arduous and expensive journey by sea and overland routes. The Dutch Royal Packet Company opened direct, fortnightly steamship service to the Arabian port of Jeddah in 1891, reducing travel time between the archipelago and Arabia to three weeks and stimulating an immediate increase in the number of pilgrims travelling from the fringe of the Islamic world. Few memories of the pilgrims' transformative experiences prior to 1891 have been preserved (Tagliacozzo 2013). In the irony of history's byways, Kartini wrote to the Abendanons requesting they ask the Dutch Arabist, Chr. Snouck Hurgronje, what in fact Islam taught regarding women (Kartini 1987, p. 146).

Appropriation may also deflect us from considering reader reception. There is little consideration here on whom the letters were written for, what the recipients wrote in response, and how they elicited such profound and intimate intercourse. The present volume cannot offer an intellectual history of Kartini and her times. The interlocutor is silent. The letters Kartini wrote to young Indonesian (she said Indies) men and women, and the letters they and Kartini's Dutch friends wrote to her are lost. Preservation of these two-way conversations is lamentably one-sided. Bijl says, in a larger context, that this book is in itself a product of the imbalance in power structures.

An earlier generation of Western academics who studied Kartini looked forward. They understood the women's organizations that were founded in the first decades of the twentieth century as a natural evolution. Cora Vreede-de Stuers, for example, studied the women's congresses and parties such as *Isteri Sedar* (Alert women) within the frameworks of modernity, emancipation, feminism and nationalism (Vreede-de Stuers 1960). Most women's movements saw their place in the social sphere. Saskia Wieringa's *Sexual Politics in Indonesia* (2002) focuses on *Gerwani* (*Gerakan Wanita Indonesia*, or Indonesian Women's Movement) that was affiliated with the Communist Party of Indonesia. *Gerwani* saw itself primarily as a political organization dedicated not only to achieving gender equality and equal labour rights, but broad structural change within Indonesian society and the postcolonial world. Wieringa (2002) describes how President Suharto's New Order linked women's political power to sexual depravity and pushed back gains made by women in previous decades. Susan Blackburn (2004) focuses on how the state engages with its women citizens. Through this prism, she examines topics of peculiar importance to women such as suffrage and education, law and order, labour conditions, political and reproductive rights. Such studies engage with developments within the wider society and the gender ideology of the state at specific times. They also show how competing demands have been reflected in the organizational history of women's movements in Indonesia.

Indonesian social commentators, from the sociologist Harsya Bachtiar to the young women Robinson interviewed, bemoan the invisibility of other role models for Indonesian women. The name of Cut Nyak Dhien (1848–1908) is most often brought forward in these counterpoints. Her almost mythical status as the leader of guerrilla bands against the Dutch in Aceh was sealed by her entry into the national pantheon of the Republic's heroes in 1964. However, serious research on her has been hampered by silence for, unlike Kartini, she left no written record of her own. The historian has to ponder, how did Cut Nyak Dhien break Islamic rules on the interaction between unrelated men and women to fight alongside men during the Aceh wars? Did her elite status allow her to break the restraints that controlled the lives of ordinary Acehnese women? The one photographic image preserved of her shows the agonizing moment of her disarray following capture by colonial forces in 1905.[5]

Among Indonesia's women's organizations, the largest and longest lived is *Aisyah*. It was established in 1917 by women for whom the wish to shape society conformable to Muslim values was a powerful motive. It was a sister organization to the men's *Muhammadiyah*, founded in 1912. Stressing gender segregation rather than class hierarchy, Islamic parties of the colonial era were separate entities for women and men. When gender segregation was contested, for example by Haji Agus Salim, a compromise allowed women to attend congresses of the men's parties albeit seated behind a curtain, unseen and excluded from debate.

It is instructive to consider this role model proposed for Muslim women who, after all, form the vast majority of women in Indonesia. The historical Aisyah was an Arab woman. As such, she was not associated with any Indonesian ethnic group, unlike the Javanese Kartini. No hint of European influence and patronage is attached to her, nor is she identifiable with any historical era in Indonesia's past or present. Born in *c.*605 CE in Arabia, Aisyah was one of the wives of the founding prophet of Islam. Being a juvenile bride in a polygamous family put Kartini's causes—opposition to early marriage and polygamy—beyond challenge by the organization's membership. This guiding principle forged an unbreachable rift with many of the colonial-era women's associations.

The historical Aisyah is the source of many of the utterances attributed to Prophet Muhammad, especially those that guided early converts to Islam in matters of ritual practice and implementation of Islam in the individual's and the community's daily life. Aisyah opposed the succession of Ali as Sunni Islam's fourth caliph and led troops against him in battle. A sixteenth-century illuminated manuscript in Turkey's Topkapi Sarayi Museum depicts this historical memory of a decisive and martial Aisyah confronting the forces of Ali unseen from within a howdah atop a camel.

The image adopted by the *Aisyah* movement for the cover of its magazine *Suara Aisjijah* in 1952 depicts a Javanese woman whose hair is covered; she is dressed in a plain blouse and batik skirt, and is reading a book to three children by her side. In the background, a farmer and his buffalo plough a rice field; the sun's rays shine upon an untroubled pastoral scene. It is an image at variance with Aceh's dishevelled Cut Nyak Dhien, surrounded by her gaolers, as much as it is at variance with the bare-headed Kartini and her sisters. Robinson notes that "Islam-friendly feminism" has its own representation of Kartini. In this appropriation, Kartini's demand for girls' education owed its inspiration to Islamic teachings of equality as much as to her Dutch education.

What do we know of the other women who are offered as models? They live on in hagiographies of barely documented deeds, constrained by the gender conventions of their day, or perhaps because individual women had no epistolary turn or found no partner in conversation to preserve what they thought and championed. Khan (2010, 2011) has devoted her research to Aceh's sultanahs of the second half of the seventeenth century, but even she cannot name the families of these four women, explain how they were chosen or by whom from among an array of candidates. She draws on scattered entries in VOC records, but documents created by the Acehnese are mostly lost or forgotten. (This lack of data holds true for many of the male rulers of Aceh too.)

Historians are seemingly left with the historical Kartini to account for great changes within Indonesian communities a century ago. There remain challenges for future students in what still might be done to give us a more complete picture. Kartini's writings have been translated into Arabic, Japanese, Russian and other languages. How has she been edited, conjured and appropriated within other language communities? Where does this volume fit in the historiographical perspective? Our authors' researches tell us that the historical Kartini is irrelevant to contemporary Indonesian society. Girls' education is an accepted fact of Indonesian life. Kartini's other great causes—opposition to child marriage and polygamy—cannot be safely championed in today's Islamic Indonesia. What this book's contributors have documented is the power of a name, a name detached from words, to lend support to diverse causes. As Robinson points out, Indonesia's Kartini Day ensures that every year there is a public airing of women's issues throughout Indonesia.

The chapters in this important book have opened doors in showing us what Kartini means to Indonesians and the Dutch, then and today. The authors have probed language, fittingly, because Kartini is really only known by words—her words and the reams of other peoples' words. The volume's contributors have taken a different approach to history, one that sharpens our sensitivity to subliminal meanings, to almost imperceptible biases within ourselves. They challenge the scholars and readers of the future. The study of appropriation of Kartini encourages us to reflect on ourselves as creators of words and to consider more deeply how we write histories.

NOTES

1. Sulastin Sutrisno translated this edition into Indonesian. See Kartini (1979).
2. Letter of 14 July 1903 to Rosa Abendanon-Mandri. It was marked *vertrouwelijk* (confidential) to warn the recipient not to share its contents or pass the letter around, as was usual, to fellow sympathizers of ethical colonialism among the Abendanons' acquaintance.
3. The photograph, probably taken in Semarang in 1900, is no. 15465 in the KITLV photographic collection.
4. Letter of Soematri to the Abendanons, 1 May 1918. Achmad's official name was Raden Ngabehi Sosrohadikoesoemo.
5. Tropenmuseum Collection, no. 10018822.

REFERENCES

Blackburn, Susan. 2004. *Women and the State in Modern Indonesia*. Cambridge: Cambridge University Press.

Coté, Joost, ed. and trans. 2008. *Realizing the Dream of R.A. Kartini: Her Sisters' Letters from Colonial Java*. Ohio: Ohio University Press; Leiden: KITLV Press.

Kartini, R.A. 1911. *Door duisternis tot licht: Gedachten over en voor het Javaansche volk*. Edited by J.H. Abendanon. Semarang: Van Dorp.

———. 1964. *Letters of a Javanese Princess*. Translated by Agnes Louise Symmers. New York: W.W. Norton.

———. 1979. *Surat-surat Kartini: Renungan tentang dan untuk bangsanya*. Translated by Sulastin Sutrisno. Jakarta: Djambatan.

———. 1987. *Brieven aan mevrouw R.M. Adendanon-Mandri en haar echtgenoot*. Edited by F.G.P. Jaquet. Dordrecht: Foris.

Khan, Sher Banu A.L. 2010. "The Sultanahs of Aceh, 1641–1699". In *Aceh: History, Politics and Culture*, edited by Arndt Graf, Susanne Schröter and Edwin Wieringa. Singapore: Institute of Southeast Asian Studies.

———. 2011. "The Jewel Affair: The Sultanah, Her Orangkaya and the Dutch Foreign Envoys". In *Mapping the Acehnese Past*, edited by R. Michael Feener, Patrick Daly and Anthony Reid. Leiden: KITLV Press.

Reksonegoro, Kardinah. 1966. "Kartini: De feiten". *Bijdragen tot de taal-, land- en volkenkunde* 122, no. 2: 283–87.

Schulte Nordholt, Henk. 2009. "Onafhankelijkheid of moderniteit? Een geïllustreerde hypothese". In *Het koloniale beschavingsoffensief: Wegen naar het nieuwe Indië, 1890–1950*, edited by Marieke Bloembergen and Remco Raben. Leiden: KITLV Press.

Suara Aisjijah 12, no. 1 (October 1952).

Tagliacozzo, Eric. 2013. *The Longest Journey: Southeast Asians and the Pilgrimage to Mecca*. Oxford: Oxford University Press.

Vreede-de Stuers, Cora. 1960. *The Indonesian Woman: Struggles and Achievements*. The Hague: Mouton.

Wieringa, Saskia. 2002. *Sexual Politics in Indonesia*. Houndmills: Palgrave Macmillan; The Hague: Institute of Social Studies.

Index

Note: Page numbers followed by "n" refer to endnotes.

www.ingramcontent.com/pod-product-compliance
Lightning Source LLC
Chambersburg PA
CBHW070242290326
41929CB00046B/2340